Consuming Silences

J. D. SALINGER

Consuming Silences

How we read authors
who **DON'T** publish

HENRY ROTH

MYLES WEBER

TILLIE OLSEN

The University of Georgia Press

RALPH ELLISON   Athens and London

Designed by Sandra Strother Hudson
Set in Minion with Syntax display by BookComp, Inc.
Printed and bound by Sheridan Books
The paper in this book meets the guidelines for permanence
and durability of the Committee on Production Guidelines
for Book Longevity of the Council on Library Resources.
Printed in the United States of America
09 08 07 06 05 C 5 4 3 2 1
09 08 07 06 05 P 5 4 3 2 1

Library of Congress Cataloging-in-Publication Data
Weber, Myles.
Consuming silences : how we read authors who don't publish
/ Myles Weber.
         p. cm.
Includes bibliographical references and index.
ISBN 0-8203-2560-0 (hardcover : alk. paper) — ISBN
0-8203-2699-2 (pbk. : alk. paper)
1. American fiction—20th century—History and criticism.
2. Authors and readers—United States—History—20th
century.   3. Salinger, J. D. (Jerome David), 1919–
—Authorship.   4. Ellison, Ralph—Authorship.   5. Olsen,
Tillie—Authorship.   6. Roth, Henry—Authorship.
I. Title.
PS379.W35 2005
813'.509—dc22   2004018186

British Library Cataloging-in-Publication Data available

for my parents

Contents

Acknowledgments

I am deeply indebted to John W. Crowley and Jackson R. Bryer for their guidance on this project.

Consuming Silences

Introduction

In 2002, recording artist Mike Batt programmed a soundless one-minute gap onto a commercial CD, cataloged it as a separate song, and later released the same track as a single for radio play. The gesture was intended as a cheeky homage to the late composer John Cage, whose 1952 composition *4'33"* instructs musicians to play nothing for four minutes and thirty-three seconds. Although Batt voluntarily paid royalties to ASCAP on behalf of Cage, Cage's publishers accused Batt of copyright infringement. Though never actually sued, Batt made a sizeable donation to the John Cage Trust as part of an unofficial out-of-court settlement. The chagrined artist reported afterward that his mother, amid the brouhaha, asked him, "Which minute of the four minutes 33 do they allege that you stole?" (Timberg F1).

Such is the absurd extreme to which silence can be commodified. That commodification illuminates this study of four twentieth-century American prose writers: Tillie Olsen, Henry Roth, J. D. Salinger, and Ralph Ellison. My contention is that these authors' disparate silences were shaped, sold, and consumed in the literary marketplace. In twentieth- and early-twenty-first-century America, unproductive writers have been able to command serious critical attention and remain literary celebrities by offering the public volumes of silence, which have been read and interpreted like any other text.

Of course, not all silences are compelling or marketable. The vast majority of literate persons do not publish, and the resulting silence goes unacknowledged. To generate a legitimate text of silence, clear proof of innate literary talent is required. For Olsen, proof came in 1932 with "The Iron Throat," a work of short fiction published in *Partisan Review.* The appearance of Roth's 1934 novel *Call*

It Sleep inaugurated another truncated career. More spectacularly, *The Catcher in the Rye* (1951) and approximately a dozen famous *New Yorker* stories placed Salinger among the firmament of America's brightest literary stars; his interrupted output has therefore been cause for nearly universal concern and speculation. *Invisible Man* (1952) performed the same function for Ellison.

Although enjoying varying degrees of fame, all four authors have been elevated to inclusion in the category Roland Barthes drolly designated "a race selected by genius." In his 1957 collection *Mythologies,* Barthes explained that a literary figure "keeps his writer's nature everywhere" in contrast to workers whose identities shift according to context. A car mechanic running down a football field is at that moment an athlete, not a mechanic, whereas a writer vacationing in the Congo remains inherently literary because "writer" is a prestigious designation that nothing can degrade. For this reason, Barthes concluded, the likes of André Gide—or Olsen, or Salinger—are writers "as Louis XIV was king, even on the commode" (27–29).

It is that insoluble essence of the writer that makes possible the literary text of silence. Silent writers remain authors even if they never write again. What they don't publish constitutes a literary product. Conversely, the critical attention paid to an author's silence serves as proof of the categorical prominence of the author in our culture: if silence exists as a literary text, there must be someone generating it; for silence to be owned, there must ipso facto be an owner. Notwithstanding Barthes's subsequent imperative in 1968 to assassinate the author and Michel Foucault's assertion one year later that the author was already dead, the author seems to have survived the twentieth century if these owned silences are a reliable indication.

The entrenched author figure whose silence is worthy of study has clear historical roots in the fifteenth century. Elizabeth Eisenstein, considering the broad shift in Europe from manuscript to print culture, observed that of the features introduced by the duplicative powers of print, preservation stands out as possibly the most important (78). In scribal culture, each single copy of a work varied from every other due to error or embellishment, neglect or emendation; but with print, standardization became the rule. The fact that errata were sometimes issued demonstrated "a new capacity to locate textual errors with precision and to transmit this information simultaneously to scattered readers," Eisenstein explained (51).

An individual author in the new print world could safely assume a work would be widely disseminated in a form that roughly mirrored the author's intentions. In turn, personal adulation might accrue. Whereas the conditions of scribal culture held narcissism in check, print culture let it loose: even facial features could now be reproduced uniformly. Publishers therefore made their books more commercially appealing by adding title pages featuring a portrait of the author. "More and more, distinct physiognomies became permanently attached to distinct names," explained Eisenstein (133). And new author-centered genres—Montaigne's essays, Pepys's diaries—eventually emerged.

In short, Eisenstein suggested that the author as a phenomenon rose to prominence simply because it could. There were no longer any material impediments holding it back. Contrary to the opinions of Roland Barthes in "The Death of the Author" and Michel Foucault in "What Is an Author?" Eisenstein implied that the natural order of things is a literary world in which writers, enabled by technology, assume their rightful place in the public sphere. Mark Rose, Martha Woodmansee, Peter Jaszi, and numerous other scholars, however, have more recently studied the rise of the author in closer harmony with the Barthesian-Foucauldian assertion that the author is not a natural occurrence but rather a cultural construct. They view the recognition of authorship as resulting directly from the enactment of legislation that establishes the author as a legal entity.

"When William Caxton introduced the printing press into England in 1476, the creation of a new form of property, eventually to be called copyright, was inevitable," wrote Lyman Ray Patterson in *Copyright in Historical Perspective*, a 1968 study consulted by most of the recent scholars interested in the rise of authorship (20). Before the advent of print, a person could own actual copies of a book, but no one held rights to the text itself. In the print world, however, entrepreneurs demanded exclusive rights to a literary product that might otherwise be counterfeited on publication. The English monarchy, viewing print technology as both miraculous and dangerous, sought an arrangement under which creativity would be encouraged and scientific ideas disseminated even while seditious or heretical books would be intercepted before reaching the marketplace. To that effect, Philip and Mary granted a royal charter on 4 May 1557 to the Company of Stationers of London. In exchange for exclusive rights to publish, Company members took it upon themselves to suppress texts that might prove objectionable to the Crown.

This arrangement lasted for over one hundred years, during which time self-serving booksellers were among the strongest proponents of censorship (Rose 15). By 1710, however, the government had grown less fearful of seditious works and non-Company printers were insisting on their right to compete in the marketplace. Faced with insolvency once a successor to the 1557 agreement lapsed, Company members lobbied disingenuously for legislation that assigned to the *author* the exclusive copyright to new works, hoping that, in practice, this copyright would be signed over to the publisher, which for a time it was. Thus, in 1710, the Statute of Anne was born, and along with this copyright act, claimed Jaszi, " 'Authorship' first entered the domain of law" (468). Ian Hamilton has suggested similarly that the statute "announced the birth of the literary profession" (*Keepers* 45). The irony, of course, is that the success of this piece of legislation in creating a legal entity known as the author was largely inadvertent. Although John Milton, Daniel Defoe, and other writers had spoken publicly in favor of authors' rights by this time, "the purpose of the Statute of Anne," Patterson has concluded, "was to provide a copyright that would function primarily as a trade regulation device" (14).

Nevertheless, the idea of the author as the owner of literary property has snowballed over the three hundred years since the passage of the statute. As Woodmansee noted ("Genius" 426), the eighteenth century gave rise to writers who sought to earn their livelihood by selling creative works to a growing base of literate consumers. Such authors cultivated the Romantic notion of the author as an individual genius. Near century's end, the United States followed England's lead by adopting a constitution that gave Congress the power to assign to authors exclusive rights to their literary works for a limited term, and the first American copyright law was passed in 1790. Another hundred years passed, however, before the United States added *international* copyright protection to the mix. The development of indigenous literature was therefore impeded and the popular profile of the American author shrouded throughout the nineteenth century. Because foreign authors—Sir Walter Scott, Charles Dickens— were not entitled to recompense for copies of their works sold in the United States, American publishers had a financial incentive to publish and promote foreign works in lieu of novels by American authors, to whom they would owe royalties.

On 3 March 1891, the U.S. Congress passed a series of amendments to the general copyright law that provided for reciprocal international copyright protection. American publishers now had to compete for the right to publish foreign works, and they had to pay foreign authors accordingly. Foreign publishers in turn owed payment to American authors. It was a win-win arrangement for writers on both sides of the Atlantic, and it helped to induce the rise of the American literary celebrity, who had previously been overshadowed by foreign authors.

Many predicted that the 1891 international copyright legislation would raise costs for the American publishing industry and harm American consumers spoiled by cut-rate editions of foreign works. As it happened, however, concurrent technological advances in both printing and transportation ignited an explosion of cheap reading materials. "These were the days during which the individual press which cranked out hundreds of copies a day gave away to steam- and electric-powered presses capable of tens of thousands of (larger) papers per *hour*," reported Christopher P. Wilson (18, emphasis in original). Book and magazine production rose dramatically, and the content therein, largely of foreign origin prior to 1891, became heavily domestic. Initials at the end of an article or a story were replaced with full bylines of commissioned American authors—Stephen Crane, Jack London, Frank Norris—whose muscular, naturalistic prose brought to an end the dominance of what Wilson called "the ideas and foreign manners of aristocratic societies" (5).

Urbanization and accompanying rises in income, literacy, and leisure time at the end of the nineteenth century spurred the introduction of a new kind of American publication: the illustrated mass-market weekly (*Munsey's, Collier's, McCall's, Ladies' Home Journal*), the cost of which was subsidized by advertising revenue. Such magazines sold consumer goods to an increasingly affluent citizenry, but they also sold authors, who were similarly branded as commodities. Publisher S. S. McClure raised Ida Tarbell to the highest level of journalistic fame and dubbed Booth Tarkington the greatest of the new generation of novelists while serializing their works (Ohmann 85). In turn, the name-brand identities of famous authors attracted magazine subscribers.

In *Selling Culture: Magazines, Markets, and Class at the Turn of the Century* (1996), Richard Ohmann considered whether promoting authors like detergent or bran flakes in the 1800s was a uniquely American phenomenon. Based on a survey of a similar British experience in the 1850s, he decided it was not. But in the matter of degree, I believe this literary commodification *is* uniquely American in that European cultures had an entrenched class system that included nobility; from their lofty perch, the noble class could observe the course of society and, when necessary, check egregiously crass public behavior. American culture, the most democratic, was free to embrace commercialism unimpeded. Ohmann is inclined to point a finger of condemnation at publishers and industrialists for cultivating consumer appetites, but such behavior seems to arise unprovoked. One is reminded of Eisenstein's observation that the phenomenon of the individual author came to dominate print cultures once it faced no technological impediments. The author as commodified celebrity may be a similarly "natural" phenomenon; it may simply have been waiting for copyright legislation and technology to set it free.

"The author is a modern character," Barthes asserted, "no doubt produced by our society as it emerged from the Middle Ages" (*Rustle* 49). Yet a trail of evidence—and simple common sense—instructs that proprietary authorship has existed since the beginning of written literature. In *The Frogs,* the Aeschylus character accuses his rival, Euripides, of literary theft. The Roman poet Martial condemned contemporaries as plagiarists when they recited his works without permission (Goldstein 39). And Cicero complained of being pestered by admiring fans who saw him less as a person than as the famous author (and owner) of his works (Braudy 95).

The year 1891, then, does not mark the inception of authorship, or even professional authorship, in the United States. William Charvat traced the rise of professional authorship in America to the 1820s and the successful attempts by Washington Irving and James Fenimore Cooper to find a paying readership (29). But notwithstanding these and subsequent cases of nineteenth-century literary success, the professional author in America was legally handicapped throughout much of the century. Therefore, although I would dispute the claim that authors did not exist until the Renaissance, or 1710, or the Romantic period, or 1891, I would still argue that fully copyrighted and commercially promoted authors differ in kind from their predecessors. There is a special purity to the Barthesian writer, who remains intrinsically literary even on the commode, and that purity seems to be recent and coincidental with the explosive rise of celebrity, a phenomenon that John Cawelti defined as "popular interest in a person beyond or aside from his works or accomplishments" (163). Such a definition is useful to this study, which examines literary figures who went decades without producing significant works yet continued to generate popular interest or, at the very least, widespread scholarly interest.

Other scholars have examined the strength of the author figure as a cultural force by using different methods of inquiry. Ian Hamilton surveyed the changing notion of literary posterity in *Keepers of the Flame* (1994). Hamilton credited chronologically remote authors such as John Donne and Andrew Marvell with showing admirable disregard for their lasting impact on the world of letters, while he exposed more recent figures as self-promoters who carefully selected the archival materials left to their estates. The manipulative agendas of Henry James and Thomas Hardy speak volumes about the growing opportunities for self-directed literary celebrity and thus about the status of the author at the turn of the twentieth century. Diverse inquiries into the phenomenon of the author tend to converge on this period of invigorating change, which made possible the rise of the silent author.

Richard Ohmann included in his study of the 1890s an anecdote about the nascent American industrialist King C. Gillette (86). Recognizing the new potential of nationwide saturation advertising, Gillette decided it would be profitable to manufacture a cheap throwaway item for daily use by millions of consumers. He just wasn't sure at first what the item would be. He settled on razor blades and poured a large percentage of his start-up costs into advertisements aimed at convincing Americans they needed such an item in disposable form.

For Ohmann, it was no mere coincidence that those advertisements, delivering a message of arguably wasteful consumption, were filling the pages of the same magazines that promoted Tarbell, Tarkington, and Crane as literary celebrities. The need for a new type of shaving device, like the rising celebrity of authors, was a PR creation. But if Gillette had suddenly ceased to manufacture his famous invention, the public would not have persisted in consuming the empty space on the pharmacy shelf where Gillette razor blades once stood. At most, they would have bought a rival brand's competing product. But a branded author's product is more elusive and yet less fungible; indeed, silence itself can qualify. Barthes seemed to allow as much when he defined the literary text as radically symbolic, irreducibly and unacceptably plural, and infinitely ambiguous (*Rustle* 59). The empty shelf space in a bookstore, then, continues to get read for the simple reason that authors have a singular hold on the imagination of the public that inorganic manufacturing concerns do not. Few consumers would invest emotional capital in the fate of a company whose products were discontinued. But the average citizen, who responded positively when author portraits were inserted into books in the sixteenth century, has a continuing fascination with published writers and their life stories. "Literary biography is a boom industry in our time," observed Peter Washington (99). "It seems that outside the academy we can't get enough of 'what the author meant.'"

David Wyatt explained why there is such a strong impulse to consider authors' careers and thereby "align literary production with the extrinsic forces which shape and are shaped by it." Doing so, he stated, "returns the author to the human community. Attention to births, marriages, friendships, letters, and budgets restores our sense of literature as written by men and women who live with particular hopes and fears, in particular times and places" (151). It is no surprise that the status of the author has itself become the focus of numerous works of fiction and is therefore the theme of several studies of twentieth-century American literature. Jack London's 1908 novel about a professional author, *Martin Eden,* is central to both *The Labor of Words: Literary Professional-*

ism in the Progressive Era by Christopher P. Wilson (1985) and Michael Szalay's recent study, *New Deal Modernism: American Literature and the Invention of the Welfare State* (2000). *Martin Eden* is exemplary but not unique. A litany of works—*The Enormous Room* by E. E. Cummings (1922), Henry Miller's *Tropic of Cancer* (1934), Jack Kerouac's *On the Road* (1957), among others—seem worthy of collective study because they feature an autobiographical narrator who, goaded by the public into constructing a fascinating author persona, places himself in unpleasant or dangerous situations.

Philip Roth's entire oeuvre might best be understood as a running commentary about his own status as an author. The novelist-narrator of *Zuckerman Unbound* (1981) enjoys commercial and critical success after publishing an irreverent novel resembling Roth's *Portnoy's Complaint* (1969). This makes Zuckerman the target of a smear campaign by Jewish leaders and intellectuals, who label him an enemy of the Jews—which also happened to Roth. A subsequent novel, *Operation Shylock* (1993), documents the life of a novelist named Philip Roth who wrote a self-revealing book called *Zuckerman Unbound,* and so on. "This is a new kind of autobiographical novel," Martin Amis observed of Roth's work (287–89). "It is an autobiographical novel about what it is like to write autobiographical novels. . . . But is it literature?"

Indeed, it is. Specifically, it is literature indicative of a culture that rewards authors for revealing themselves to the public. In turn, these authors are so vivid as personae that, should they cease to write, their silence would continue to speak for them. Truman Capote, himself a silent author for much of his final two decades, claimed to have invented a new genre, the nonfiction novel; his personal involvement in *The Muses Are Heard* (1956), *In Cold Blood* (1965), and the novella "Handcarved Coffins" (1980) is so prominent that the works, though obviously fictionalized, no longer qualify as fiction by the author's definition. Edmund White's autobiographical novels are indicative of the broad generic association frequently made between literature and specific sexual or ethnic identities (White is homosexual). For there to be gay authors, or Native American authors, or immigrant authors, there must first be authors. The incentive to build a public identity in one's fiction is therefore very strong.

Public fascination with literary lives increases commensurate with exposure to name-brand authors. The development of electronic media—film, radio, and television—has given famous persons of all professional stripes exponentially greater exposure than before, so much so that the celebrity persona had to be granted legal protection against unauthorized use in commercial endorsements (Coombe 102). But less heralded writers have felt the effects of the new author fixation as well. With the rise of English as a discipline within American institutions of higher learning, commercially marginal authors became branded for the purpose of academic investigation. So firmly was the professional category of American author fixed by the time of the Great Depression that persons who had never actually published were assigned the label "unemployed poet" by government-assistance projects (Szalay 62). Already, a literary figure did not need to produce anything to belong to the race selected by genius. The silence of someone officially designated an author would soon induce public curiosity as well as serious critical attention. And that silence would inevitably be placed within a career narrative, even if a proper career hardly existed.

The phenomenon of the silent author has subsequently entered the realm of fiction. Jay McInerney's 1992 novel *Brightness Falls* features a character named Victor Propp who achieves literary celebrity owing solely to public boasts about a novel-in-progress that never appears. While his contemporaries see their literary reputations rise and fall commensurate with the popularity of their latest books, Propp's stature is unshakable, thanks to the uniform quality of his extended nonproductivity. More recently in *The Book of Illusions* (2002), Paul Auster's literature-professor narrator publishes a scholarly tome that more than superficially resembles my own study. It is described as a book about several writers, including J. D. Salinger, who gave up writing—"poets and novelists of uncommon brilliance who, for one reason or another, had stopped." It is, the narrator explains, "a meditation on silence" (14).

But that is precisely what my study is not. This is not a meditation on silence. While conducting my research, I read numerous such meditations, the best of which provided invaluable context for my work. But the focus throughout this project is on the linked transactions of producing and consuming silence, not on the mysterious and sublime qualities of silence itself. I direct those seeking such meditations to *The Treasure of the Humble* (1910) and *Before the Great Silence* (1936) by the Belgian playwright Maurice Maeterlinck, Swiss philosopher Max Picard's *World of Silence* (1948), Yasunari Kawabata's 1968 Nobel Prize acceptance speech *Japan the Beautiful and Myself,* and John Auchard's scholarly monograph *Silence in Henry James* (1986). They are the most useful and beautifully written of the books I consulted.

In response to the rise of the copyrighted author and the exploding popularity of literary biography, there was a critical reaction against the author, culminating in the New Critics' concentration on the text itself and a more virulent eschewing of biographical information by subsequent theorists. Barthes and Foucault were continuing an existing debate when they spoke against what they considered the naive belief in a deep or psychologically consistent person responsible for a text. "None of this is recent," Foucault wrote in 1969; "criticism and philosophy took note of the disappearance—or death—of the author some time ago" (103). And, indeed, as early as 1923, in the essay "Literature and Biography," Boris Tomaševskij made many of the same points Barthes and Foucault were to repeat a half century later. Tomaševskij lamented the rise of the bad-boy literary hero, an explicitly autobiographical figure popular among the Romantic poets that has carried over in creative works ever since. And like Barthes and Foucault, Tomaševskij considered the actual flesh-and-blood person who drafts a manuscript to be inaccessible in any meaningful sense; he scoffed at the idea of a scholar sniffing around archives to construct the sort of biography one might write about a politician or military leader (117). But Foucault and Barthes differed from their predecessor on how to handle the pesky copyrighted entity assigned to a text. Tomaševskij was resigned to addressing what he called the "author legend" found within creative works. Author legend referred to a narrative generated by the autobiographical figure—someone like Wayne C. Booth's "implied author" (211)—who was now appearing in most oeuvres, and whom Tomaševskij ultimately accepted as an unwelcome literary fact. Foucault and Barthes made no such concession. Foucault coined the term "author function" to refer to the shaggy amalgam of writer, editor, publisher, publicist, critic, and scholar that he deemed "the result of a complex operation which constructs a certain rational being that we call 'author'" (110). By so doing, Foucault has provided me with an extremely useful tool with which to examine the professional lives of silent American authors. By comparing two versions of each author's career narrative—one, the author legend contained within each writer's published works; the other, a narrative provided by the unwieldy, complex operation called the author function, which often includes idle speculation by critics and other readers—I am able to tease out the workings of a literary community that consumes and interprets silence.

For Tillie Olsen, it is literally true that the author offered the public a text of nonproductivity: she published her *Silences* in 1978 with Delacorte Press. That book, her third, ironically fulfilled a chilling prediction Olsen made in 1962 that she might become a "one-book silence." But Olsen guided the reception of her work to conform to that reading. In subsequent years she published only works that supported her prescient self-assessment: an unfinished novel, an unfinished short story, brief essays about her status as a silenced writer. At the same time, she was awarded residencies at writers' colonies and numerous fellowships that provided her the resources necessary to continue writing nothing full-time.

In her author legend, Olsen established herself as the representative silenced female author. Illiterate or oppressed groups do not produce a text of readable silence the way an individual author can. Working-class women or Jewish immigrants or political activists may find themselves silenced en masse by forces emanating from the dominant culture, but only an exemplary immigrant, activist, or worker can author a specific, readable text of silence. The problem in the case of Olsen is that among the credentials she used to establish her identity as a silenced author of genius was the receptivity of the literary world to her few published proletarian works in the 1930s. This enthusiastic reception served as proof of her talent and the particularly tragic nature of her abbreviated career. But the same evidence, particularly a publishing contract with a monthly stipend, suggests that Olsen forfeited the opportunity to pursue a career as a professional writer. Since the mid-1950s, when she resumed writing, Olsen has received a steady stream of encouragement, praise, and adoration. There is therefore a fundamental contradiction in her author legend. A talented writer who was given widespread institutional support has been resold as an unfairly neglected artist.

This was possible because the career narrative constructed by Olsen's author function carefully matched Olsen's author legend. That is, members of the critical and scholarly establishment and the writing community accepted and repeated the story Olsen provided them in her essays and interviews. Her story was internally incoherent, but the literary community—particularly feminist scholars—ignored its unsustainable logic out of a desire to promote the inspiring and iconic figure of Tillie Olsen.

Like his 1934 novel *Call It Sleep*, Henry Roth's silence has been read as a complex work of high modernism, stylistically influenced by James Joyce and T. S. Eliot. This silence took physical form in *Shifting Landscape* (1987), a collection of miscellany that emphasized two root causes for Roth's decades of nonproductivity: the loss of a Jewish homeland when the author's family moved from the Lower East Side of Manhattan to Harlem, and restrictions imposed on him by the Communist Party. But a fractured litany of other impediments, from laziness to a sore elbow, was raised as well. In *Shifting Landscape* and throughout the interviews excerpted therein, Roth made his case for appreciating *Call It Sleep* as a densely layered narrative of great psychological and structural complexity (not a "message" novel), and as a work most comfortably situated among the elite brotherhood of high-modernist classics. He suggested that his silence should be read the same way.

With *Mercy of a Rude Stream*, a four-volume novel sequence published in the 1990s, Roth revised his text of silence, issuing new instructions on how his sixty-year gap in productivity should be understood. Abandoning Joyce's politically uncommitted modernism, Roth simplified the narrative of his frustrated career into a personal horror story of incest and authorial guilt. He had been unable to continue writing fiction, the octogenarian now admitted, because he was an intrinsically autobiographical novelist who was moving chronologically through his own personal history. At the end of *Call It Sleep*, Roth neared the point in his own life when he sexually abused his younger sister. Subsequent material had therefore been off limits until this late date, when the author chose to issue a *mea culpa*. The literary community, comfortable with the complex high-modernist reading of Roth's silence, rejected the revised version. In effect, Roth had attempted to seize control of his own biography, but the critical consensus ruled that the author legend coming from the pen of an elderly Henry Roth was inferior and should be ignored; instead, the more palatable author-function version of events, arrived at with significant contributions from the critical establishment, was retained.

J. D. Salinger's status as a professional author remains secure though he has chosen to publish nothing since 1965. At nearly the same moment that Salinger ceased to publish, Susan Sontag examined the arrogant gesture whereby the supreme modernist artist disappears into silence. She meant the near silence of virtually inaccessible prose, à la Joyce's *Finnegans Wake;* a writer cannot literally go silent and remain an artist, she claimed (*Styles* 11). Yet Salinger has proven her wrong. Biographers and critics now speculate about his careful and strategic refusal to produce anything; they read his silence as a puzzling masterpiece. Salinger's author legend has reached its self-declared end, but the author function grinds on.

Finally, after delivering a masterpiece in *Invisible Man*, Ralph Ellison was unable to complete a second novel. All subsequent texts issued during Ellison's lifetime—essays, essay collections, interviews, short stories, novel excerpts—served as paratext to the one great book. The author's stopgap texts—his articulated "silence"—continue to provide a threshold to his masterpiece and comment on its missing successor. Unable to deliver a second book of fiction, Ellison constructed instead a complicated paratextual apparatus to guide his novel's subsequent reception.

U.S. copyright law, responding to technological developments in the entertainment industry, has been amended in ways that shift proprietary rights away from the individual writer toward corporate entities (estates, publishers, film studios, conglomerates)—the forces composer Mike Batt ran afoul of with his cheeky homage to John Cage. Perhaps the claims of Barthes and Foucault about the dead or disappearing author were only somewhat premature if legislators are now abandoning the creative individual in favor of the inorganic corporate owner. It is uncertain that the phenomenon of the silent author will survive the coming century if legislative and technological trends continue—a possibility I take up in this book's conclusion.

CHAPTER ONE   Tillie Olsen and the Question
of Silenced Literature

The elderly protagonist in Tillie Olsen's story "Tell Me a Riddle" balks at her husband's suggestion that they move to a retirement community. The husband tries to entice her with news of a reading circle, something she had wanted to join decades earlier, but the offer comes too late. "And forty years ago when the children were morsels," she charges, "and there was a Circle, did you stay home with them once so I could go? Even once? You trained me well" (66).

What the husband has trained her to do well is to subsist without activities of the mind, activities in which the protagonist has deserved to participate all along. More important, the husband has inadvertently trained her to refuse opportunities to participate in such activities once they are made available.

In more than forty years since the initial publication of "Tell Me a Riddle," Tillie Olsen has constructed for herself a career as an author similarly characterized by nonparticipation and a stubborn refusal to enter into the processes of writing and publishing. She has done so even though the opportunities (fellowships, encouragement from critics and other authors, time to write) were made available after two decades during which, according to the author, those opportunities were brutally denied her. In fact, the works Tillie Olsen has published since 1960 seem designed to underscore her inability or refusal to create and disseminate works in the manner expected of a functioning author. Olsen has built a singular career by producing—and rarely at that—only works that address her inability to write, which she claims is the result of the damage done to her by male-dominated social, political, and familial institutions. So closely did this point become associated with the nature of Olsen's career during the 1960s and 1970s that, following the publication of the essay collection *Silences* in 1978, the author was able to reaffirm that association by not elaborating on it further in print. Olsen has extended her literary life and even solidified its importance by not writing at all, by remaining silent.

As early as 1974, John Alfred Avant described Olsen as "the least prolific" and "among the least read" of "major living American writers" (28), asserting that a dearth of published works had not hindered her ascent in the literary world. And indeed Olsen's four completed works of fiction (the stories that compose the 1961 collection *Tell Me a Riddle*) have received considerable scholarly attention and been included in most of the widely disseminated anthologies of twentieth-century American literature. In addition, the author herself commands tremendous respect—"reverence" to use Margaret Atwood's term (250)—from other writers, especially women writers.

Still, it is difficult to ignore the obvious kinship between Olsen and writers who have been labeled "minor." A prime American example is Sarah Orne Jewett, particularly in the wake of Louis A. Renza's 1984 monograph *"A White Heron" and the Question of Minor Literature*. Renza's thesis is that Jewett's preference for loosely plotted stories or sketches in the face of patriarchal proscriptions against major works by female authors became "a supererogatory aspect of her writing 'A White Heron' " (163), a story that "defines itself as a benign or less ambitious version of major American literature" (4). Not only is the piece short, sketchlike, and, as the author herself admitted in a letter, rather ill suited for publication, its plot and thematic emphasis seem to address the issue of minor literature: the story's white heron stands in obvious and rather meager contrast to Melville's great white whale; the main character, Sylvia, never matures beyond her nine-year-old point of view; and, most important, the child refuses to speak even about that which she does know, thereby making herself more marginal to the adult world than need be. The city-bred male hunter who plans to shoot and stuff the title bird for his taxidermy collection has offered Sylvia ten dollars—an impressive sum to her and her grandmother in rural, postbellum New England—but the girl decides not to provide him with information about the heron's whereabouts. "[S]he cannot tell the heron's secret and give its life away," the narrator explains (Jewett xxii).

The obvious parallel between Sylvia and the author is that Jewett refused to write in a way that would reap substantial financial or professional benefits from the industrializing, male-controlled world, for fear of giving "its" life away—

the exact nature of "it" being unclear, or just all encompassing: "it" is the very source of major literary material, the inspiration for the great works, the cause of all conflict and resolution—life itself.

If all this suggests an unusual delicacy, even timidity, in Jewett's approach to writing about the human condition, that only points up the inverse side of her—and Olsen's—response to the constrictions of the dominant order: those short, sketchlike works Jewett deliberately offered as bold resistance to the proscriptions of the literary establishment (and the silences offered by Olsen) are, at the same time, capitulations to that order. Just as there is sometimes a fine line, perhaps impossible to draw, between censorship and self-censorship, there is here a line equally impossible to draw between diminution and self-diminution (in Jewett's case), between silencing and self-silencing (in Olsen's). But whereas one can quite easily understand that Jewett could derive satisfaction and professional acclaim from publishing her sketches, it is much more difficult to see— and I will attempt in this chapter to illuminate—what rewards Olsen can derive from publishing nothing. The conventional view would hold that muffled expression and muteness are much more chilling diminutions of a writer's career than is strategic modesty of execution à la Jewett, and yet Olsen's professional status rests on that very characterization and seems to have been helped rather than hurt by it.

If, as Renza suggested, Jewett sought to construct an author's career in which only the peripheral, minor works were written—as if Virginia Woolf had composed only her letters and notebooks and nothing else—then Olsen has gone one step further by constructing a career that consists of gaps between even the minor works. These represent the times, to continue the Woolf analogy, when the author's room was no longer her own, when she was neither writing a novel nor composing a letter, but was cleaning, cooking dinner, entertaining her husband's guests, or working outside the home. And if, as Renza further suggested in his book's epilogue, it was almost by unfortunate accident that Jewett ended up compiling the sketches in *The Country of Pointed Firs* (1896), which present-day critics generally categorize as a major work, then it is likewise hazardous to Olsen's career design when she publishes anything at all, even if it is only the sort of brief piece Jewett published regularly in *Harper's* and the *Atlantic Monthly*. But Olsen herself would no doubt counter with a very different interpretation: she has written only the gaps and silences because the male-dominated world has prevented her from writing more. In fact, her entire oeuvre can be read as insisting on that point and making almost no other.

Olsen's first published fiction—the only fiction she published before the

1950s—was "The Iron Throat," which later became the opening chapter of the unfinished novel *Yonnondio: From the Thirties.* The excerpt received wide exposure in 1934 as the lead piece in the second issue of *Partisan Review.* Robert Cantwell, in a survey of literary magazines published in a 1934 issue of the *New Republic,* singled out "The Iron Throat" from among some two hundred works of short fiction published in small literary journals, describing it as "so fresh and imaginative that even a cautious critic can call it a work of early genius" ("Little Magazines" 295). Granville Hicks, who included "The Iron Throat" alongside works by John Dos Passos, James T. Farrell, Michael Gold, and Josephine Herbst in his 1935 anthology *Proletarian Literature in the United States,* noted that Olsen's very first work of fiction had "catapulted her into prominence" (*Great Tradition* 319).

As one of the few women of working-class origin writing in the 1930s, Olsen was sought after by organizations in need of proletarian credentials (Rabinowitz 125). As a result, she attended the first Congress of American Writers in April 1935 and was the youngest of two hundred delegates gathered to organize the League of American Writers, an affiliate of the International Union of Revolutionary Writers (Nelson 1). And, according to Cantwell ("Literary Life" 49), no fewer than four book publishers were pursuing Olsen after the appearance of "The Iron Throat"—a competition won by Bennett Cerf at Random House, who offered a monthly stipend in exchange for progress on the novel (Martin 10).

In her "Note about This Book" published as a preface to *Yonnondio: From the Thirties,* Olsen stated that the novel was begun in 1932 in Faribault, Minnesota, when she was nineteen. She ultimately abandoned the manuscript, according to *Silences,* because of the time and energy demands of domestic chores and wage labor outside the home. But the demands of political activism were a greater impediment. In fact, not until illness forced Olsen to abandoned her Young Communist League work in 1932 did she find herself with enough free time to begin writing a novel, having postponed her political work long enough to recover from incipient tuberculosis ("to be a good Bolshevik I need health first" Olsen wrote in her journal). Olsen was productive during this recovery period in 1932 and another period of withdrawal from political activity in 1935, which Olsen called her other "good writing year" (Rosenfelt, "From the Thirties" 382). During the latter period, she received the stipend from her publisher. Like many writers facing a blank page, however, Olsen grew restless. She relocated to southern California, hoping to complete the manuscript there. But while socializing with Tess Slesinger and other writers who admired her work and shared her political sympathies, Olsen—then unmarried and named Tillie Lerner—began to lose interest in the novel. "The young Lerner was further lionized by Lincoln Steffens and his coterie of important intellectual socialists in Carmel," Nora Ruth Roberts reported. "All this seems to have done more to harm than to further young Lerner's progress" (75).

If I understand Roberts's observation correctly, the more Olsen was praised, the more she felt pressured to deliver exceptional work. "It is yet to be demonstrated," Granville Hicks intoned in 1935, "whether Tillie Lerner can sustain the burden of unifying, through an entire novel, what her extraordinary insight gives her" (*Great Tradition* 319). Some authors are invigorated by the challenge of raised expectations, while others wilt under the pressure. The latter may apply to Olsen. In any event, she was certainly not crushed by critical or editorial discouragement—if anything, the opposite is true. Olsen eventually took on organizational work again rather than write (Martin 10). Finally, having forfeited her contract with Random House and the subsidy it provided, she moved to San Francisco, to a life served under those conditions that she would later fault for silencing her.

Deborah Rosenfelt, whose 1981 essay "From the Thirties: Tillie Olsen and the Radical Tradition" was written with Olsen's close cooperation and has provided the blueprint for all subsequent biographical scholarship on Olsen, explained that "Olsen's political work came first throughout the early and mid-thirties—along with the burdens of survival work and, increasingly, domestic work" (382). This point must be made delicately, as it risks undercutting or even disproving the central theses of Olsen's primary texts and entirely upending her professional identity. Olsen is a radical proletarian writer—this, along with her unique status as a silenced major author, is key to her appeal among readers and scholars. But she is also someone who forfeited a chance at conventional literary success, then charged the supportive literary establishment with soulless indifference. Because Olsen's abandonment of a literary career is intimately tied to her proletarian identity and sympathies, the result is a complicated muddle of facts and interpretive statements that, on the one hand, emphasize her working-class origins and blame the bourgeoisie for preventing her rise as a writer (this is the explicit theme of *Silences*) but, on the other hand, credit the bourgeoisie with recognizing her obvious talent (the implication of much Olsen scholarship, produced with the author's cooperation).

After setting the novel aside, Olsen raised a family with Jack Olsen and continued her political and labor-organizing activities—picketing with strikers, handing out leaflets to workers—while writing occasionally for various leftist publications and the Federal Writers Project (recording life stories of Slavic, Filipino, and Mexican workers). According to Rosenfelt (380), Olsen remained an activist throughout the 1940s as she raised her children, organizing war relief work as president of the California Congress of Industrial Organization's Women's Auxiliary. Though she briefly wrote a cheerful column for the *People's World* in the 1940s, during which time *Yonnondio* remained shelved, she did not publish any more fiction before the mid-1950s.

Attempting to mesh the historical record and passages from Olsen's journal from the 1930s with Olsen's subsequent conflicting statements and central assertions in *Silences*, Rosenfelt suggested in her 1981 essay that, although time devoted to activism hindered Olsen's literary progress, "the atmosphere of the Left as a whole" actually encouraged Olsen as a writer by providing venues for intellectual discussion, giving her a sense of broader community and recognizing and valuing her talent (387). This line of argument permits the antagonistic forces cited in *Silences* to retain their stain of guilt, but ultimately this strategy fails. For one thing, those persons recognizing and valuing Olsen's talent were intellectuals who stood outside the party's central hierarchy, which was fairly indifferent to literary radicalism (Rabinowitz 19). For another, the deeper Olsen involved herself in "the atmosphere of the Left as a whole," the less productive she became as a writer. It is unclear to what extent Olsen, realizing her writing project was failing, embraced labor and party activism to fill the creative and emotional void or, reversing the chronology, to what extent she caused her writing project to fail by embracing activism. But the relationship between the two is clearly inverse.

Between the end of the war and 1953, when Olsen began working on the story "I Stand Here Ironing," the changing political environment forced the retreat of the Communist Party in the United States. This had ramifications for Olsen's political life and, though she is careful not to mention them in her work, for her writing career as well. Enduring "the soul-destroying harassment typically directed at leftists and thousands of suspected leftists during the period," as Rosenfelt put it (380), Olsen ended her activism and began writing. The painful irony here, which Rosenfelt never acknowledged explicitly, and which Olsen disguises in *Silences*, is that the author seems to owe the recommencement of her writing career, at least in part, to McCarthyism. In *Silences*, Olsen raged against the silencing that results from government censorship but rarely touched on the sort of political silencing that applied most directly to herself: the sapping by political activism of time and energy that could have been devoted to literary pursuits, which is actually a form of self-silencing. Not until

Olsen gave up her political activism, under pressure from the extreme Right, did she enter her most productive period of fiction writing.

At the same time that the McCarthyite threat pressured Olsen and many others on the Left to curb their political activities in the early 1950s, Olsen's youngest daughter entered elementary school. Freed of two substantial time burdens—activism and full-time mothering of a toddler—Olsen enrolled in a fiction-writing course at San Francisco State University in 1954 (Rosenfelt, "Tell Me" 8). Based on her work in this course, she received a Stegner Fellowship in creative writing to Stanford University, where, according to Mickey Pearlman and Abby H. P. Werlock, she was "the only 'unknown' among the group that year [1955–56], which included James Baldwin, Bernard Malamud, Flannery O'Connor, and Katherine Anne Porter" (29). "I Stand Here Ironing," Olsen's first published work of fiction in over twenty years, was included in the Best American Short Stories anthology of 1957, the year her stories "Hey Sailor, What Ship?" and "O Yes" were also published. A two-year Ford Foundation grant in literature facilitated the completion of Olsen's fourth story, "Tell Me a Riddle" (published in 1960 and awarded an O. Henry Prize), and the appearance of Olsen's collection of the same name in 1961, marking the author's debut in the world of book publishing and bringing to a definitive end that period which she would later refer to as the "most harmful" of all her silences (Silences 21).

But the following year, less than a decade after her return to writing, and while her first book was still being reviewed—often ecstatically—Olsen delivered a lecture at the Radcliffe Institute that would set the agenda for her career to follow. This agenda would require that she cease publishing complete works of fiction, even at so slow a rate as one slim book of stories each half decade. In this lecture, later edited from a taped manuscript and published as "Silences: When Writers Don't Write" in the October 1965 issue of Harper's, Olsen described her two-year Ford Foundation Grant as coming "almost too late" (Silences 20). She had wanted to write and been denied the opportunity for decades, she claimed, but now that the opportunity had finally presented itself, she felt dazed by the prospect of writing. She later expanded on this in a passage quoted by Abigail Martin (11): "I am a partially destroyed human who pays the cost of all those years of not writing, of deferring, postponing, of doing others' work—it's in my body too (deafened ear from transcribing), etc." In 1974, she told a group of young writers, "You see, I am a destroyed person" (Boucher 30). Olsen cautioned those listening in 1962 that she had "not yet recovered" from the years of overwork and silencing (21). More ominously, she predicted—quite accurately, as it turned out—that she might become a "one-book silence" (21), by which she meant a writer who just managed to eke out a single book's worth of material, only to be swallowed up again, forever, by the forces that work against creativity and publication.

In fact, Olsen's entire output of new fiction, in the more than forty years since she gave this lecture, amounts to exactly one unfinished story, "Requa," published in 1970. It is my thesis that Olsen has solidified her unique place in the literary canon by maintaining her status as a one-book silence. She has done this by subsequently publishing only old work (*Yonnondio*), unfinished work ("Requa," *Yonnondio*), and other people's work, either as a compilation of fragments padding one of her own books (the final 170 pages of *Silences*) or as a "reclaimed masterpiece" around which to wrap her commentary (the reissue of Rebecca Harding Davis's *Life in the Iron Mills*). Olsen's one book of completed fiction, the 115-page *Tell Me a Riddle*, established her career as a writer; the absence of work since, far from harming her career, has sustained it, nourished it, *become* it. The method of canonization for short-story writers rests primarily on anthologization, often with the inclusion of only one story per anthology. The fact that Olsen has written a total of only four and a half stories merely makes the anthologizers' job of selection easier. If, by now, Olsen had published fifty or one hundred stories, she could realistically hope to do no better than one story per anthology anyway, and a Tillie Olsen who could write and publish fifty or one hundred stories would not be the Tillie Olsen we were introduced to in the early 1960s—the Tillie Olsen who wins prestigious fellowships based on her unique history and who for forty years has been invited to lecture at universities about her experiences as a silenced writer. Rather, this would be a Tillie Olsen who, stripped of her special muted quality, might prove less attractive to editors who select authors for anthologization, and who certainly would prove much less useful to feminist scholars and university instructors.

If, in the decades following the appearance of *Tell Me a Riddle*, Olsen had published another book of new fiction—or perhaps even a single completed story—she would have seriously altered the definition of her literary career that she herself set forth in "Silences: When Writers Don't Write." For her to begin, at a later point, publishing in the manner of a conventionally productive author would only confuse the reading of her author legend.

By the 1970s, that reading was accepted almost universally. Even Joyce Carol Oates, in a negative review of *Silences*, accepted Olsen's explanation for her twenty-year hiatus from writing prior to the publication of "I Stand Here Ironing." Oates lamented that, during the time when Olsen was silenced, "[s]ome stories died. Deprived of the time and energy to imagine them into being . . .

Tillie Olsen lost them forever" (246). The implication, of course, is that the four that lived (one for each daughter?) are all the more precious and remarkable for having done so. Annie Gottlieb, referring to *Tell Me a Riddle* in her 1974 review of *Yonnondio: From the Thirties,* made this point explicitly. She wrote that Olsen's "close brush with a final silence left its indelible mark, for those four stories reverberate with wonder at the human urge to create and with pity and pain at its crushing, again and again, by the circumstances of life" (5). Elaine Orr added: "One marvels at the way Olsen's vision seems to hover on the brink of expression" (135). *Tell Me a Riddle,* then, is not merely a collection of four stories—or even a collection of four very good stories—but is instead nothing less than a literary miracle. The stories included therein are cause for celebration, not for aesthetic reasons first and foremost, but because of the manner in which they were produced. But if the awe one feels for the stories' very existence should somehow translate into admiration for the quality of the prose—and it seems to have done just that among most of her readers and critics—then that does Olsen's career no harm either. And Olsen's deliberate instructions on how to read her work suggest that she herself does not oppose a blurring of distinctions.

Of course, to say that Olsen is a one-book silence is not technically accurate, in that she has published subsequent books. The novel *Yonnondio: From the Thirties* appeared, unfinished, in 1974, but as the subtitle suggests, it was entirely old material written in the 1930s and uncovered by accident in 1972. Olsen spent five months at the MacDowell Colony putting the work in order— omitting scenes, reordering sections, choosing which draft to use when multiple drafts of a passage were available—but she assured the reader in "A Note about This Book" that "it is all the old manuscripts—no rewriting, no new writing" (*Yonnondio* n.p.). Olsen, according to Martin, realized that "from the very nature of things, youth and inexperience cannot really collaborate with middle age and the viewpoint of middle age. The whole tone of the novel would have been spoiled, would have jangled into confusion if she had started to revise, to interpolate" (17). So, Olsen reported, "Not a word was added or changed, and the story remains unfinished" (*Yonnondio* n.p.).

The novel's appearance in the marketplace, then, did not imperil the uniqueness of Olsen's career. Rather, it served as direct evidence of a period in the 1930s when the forces working against creativity triumphed and as evidence of Olsen's obvious literary talent at the time. Also, the book's story chronicles the lives of working-class people who struggle to stay afloat and together, who try to secure an education for their children, giving loosely autobiographical urgency to Olsen's own struggle to overcome silencing.

In 1978, Olsen published the nonfiction book *Silences,* which contains the title essay from the early 1960s, the 1971 essay "One Out of Twelve: Writers Who Are Women in Our Century," and "Rebecca Harding Davis," which originally served as an afterword to the Feminist Press's 1972 reprint edition of *Life in the Iron Mills* and which is Olsen's longest published piece of nonfiction.

Still, the three pieces together constitute less than two-fifths of the volume. Olsen concludes by excerpting from *Life in the Iron Mills* and Baudelaire's *My Heart Laid Bare.* The vast bulk of the book, however, is a long middle section that the table of contents lists as "Acerbs, Asides, Amulets, Exhumations, Sources, Deepenings, Roundings, Expansions" and that even the most laudatory reviewers and scholars described as "a grab bag of excerpts" from the diaries, journals, letters, and other autobiographical work of other writers, with brief conclusions by Olsen, which are "not always in sentences" and which give the book a "condensed and fragmentary quality" (Atwood 250; Orr 144). Oates, less equivocally, made reference to what she called the book's "editing, or lack thereof" (246), citing an absence of collation throughout the book, which too often results in a repetition of statements among the various essays and the "gnat-like presence" of inconsequential footnotes at the bottom of many pages, which Oates took as a sign of haste or editorial indifference. Margaret Atwood more charitably noted that there are footnotes "blooming on every page as if the author, reading her own manuscript, belatedly thought of a dozen things too important to leave out" (251)—but evidently not important enough to integrate into the text proper.

I suggest that the book is presented this way not due to spontaneity, haste, or editorial neglect, but rather by authorial intent. As even Oates acknowledged (246), if the book is uneven, it is "necessarily" so—for its own purposes and, it is now clear, for the purposes of Olsen's career. Or, as Elizabeth A. Meese phrased it, "The book is what it can be" (109). The scattered and fragmentary pieces that make up most of the text are, like the unfinished *Yonnondio,* illustrations of Olsen's main point that poverty, illness, family responsibility, political censorship, religious censorship, and other obstacles prevent many writers, especially women writers, and Olsen in particular, from writing complete and traditionally coherent works of literature. If, instead of the *Silences* that exists, Olsen had issued a sustained, unobstructed, three-hundred-page work systematically laying out her thesis, the book's very nature would negate its own point and confuse our understanding of Olsen's career. As it is, that long middle section, as muddled as it may seem, provides clear enough instructions on how to read Olsen's one real book, *Tell Me a Riddle.* Atwood observed: "Reading this section may be hazardous if you are actually writing a book. It's like walking along a sidewalk only to be shown suddenly that your sidewalk isn't a sidewalk but a tightrope over Niagara Falls. How have you managed to do it at all?" (251). More to the point, how has Olsen managed to do it at all? The long middle section, in its existing fragmented form, is meant to heighten our awe at what Atwood called "the near miracle of her survival" (250) without detracting from the uniqueness of *Tell Me a Riddle* by adding a second full book to Olsen's oeuvre.

And again, as in the case of *Yonnondio,* even the part of *Silences* that does exist as polished prose from Olsen's hand is qualified in nature. Whereas *Yonnondio* was an old, presilence manuscript to which Olsen resisted adding a word, the first two essays here, "Silences" and "One Out of Twelve," were each, as their prefaces note, originally "an unwritten talk, spoken from notes," and not, as it might appear, a traditional essay composed by an author who had the luxury of a fixed income and a room of her own or, if she did have these things (thanks to the Stanford Fellowship [1956], the Ford Foundation Grant [1959–60], a Radcliffe Fellowship [1962–64], a National Endowment for the Arts Grant [1967], five months at the MacDowell Colony [1972–73], a Guggenheim Fellowship [1975–76], and visiting professorships at Amherst [1969–70], Stanford [1972], MIT [1973–74], and the universities of Massachusetts and California at San Diego [1974]), then an author who had survived into middle age with a clear, undazed mind with which to compose such works. And even the third essay, though longer and originally written, not spoken, does not seriously violate our expectations of a work by Tillie Olsen nor alter our understanding of her career. The piece is safely secondary, serving as mere accompaniment to the real work at hand, Rebecca Harding Davis's *Life in the Iron Mills.* It is presented as an essay performing much the same purpose for that nineteenth-century author that the rest of *Silences* does for Olsen. But by first eliciting admiration for Harding Davis (at such length in the original Feminist Press reprint that it dwarfed the novella itself) and then drawing an obvious kinship between Olsen and the earlier silenced writer, the essay reflects admiration back on its author as well, thus serving, though at greater length and in what is for Olsen a dangerously sustained and coherent manner, the same purpose as the rest of the collection.

Like *Yonnondio,* then, *Silences* does not disqualify Olsen from the category she has constructed for herself, that of the one-book silence. Its contents (explicitly) and its form and style (implicitly) tell us as much. Olsen is a one-book author whose second and third books confirm that point.

And, likewise, Olsen's other miscellaneous works contribute to this understanding of her career. Chiefly, her short story "Requa," published unfinished in 1970 and not yet completed, serves by its very nature of incompleteness the same function as *Yonnondio* and by its fragmented style a function similar to that of the middle section of *Silences*. The story, set in the 1930s, is about a working-class boy who seems to be descending into a psychotic depression. On the basis of this piece, Martha Foley described Olsen as "one of those authors experimenting with typographical appearance and spacing" (x). Blanche H. Gelfant called the story's form "discontinuous" and described its text as "broken visibly into fragments separated from each other by conspicuous blank spaces, gaps the eye must jump over and the mind fill with meaning" ("After Long Silence" 61, 67). The story, Gelfant noted, is "the repository of bits and pieces: sentences broken into words, words isolated by blank spaces." With even the typography discontinuous, the text seems "a mosaic of oddly assorted fragments." Clearly, the effect of the story is that the reader must take note of and interpret the silences in the text—the blank patches on the page—just as the reader is expected to read the silences in Olsen's career. "Requa," like her second and third nonbooks, does not detract from but in fact accentuates the specialness of Olsen's career, as she has presented it.

And Olsen has published nothing in the last two-and-a-half decades that would disrupt this presentation. Her works since *Silences* have included no fiction and only a few short essays. It would be understandable that a writer, upon reaching Olsen's advanced age, might slow down her work schedule or even retire, but reports indicate that Olsen continues to battle the forces that would keep her silent. Blanche H. Gelfant in 1984 (69n), Elaine Orr in 1987 (135n), Mickey Pearlman and Abby Werlock in 1991 (35), and Joanne S. Frye in 1995 (176) all noted that Olsen continues to work on her fiction, specifically her story "Requa," attempting to complete it to novella length. Olsen, then, seems determined to continue extending her career as an author. But whereas for other writers that would mean continuing to publish, in the case of Olsen, whose position is peculiarly like no other, one is tempted to say that the extension of her career requires that she diligently continue *not* to publish—as long as she is able. Or, at best, that she make only slow progress on the work in question. "Even if 'Requa' is completed," added Orr (130), "we can say that Olsen's words to us are brief, her style fragmentary, almost hesitant." And, indeed, it is probably safe to say that the publication of "Requa" as a novella (which would be Olsen's first completed work of fiction since 1960) would not challenge the general understanding of the author's career or revise the text of silence she has produced over the last half century. Four decades is a long time between stories—it spans the years from the Eisenhower to the second Bush administration—and is certainly ample testimony to the severity of the author's struggle to write in spite of the obstacles placed before her. Forty-plus years would certainly distance her sufficiently so that, rather than detract from her professional uniqueness, a completed "Requa" might serve as another reminder of it, a second peak to her career, perhaps an inspiring ending.

Significantly, Orr further noted that, "looking at Olsen's canon—a partial novel, a thin book of three short stories and a novella, a prose book of reflections on the subject of silence, a later partial novella, and an essay on her mother— we sense that she has not told all" (36). Either Orr was displaying a perverse gift for understatement, or she merely has an extremely faulty understanding of the author, whose entire career has been spent cultivating the notion that she was nearly prevented from telling *anything*.

Orr's comment does raise a larger issue—what has Olsen not told in *Silences*?—which strikes at the very foundation of Olsen's special status in the field of literature. If *Yonnondio* was a novel "abandoned by necessity" in the 1930s, the causes of that necessity are plainly not limited to those offered by Olsen in *Silences,* which she has used to construct the widely accepted reading of her work and career. Near the end of the title essay, Olsen stated: "In the twenty years I bore and reared my children, usually had to work on a paid job as well, the simplest circumstances for creation did not exist. Nevertheless writing, the hope of it, was 'the air I breathed, so long as I shall breathe at all' " (19). Yet in her journals from the 1930s, as quoted by Rosenfelt, Olsen condemned herself for the paths she has worn of "inefficiency, procrastination, idle planning, lack of perseverance," adding, "Only in my League work did these disappear, I have that to thank for my reconditioning" ("From the Thirties" 382). She expressed her wish to write in a more disciplined way, but added, "I must abolish word victories. . . . let me feel nothing till I have had action—without action feeling and thot [*sic*] are disease" (382–83, ellipsis in Rosenfelt).

Even if one dismisses Olsen's comments about "inefficiency" and "procrastination" as the self-flagellation of a young and insecure woman, a contradiction remains in the two passages concerning the urgency, in the 1930s, that Olsen should write at all. The disdain that the author seems actually to have felt at the time for what the revisionist Olsen of *Silences* called the air she breathed appears elsewhere in Olsen's work from the 1930s. In a 1934 essay from *Partisan Review* about the San Francisco dockworkers strike, Olsen apologized— bragged, really—that her words are "feverish and blurred. You see, If I had time, If I could go away. But I write this on the battle field" ("Strike" 144). She further apologized for bothering with the typewriter at all—"I sit here making a metallic little pattern of sound in the air, because that is all I can do, because that is what I am supposed to do" (142)—when she should have been down at the "battle field" performing legitimate work, even if such activity should leave her "dazed" and unable to place the sequence of events into "neat patterns of words" (138). (There is, of course, a clear irony here in that the demands of others—party leaders, the editors of *Partisan Review*—"forced" Olsen to write this piece when she would rather have stuck to what she considered more legitimate work: picketing and protesting.)

Olsen's scorn for mere wordplay and her refusal to recognize writing as valid action, while perhaps common among party members, had grave professional consequences for any activist who had hopes of becoming a writer—unless, of course, the activist were later able to present her lack of output during this period as an unchosen "silence" imposed from without. Clearly, the factors Olsen emphasized in *Silences* as impediments to a writing career—particularly the need to earn money—were not the only obstacles, or even the chief obstacles. Omitted from *Silences* is any mention of the influence the Communist Party had over her: the demands it made on her time, the way it shaped her scornful attitude toward the activity of written creation, and the restrictions it placed on the suitability of what should get written and published by committed Communists.

In light of party preferences, Olsen planned to extend the manuscript of her first novel, a family saga, to include such events as a Midwestern packing-house strike and labor-organizing activities in California. But she recorded in her journal in the mid-1930s: "Now it seems to me the whole revolutionary part belongs in another volume. . . . and I can't put out one of those 800 page tomes" (393, ellipsis in Rosenfelt). Why exactly she couldn't "put out one of those 800 page tomes" isn't clear. She may have felt that she lacked the kind of writing time necessary for a novel of that length—perhaps there were limits to the largesse Bennett Cerf was willing to bestow on the young first novelist. Or she may have dismissed the idea of a long novel as bloated and artistically unsuccessful. In any event, the whole project became unfeasible, according to Rosenfelt, once Olsen had "so fully internalized the Left's vision of what proletarian literature could and should do to show the coming of a new society that she did not even consider then the possibility of a less epic and, for her, more feasible structure" ("From the Thirties" 394). And the novel, of course, was never completed.

Illuminating comparisons can be drawn between the fate of Tillie Olsen and that of an author whose work she greatly admired, Henry Roth. Both writers faced the party's proscriptions about literature in the 1930s. Both had major publishing contracts for a novel that neither finished. And both produced very little in the decades that immediately followed. But there is a significant dissimilarity between the two authors: whereas Roth attempted for some time to explain his troubles as stemming from the excesses and failures of a political cause to which he was devoted (see chapter 2), Olsen has never done so. In fact, she disguised her involvement in Communist Party activities throughout *Silences,* making only one brief, oblique, and seemingly impersonal entry related to this and tucking it away in the convoluted middle section of the book, under the heading *Involvement:* "When political involvement takes priority, though the need and love for writing go on. Every freedom movement has, and has had, its roll of writers participating at the price of their writing" (140).

Rosenfelt observed that Olsen has spoken little of silences caused by political commitments compared to other kinds of silences, which have received more full analysis; Rosenfelt suspected, quite generously, that this is because Olsen "has not wanted to be misread as encouraging a withdrawal from political activism for the sake of 'art' or self-fulfillment" (381). More likely, though, Olsen was motivated by professional self-interest. By dressing her silencers in the garb of the capitalistic male establishment, she set herself apart from the crowd of discredited Stalinists and constructed for herself an important and lasting place in American literature, a place that almost certainly would not have existed had she not retroactively, and carefully, served as its architect.

One can accept that the time demands placed on Tillie Olsen as a working-class wife and mother during the 1930s and 1940s diminished the vigor with which she was able to pursue her personal interests outside the domestic sphere. But when she writes, "The years when I should have been writing, my hands and being were at other (inescapable) tasks" (*Silences* 38), one must respond with incredulity. (Her involvement in party work was inescapable? She didn't choose it, *it chose her*?) As Rosenfelt explained, "The point is not, then, that insensitive and rigid communist bureaucrats imposed unreasonable demands on party members, but rather that rank-and-file communists made these demands on themselves, because they believed so deeply in the liberating possibilities of socialism" (383). Of course, the insensitive and rigid party bureaucrats were for the most part male, and to the extent that they did impose demands on party members, their impositions might conceivably be made to fit Olsen's larger framework of male silencers. But the fact that Olsen omitted explicit reference to their influence on her life and career suggests that she herself had difficulty fitting them into that framework or could not risk including them without suggesting that much of the silencing she has suffered has actually been self-silencing—that she was duped by Socialist utopianism, not crushed by capitalist oppression.

Equally suspect is the explanation Olsen gives for her silences *since* the 1950s. Her obvious and strategic omission of details about previous decades harms her credibility as a witness to more recent times. When she claims to be dazed by the responsibilities of daily life and by patterns still imposed on women, it seems equally likely that she may be omitting reference to idle distraction, waning interest, the political disillusionment she no doubt shares with an entire generation of former party members, or other factors that have kept her lethargic and unproductive and necessitated the delivery of the original "Silences" lecture and subsequent documentation to instruct others to read her few published works as heroic feats performed despite the crippling demands of housework and mothering.

As noted, once the instructions she offered about how to read her career were widely accepted, Olsen was bound not to become undazed and suddenly produce like a nonsilenced writer. Adrienne Rich, noting that "women's struggle for self-determination has been muffled in silence over and over," complained that "women's work and thinking has been made to seem sporadic, errant, orphaned of any tradition of its own" (11). Sadly, Olsen seems to have muffled her own struggle for self-determination and has certainly contributed more than anyone else to promoting the interpretation of her own work as sporadic and in the errant tradition of silence itself.

Still, in spite of her peculiar method of self-muffling or (frightening thought) *because* of it, Olsen remains a seminal force in women's literature, "a catalyst for many younger writers both as an example and as a great source of personal encouragement" (Gottlieb, "Feminists" 51). That a woman who has contributed significantly to her own silencing, and instructed others to recognize her as a textbook example of the patriarchy's victim (having first skewed her personal record to make the point credible), serves as a source of inspiration to the women of today suggests that the patriarchal stranglehold on women writers is even stronger than Olsen would have us believe or is herself aware of or willing to admit.

The fact that, for many, Tillie Olsen's *Silences*—like her silences—does not have the effect of weakening Olsen's claim of victimhood is puzzling. Just how did Tillie Olsen manage to win widespread acceptance within the scholarly community for an autobiographical legend that was internally inconsistent? We can begin to answer that question by returning briefly to pertinent essays by Roland Barthes and Michel Foucault who, at the very time Olsen was constructing her legend, dismissed the concept of the author as a weakened irrelevancy whose disappearance was imminent.

In fact, nothing could have been further from the truth, as Olsen's career demonstrates. The post–World War II author, even in academia, was still an ascendant celebrity whose sustained existence no longer required the production of published works—or even "texts," to honor Barthes's distinction—with one exception: the text of silence itself. But silence, by its very nature, must be attributed to a clearly identifiable author for it to be read coherently. The categorical silence of working-class women is too vague a concept to permit useful textual analysis, raising as it does a series of questions: (1) Do such women really constitute a chorus with one consonant voice? (2) Who can meaningfully interpret the void of nonwriting they produce? And (3) how do we even know if, given the tools and opportunities, they would choose to pursue writing and prove sufficiently skilled at it?

Tillie Olsen provided a solution to this quandary: she offered herself as an emblematic working-class woman who produced just enough nonsilent text to (1) give specific voice to the group, (2) allow for conventional literary interpretation (i.e., close readings), and (3) prove conclusively that great talent is latent among the silenced. But by so doing, she disqualified herself from membership in the group she was meant to represent: silenced working-class women or, more generally, silenced authors. The proof of her considerable talent—critical praise, publishing contracts and advances, literary prizes, fellowships and grants—removed her from the roster of neglected potential authors and placed her instead on a list of the conventionally encouraged and, despite her humble origins, privileged.

This was unavoidable. While it is logically conceivable—if not empirically verifiable—that there exist a plethora of unrecognized authors producing silence, Olsen's project required the production not merely of texts, a nebulous category among which silence can be included, but also of authored works—*Tell Me a Riddle, Silences,* the published fragments of *Yonnondio* and "Requa"—and the creation of a full-fledged Foucauldian author function, boasting a publisher, editors, avid readers, devoted scholars, and so on. A silenced writer is not an inherent contradiction, but a fully silenced author function, whose published works attract general acclaim and considerable scholarly attention, is. Olsen's mistake, if I can call it a mistake in view of her considerable success as a literary figure in defiance of this oxymoronic trap, is that she believed that an example of the silenced-yet-successful author function *did* not exist, when in fact it *could* not exist. If such an author function merely *did* not exist, Olsen reasoned, she just had to be invented.

Joan M. Jensen, writing in 1997, cataloged the string of fellowships Olsen received immediately following the publication of *Tell Me a Riddle* and deemed them "long overdue" (149). But consider Olsen's actual history: she received advances on a novel based on a single published excerpt; she was awarded a Stegner Fellowship prior to completing a single new work of short fiction; and she won a two-year Ford Foundation grant prior to completing her first book. This string of good fortune, had it benefited any other writer, would be deemed *premature*—quite accurately so in the case of the Random House advances, which the young author never delivered on. Olsen's career narrative is simply a mass of contradictions. Her enviable track record regarding institutional support cannot be denied—it is a matter of public record. Nor does Olsen hide her success as a grant recipient. In fact, the fellowships serve as a reminder that she should have been receiving support all along, even when she showed no interest in writing.

It is no surprise, then, that scholars are sometimes confused. Nolan Miller wrote in a sympathetic 1978 review of *Silences:* "There is a good reason for this writer's low production. For more than forty years she has been a wife and mother, a family wage-earner at dull and time-sapping menial jobs" (252). Miller had his facts wrong—Olsen's "menial" employment ended some twenty years prior to 1978—but he was correctly reporting the *spirit* of Olsen's book. To be fair to Miller, one could not sympathetically and faithfully summarize Olsen's thesis and still stick to the documentary record. The two are incompatible. And any honest attempt to reconcile the two risks indicting Olsen for squandering her singular talent and the numerous opportunities handed to her.

One of the few critics to issue an indictment is Doris Grumbach, who published a blistering front-page review of *Silences* in the *Washington Post Book World.* Olsen scholars generally acknowledge that initial reviews of *Silences* in the popular press were mixed or largely negative. Brigette Wilds Craft concluded in 1993 that critics were particularly displeased with the structure of the book (191) or what Karen L. Polster called Olsen's "experimental narrative form" (248). Summaries of the book's 1978 reception almost invariably cite a two-sentence mininotice by Phoebe-Lou Adams in the *Atlantic Monthly* that deemed Olsen's analysis "a discussion with more eloquence than logic" (96). Routinely passed over is Grumbach's extensive, wholesale rejection of what she calls "truly a terrible nonbook" (1). *Silences,* according to the flummoxed reviewer, was "a scrapbook of notes, half-digested ideas, 50 [*sic*] pages of quotations from other writers, bits and pieces from what [Olsen] calls 'unwritten talks' which are still unwritten as she heaps them on paper"—all of which is made more galling by Olsen's enviable record as a recipient of institutional largesse (1). What does this three-hundred-page "pasticcio" prove? Grumbach asked. "Nothing that we don't already know—that women writers have not been as plentiful as men due to a variety of cultural causes, [and] that this situation is righting itself (only the footnotes indicate that)" (4). She concluded her piece by faulting Olsen's tone, which she claimed hasn't changed in the twenty-two years since "I Stand Here Ironing" was first published. "It is still compounded of *kvetch,* self-pity, rationalization, and rage against patriarchic culture, men, the Fates. Such a wasteful, useless, synthetic book from the author of 'Tell Me a Riddle,'" she lamented. "A pity" (4).

Other critics also took issue with Olsen. Isa Kapp wondered why Olsen so vehemently decried the fact that Christina Stead, author of *The Man Who Loved Children,* had to work in a bank for a living when the job equipped her to write a novel about world banking (5–6). But no one else was as unshaded and wholesale as Grumbach in critiquing Olsen's general approach to the subject of impeded careers and authorial frustration. More often, reviewers voiced their misgivings about the writing while ultimately making goodwill gestures toward the project and its author.

Typically, Joyce Carol Oates found the book "marred by numerous inconsistencies and questionable statements offered as facts," yet allowed, "One feels the author's passion, and cannot help but sympathize with it" (248). In the *Nation,* Joan Peters called the book's argument "weak," its demands "extreme, almost silly" (282), but conceded that, "as a lament for lost art and for the struggles of artists, *Silences* is powerful" (281). Valerie Trueblood admitted that at first she quibbled with the book's repetitious argument and jumbled language, but she ultimately found herself coming under the book's spell (254). Similarly, Iris Tillman Hill debunked Olsen's utopian views (of a writing community freed from market considerations), yet she concluded that *Silences* was "a remarkable meditation on the conditions that make serious writing possible" and a "curious, compelling work" (958). And John Leonard, a friend of Olsen's assigned to review the book in the *New York Times,* found the text "worried" and "harried" by footnotes and a hodgepodge of undigested quotations, yet pronounced: "I've no doubt *Silences* will become an important text in women's studies programs at various colleges" (c15).

This ostensibly prescient observation was in fact an easy call. As Sandy Boucher observed, Olsen's two "unwritten" talks in mimeograph copies had by this time become "staples in the teaching of women's studies courses throughout the country" (29). After the talks' initial publication in journals, feminist scholarship in the United States began to take seriously "the roles of silence and anger in the lives and literary production of women," according to Deirdre Lashgari (1). More important, Olsen's reading lists of women writers and her direct intervention in the publishing industry set in motion a trend that made possible the realization of what Adrienne Rich, in her 1975 essay "Toward a Women-Centered University," called "a reorganization of knowledge, of perspectives and analytical tools that can help us know our foremothers" (141). Olsen convinced Florence Howe of the Feminist Press to redirect that organization's mission in the early 1970s away from producing short, biographical pamphlets about women of distinction and toward reissuing out-of-print works by women writers (Fishkin, "Reading" 27). She specifically initiated the republication of *Life in the Iron Mills*, Agnes Smedley's *Daughter of Earth*, and Charlotte Perkins Gilman's *Yellow Wallpaper;* the success of subsequent reissued Feminist Press works by dozens of other authors and the spread of similar lists to other publishing houses also followed from Olsen's example.

It is therefore no surprise, considering Olsen's impact on a burgeoning academic field and tandem developments in the field of publishing, that a book putting Olsen's pioneering talks between hard covers would be immediately recognized by some as indispensable to women's studies courses. In 1997, Karen L. Polster observed that "Olsen has become more well known for her inspiration to other women than for her own fiction" (243). The same probably held true already in 1978. Pearlman and Werlock, who had made an earlier pronouncement similar to Polster's—"Olsen is known and admired more because of what she represents than because of what she has written"—credited Olsen's "constant attention to those on the margins of society" with ennobling the author to other writers, in and out of academia: "This is her most powerful and empowering legacy" (xii–xiii). Elaine Hedges and Shelley Fisher Fishkin expanded this legacy from the personal to the professionally academic: "Olsen pioneered a whole new critical territory," they claimed (4). "The women's movement was making the case for taking women's experiences seriously," wrote Fishkin in a separate essay ("Reading" 25), "and here was Olsen handing out road maps on how to do just that in the study of literature."

The problem is that Olsen's road map led readers ultimately back to a single brutalized author, Tillie Olsen. "[T]he flaws of this book itself," a critic wrote of *Silences*, "testify to its reality" (review of *Silences, Yale Review* x). With such an enigmatic text, at least one reviewer who admired Olsen's short fiction, Grumbach, could dismiss the work as a travesty while others embraced its appearance as, in the words of Alix Kates Shulman, "an occasion for rejoicing" (528).

Books, particularly ones as politically freighted as *Silences,* can generate extreme responses, both positive and negative. But the responses to *Silences* often contained both extremes in a single review. As noted earlier, critics who admired Olsen's tenacity at arguing for the reclamation of other authors' works lauded the book yet also felt compelled to express misgivings about its abbreviated and jerky commentary, its lumpy text, its cryptic and strained language—all rhetorical gestures supporting Olsen's claim of having been silenced for two decades and permanently damaged as a result. Doris Grumbach alone chose to disregard Tillie Olsen, the powerful and laudable academic force, and focus instead on Tillie Olsen, the absurdly incoherent author. While other reviewers were merely uncomfortable with Olsen's "experimental narrative form," Grumbach came the closest to citing explicitly the self-imploding nature of Olsen's entire project. *Silences* was a meticulous tour de force of incoherence by an author ostensibly unable to produce meticulous work. But Grumbach's impolitic assertion that the empress had no clothes went unheeded, and the crowd of supplicants continued to voice their adoration for Olsen's imaginary garments—more loudly than before, in fact. "Despite antagonistic postures," Kay Hoyle Nelson observed of the book's reception, "critics did agree that *Silences* revitalized interest in Olsen" (15).

With an even less critical eye than the reviewers in the popular press, the community of feminist scholars, who were devoted to Olsen and supportive of her efforts to reshape the university curriculum, accepted Olsen's confused, self-contradictory career narrative unquestioningly. Yet the narrative details that should have cast doubt on the story's plausibility originated from a friendly source, Tillie Olsen, who has made herself widely available to scholars (Pratt 130), nearly all of whom thank the author profusely for the access afforded and assistance given to their work. Elaine Orr's acknowledgement is exemplary: "Tillie Olsen has talked with me, written letters, shared notes, stayed up late over the phone and in person. Her spirit and faith give me hope" (xi). Joanne S. Frye's acknowledgment is similarly effusive: "I owe my deepest gratitude to Tillie Olsen herself, for her openness in conversation, her generosity of spirit, her love of language. I am extraordinarily grateful for the many hours she contributed to the development of this project" (xv).

There is a twofold danger in this symbiotic relationship between scholar and subject. First, it permits the author to direct the scholarship examining her own writing. "Olsen herself is an active guide to the fractured nature of her own work," Janet Goodwyn observed in 1993 (74). "The best commentator on Olsen's fiction is Olsen herself," Deborah Rosenfelt concluded, discounting the perils of autointerpretation; "passages from *Silences* provide both a context for the writing of the fiction and a more direct articulation of many of its themes" ("*Tell Me*" 16). But the larger peril is rooted in the personal sympathy Olsen evokes. "Since her short story collection *Tell Me a Riddle* was published in 1961," Alix Kates Shulman wrote in a review of *Silences*, "Tillie Olsen has occupied a special place in the consciousness of American women writers" (527). Lydia A. Schultz observed in 1997 that women still treated Olsen with "reverential awe" (127). According to Blanche H. Gelfant (review of *Tillie Olsen* 237), the veneration Olsen receives has turned her into an "icon." And Orr explained in her monograph on Olsen that the author's artistic vision is "a resounding affirmation of life" (xiv), whereas the silence Olsen has combated her entire career is "a kind of death" (151). "To be circumstantially and historically denied the opportunity to create is a denial of sacred being," Orr further concluded, expanding the case for her subject's martyrdom to include possible deification (153). At the very least, Olsen can anticipate canonization: "Among women writers she is something of a saint," observed David Dillon (106). Novelist Alice Walker described Olsen as "a writer of such generosity and honesty, she literally saves lives" (14). And Jules Chametzky concluded in 1994, "'Tell Me a Riddle' has become almost a sacred text" (118).

The intimate relationship between Olsen and an admiring community of scholars and writers may have helped to facilitate individual research projects, but it thwarted the pursuit of objective scholarship. Gelfant acknowledged in a footnote to her 1984 essay: "This reading of 'Requa' is based upon a talk honoring Tillie Olsen. The occasion was a conference on women writers held by the New England College English Association at Wheaton College in October 1982. Tillie Olsen was the guest speaker" (214). Such an occasion does not facilitate careful, scholarly interrogation of a work that can be understood only in the context of a suspect author legend designed by the guest of honor. At times, Olsen has presented her early adulthood honestly—that is, she has acknowledged abandoning a promising writing career to perform political work and, subsequently, raise a family. But this theme is not developed in her primary texts; rather, it is secondary information offered to sympathetic scholars whose affection for Olsen only grows upon hearing of her commitment to political causes. Olsen does not own up to the contradiction of her story, nor do most scholars detect one. Instead, they contribute to the groundswell of Olsen hagiography.

"Olsen would be the first . . . to object vehemently to both the almost religious fervor of her followers and the exalted status that has been accorded her relatively small body of work," Pearlman and Werlock asserted (ix). But because Olsen herself spun the myth of the silenced author from which this veneration originates, one is inclined seriously to question that assertion. "Part of Olsen's present high reputation in America admittedly springs from her role as heroine of her own life," Helen McNeil observed (1,294). Olsen, in fact, has worked tirelessly and with intense focus for more than four decades to solidify her position as a heroine-author suffering from debilitating fatigue and a tragic inability to focus long enough to complete a work of fiction. The adulation she receives from scholars and critics helps to prolong the viability of this incongruous career narrative in the face of inconsistencies that would sink a text approached by more clear-eyed, less loyal readers.

So complete is Olsen's emphasis on the impediments to writing that perusal of contrasting views can be startling: assertions that the writing process is not utterly debilitating can be read as the irresponsible mishandling of material best left to the maligned and defeated. Patricia Highsmith offered the following common-sense advice in *Plotting and Writing Suspense Fiction*: "If you are trying to write while holding a job, it is important for you to have a certain length of time every day or every weekend which is sacred, and during which there are no interruptions. In a way, this is easier to arrange if you live with someone, because that person can answer a doorbell or a telephone" (76). Highsmith's statement may seem callous to those raising a family—Highsmith was childless—but her advice offers an interesting corrective to Tillie Olsen who, in *Silences*, demands financial subsidy for writers deemed deserving of support. (Deemed so by whom? Based on what criteria? It is never made clear.)

"Economics are always a problem, and writers are always preoccupied with it," explained Highsmith, "but this is part of the game. And the game has its rules: the majority of writers and artists must hold two jobs in their youth, a job to earn money and the job of doing their own work" (144). Following the success of *Strangers on a Train* (1950), Highsmith was able to support herself by writing, but she recounted that, in her twenties, she had to do her own writing in the evenings, because her "days were taken up with jobs or hack work" (51). The irony is that Highsmith, who was not the early beneficiary of a publisher's advance, stoically accepted the trap of double employment for a young author, whereas Tillie Olsen, who forfeited a subsidy, rails against the "rules" faced by most young artists and writers and claims she was silenced by them for decades.

A more startling voice in this context is that of Brenda Ueland—like Olsen, a single mother in the 1930s—who was forced to abandon a faltering freelance writing career in New York City at the height of the Depression and return to Minneapolis, where she wrote for local newspapers, published two books, and offered creative writing seminars through community organizations. She wrote of her teaching experience:

> I would say to the worn and hectored mothers in the class who longed to write and could find not a minute for it:
>
> "If you would shut your door against the children for an hour a day and say, 'Mother is working on her five-act tragedy in blank verse!' you would be surprised how they would respect you. They would probably all become playwrights."
>
> They look at me wistfully and know it is true. (*If You Want* 100)

This passage from 1938 reads like a provocative rebuttal to *Silences,* published forty years later. Olsen and Ueland, in fact, are at loggerheads on most issues involving money, writing, and women. For Ueland, who confessed to being a lazy freelance writer, poverty spurred productivity (*Me* 209). Marriage and family, at the root of Olsen's original two-decade silence, were for Ueland impediments one wisely shed or made accommodations for, though not at the expense of one's writing career (*Me* 185). In short, Olsen and Ueland espoused two very different forms of feminism. "In Olsen's feminism," Catherine R. Stimpson observed, "what binds women together is loss." Some women may be wealthy, others poor, but "all women can share a sense of violation of the potential self, of deprivation" (74). Already in the 1930s, Ueland espoused a feminism of plenitude, considered aggrieved feminism "old-fashioned," and said of the limitations faced by women: most are "our own making and not imposed on us" (*Me* 5).

My interest here is not the authors' contrasting points of view per se but rather the hugely divergent levels of interest in these two women within the academic community. Olsen, who has published a total of four completed works of short fiction, is the subject of more than a dozen scholarly monographs and other book-length studies and the object of intense sympathy and adulation. Ueland's output of published fiction and nonfiction is estimated to total between five and six million words (Perlman ix). She was the first woman reporter hired by the *Minneapolis Tribune* (Toth xiv), an early antivivisectionist and animal-rights advocate, the recipient of a Knights of St. Olaf medal from the Norwegian government, and a posthumously best-selling author, yet she remains a nonentity among academic feminists despite the fact that an extensive archive of her papers is conveniently housed at the Minnesota Historical Society. A search of the MLA Bibliography Database, admittedly an inexact science, yields 142 hits for the keywords "Tillie Olsen"—22 fewer than "Truman Capote" but 38 more than "Gore Vidal." A search for "Brenda Ueland" yields zero hits.

A partial explanation for Olsen's popularity among scholars lies in the quality of her fiction, which receives widespread praise inside and outside academia. In addition, her success stems from personal charisma. "Wherever Olsen goes," reported Marilyn Yalom, "her impact on the public is tremendous" (65). Most important, though, is the fact that Olsen has succeeded at both writing *and* embodying current theories about silenced female authors. This is a demanding task that Olsen has met by insisting on an association between herself and women who actually never had a chance to pursue writing as a career, and by involving herself directly in the shaping and presentation of Olsen scholarship, which might otherwise have seriously questioned her inclusion in that neglected group. The sympathy that academics naturally feel for underdog artists and a self-interest in their own professional advancement compel them to embrace Olsen's self-fulfilling narrative of defeat and silencing—embrace it so intensely, in fact, that it no longer matters that the text in question is self-contradictory. "Tillie Olsen is living proof of the death of craft," wrote Kay Mills, apparently missing the full extent of her own irony (3).

Olsen's is not the only case of a carefully designed yet utterly implausible author function enjoying public success. In 1993, Crown Publishing issued *A Rock and a Hard Place,* a harrowing memoir by a fifteen-year-old sexual-abuse victim named Anthony Godby Johnson. Now in its fifth printing, the book features an afterword by Fred Rogers, the late host of the PBS television series *Mister Rogers' Neighborhood,* and a glowing blurb on the jacket cover by best-selling novelist Armistead Maupin. Both Rogers and Maupin befriended the young author over the telephone, as did National Book Award–winning memoirist Paul Monette, who wrote the foreword to Johnson's book and who, like the ailing teen, suffered from AIDS. Monette, prior to his death in 1995, encouraged his young friend to go public with his horrific story of sexual abuse at the hands of a New York City policeman father and a sadistic ring of pedophile accomplices (Friend 89). Child abuse and pediatric AIDS were important issues that needed exposure, Monette reasoned, and a fifteen-year-old victim—a tested survivor—was the authentic, inspiring voice that could best bring them to the fore.

The problem was that no such person existed. "Anthony Godby Johnson" was an author function in its purest form. Following investigative journalistic pieces by Michele Ingrassia in *Newsweek* and, later, Tad Friend in the *New Yorker*, it became apparent that the teen author was the invention of a middle-aged woman who had always wanted to be a writer. She created Tony Johnson, then spent hundreds of hours on the telephone with Monette, Maupin, and other concerned celebrities impersonating him. It is she who wrote *A Rock and a Hard Place*.

Obviously, the parallels between Anthony Godby Johnson and Tillie Olsen are inexact, to say the least. There is an actual woman, born Tillie Lerner, who did stop producing fiction from the late 1930s to the early 1950s, as she claims. But the disparity between Tillie Olsen, the person who raised four daughters during the 1940s and has received institutional support ever since, and "Tillie Olsen," the author function who cataloged spirit-deadening setbacks suffered at the hands of the patriarchy, is so stark that it permits a useful comparison to Tony Johnson's story, especially in the particulars by which readers and admirers slipped into a state of denial when confronted with an increasingly implausible autobiography. As the litany of Tony's AIDS-related maladies expanded, a core of believers grew more staunch in defense of the story's veracity. Armistead Maupin had doubts but chose to proceed as if he did not. "I broke my brain down the middle," he explained (Friend 93).

In general, supporters of Tony Johnson believed they were aiding the fight against pediatric AIDS and defusing prejudice against the infected by remaining loyal to an obviously falsified story. A good deal of coercion went on behind the scenes as well. When approached by a journalist about the possibility of a hoax, David Groff, Tony Johnson's editor at Crown Publishing, sniffed, "To me, what's really interesting is how little people allow themselves to believe" (Friend 89). A friend of the disguised author made the key point more explicitly. "If a journalist discredits Tony's experiences," she charged, "he does the same for hundreds of others" (Friend 98). That is, he does so for children who actually do exist, who actually do suffer from AIDS. This appears to have been the reasoning of Paul Monette, whose repeated requests to meet with Tony in person were rebuffed, but who remained loyal to the utterly implausible story until his death. His companion at the time, Winston Wilde, told Friend that Monette defended Tony out of love, and because he worried about appearing to have been duped; but, Wilde added, Monette also believed the voice of a child with AIDS was important for people to hear "even if it might be fiction" (92).

That statement usefully summarizes the reasoning of an entire community of feminist scholars who have been moved and inspired by a survivor named

Tillie Olsen whose autobiographical story seems dubious in many of its particulars. They have developed a great deal of personal affection for Olsen, they fear exposure of their own gullibility (and the discrediting of their previous scholarship), and they hold the broader phenomenon of silenced women writers to be of paramount importance. If they are required to issue what are in effect public declarations of allegiance to a fraudulent story, so be it. To question Tillie Olsen on the veracity of her autobiographical statements would mean discrediting millions of other women who have suffered much worse.

Not surprisingly, there exist works of literary theory that, while not addressing Olsen specifically, guide scholars toward respecting dubiously constructed author functions as long as they are gendered female. The reason for this is obvious: as Linda Wagner-Martin commented to Fishkin, "It would be hard to find a feminist critic [of our generation] who was not influenced in key ways by *Silences*" ("Reading" 31). Moreover, feminist scholars sometimes place themselves within Olsen's category of victimized authors. "Scholars, like other writers, face the same problems of silencing," claimed Joan M. Jensen in 1997. "They usually must teach to support themselves and their families" (148). It follows, then, that members of the academic community would allow fiction writers considerable leeway in shaping their autobiographical narratives: they are all in it together.

In her essay "Arachnologies: The Woman, the Text, and the Critic," Nancy K. Miller took exception to arguments presented in several works by Roland Barthes (not merely "The Death of the Author" and "From Work to Text," but also *The Pleasure of the Text* and *S/Z*) and, in the process, encouraged scholars, critics, and readers to accept career narratives *by women* regardless of their suspect composition. She stated that "the 'Death of the Author' himself"— the only instance in which Miller used a masculine pronoun generically—is "in so many ways, long overdue" (271). But she objected to the erasure of the female author.

Miller applied to Barthes's writings an earlier criticism of Jacques Derrida's work by Gayatri Chakravorty Spivak. In "Displacement and the Discourse of Women," Spivak summarized her attitude toward Derrida's deconstructive theories thus: "[F]irst, deconstruction is illuminating as a critique of phallocentrism; second, it is convincing as an argument against the founding of a hysterocentric to counter a phallocentric discourse" (184). But if a scholar's mission is specifically to found a hysterocentric discourse, her relationship to deconstruction necessarily will be confrontational, no matter how warmly she welcomes its usefulness as a method for critiquing phallocentrism. The same applies to Miller's relationship to Barthes's theory of the text. Miller used Spivak's phrase "double displacement" to describe Barthes's process by which the author, male or female, is erased and replaced by a process of textual examination performed by male critics—Barthes, Foucault, Derrida—using ostensibly genderless but actually male-gendered signifiers. Lost in the process, then, is our admiration for the female author.

This is especially alarming in Olsen's case because, minus admiration for the author, there is precious little there. And the text that does exist (Olsen's *silences*) withers under scrutiny unless fortified by a cult of admiration for the author. Some admirers are tempted to allow Olsen as much flexibility in constructing her author legend as one allows a novelist plotting a work of fiction. A sense of entitlement and simple fair play is at work here: Jack London, once a bookish boy, sold himself to the public as a rugged outdoorsman; Ernest Hemingway, a careerist who cut a trail of personal disloyalty to facilitate his professional advancement, managed to refashion himself as a self-sacrificing friend and colleague who valued art and loyalty above all else. One could argue it is high time Tillie Olsen and other female authors were permitted to write a personal narrative that is similarly self-serving. But there are numerous problems with that argument, beyond the fact that male authors are now subject to much harsher scrutiny than they were eighty or one hundred years ago.

First, Tillie Olsen's case is unlike any other. The contents of *A Moveable Feast* may not jibe with all the facts, but nowhere does its author insist that the book we are holding never got written. In the case of Hemingway, London, or other authors who manipulate the details of their lives, we can refute the veracity of their narratives through inductive reasoning, while Olsen's narrative refutes itself, deductively.

More important, though, is the plausibility of Olsen's identity as a pioneering truth teller. In her essays, according to Elaine Orr, Olsen seeks "to tell the truth about silences, the breaks, absences, and discontinuities in literature and history" that tell us something about the circumstances of lives spent in menial work or parenting. "Olsen is concerned with the truthful depiction of such lives in order that political and cultural change occur," Orr explained (145–46). And she offered a definition: "We can say that for Tillie Olsen truth is whatever understanding or insight leads to a more inclusive, more coherent, more fruitful way of living" (161).

I don't take issue with Orr's definition of truth as it applies to Olsen; but I feel compelled to point out that this definition conflicts with a more conventional one, which holds that truth is the representation of events as they actually happened. We have a long tradition in our slave narratives of authors inventively shaping or acquiring details for their autobiographies in order to undermine the system of slavery and, in turn, bring about "a more inclusive, more coherent, more fruitful way of living." If one had been brutalized by a slave owner for what seemed a very long time, one might claim the brutalization lasted seven years, to give the text biblical resonance. Or, if one had heard of another slave who was brutalized, one might claim that brutalization as one's own. One did this to further the abolitionist cause, not to qualify for fellowships and grants or attain the status of a major author. I'm not convinced that the ends justify the means in Olsen's case. In fact, I'm not even certain the chosen means assist the achievement of the desired ends.

"Tawana told the truth" reads a line of street graffiti in Spike Lee's 1989 film *Do the Right Thing*. The text refers to Tawana Brawley, a Wappinger, New York, teenager who fabricated a story of physical and sexual assault at the hands of six white law-enforcement officials in 1987. The implication of the graffiti is that, though discredited in a literal sense, Brawley's accusations spoke of a larger and more valuable truth about our culture. But few would argue that, in the aftermath of the episode, sympathy was generated for victims of racist police brutality. Rather, the incident cast doubt on the veracity of future claims.

Such may be the legacy of Olsen's works, though her story has shown amazing resilience so far. Even a reviewer of *Silences* who deemed the book dangerously solipsistic, annoying, tedious, and limited in scope, depth, and credibility reported, "When, in the 'fifties, [Olsen] finally found scant time to write, her energy and imagination had diminished" (review of *Silences, Yale Review* vi). Thus, the most incredulous critics still repeat almost verbatim Olsen's claims of permanent authorial damage even though Olsen's text of silence features a meticulous design that one could reasonably assume required considerable artistic stamina and undiminished talent. The power of Olsen's narrative to defy academic scrutiny, despite its obvious contradictions, is perhaps attested to most succinctly in the comments of Elizabeth A. Meese, who deemed Olsen a talented writer who "refuses to impose coherence as a way of achieving the conventional unicentered voice one expects in a book." As a result, "the interpretive dilemma grows more complex," Meese conceded. But not too complex, for in the end, she concluded, "it matters little whether Olsen won't or can't order her words" (109–10).

Of course, it matters greatly whether Olsen *won't* order her words—and freely elects to appear incoherent and impaired—or *can't* order her words, which implies a legacy from past suffering. It determines, in fact, whether Olsen is primarily an opportunist or a victim.

But, indeed, it has mattered little to those scholars who share Olsen's professed passion for "documenting the experiences of those who cannot tell their own stories" (Fishkin, "Borderlands" 152). Like Armistead Maupin, such scholars seem to have broken their brains down the middle. For decades, a polite silence was observed toward Olsen's obvious manipulation of her own personal history. Only since 1990 or so have admirers of Olsen finally begun to question the author's willful retreat from writing. Even so, as Kay Hoyle Nelson observed, "their speculations rarely emerge as a discernible thread in the critical record" (4). Gestures toward dismantling Tillie Olsen's career narrative have been at best tentative and fitful.

In the introduction to their 1991 monograph *Tillie Olsen*, Pearlman and Werlock promised to challenge extant criticism and scholarship that they found "so adulatory that it impedes rather than enhances a straightforward understanding and appreciation of [Olsen's] work" (ix–x). They specifically sought to question why Olsen was not forthcoming about events in her life since the publication of "Requa" that might explain why she had completed no new fiction since 1970. Gelfant was even more direct the following year: "What remains inexplicable is why Olsen did not write, or write more productively, during the interims in which she was supported by prestigious national fellowships and grants to artists' colonies" (review of *Silences* 236). But Gelfant's important observation is one minor remark included in a review of Pearlman and Werlock's book. It is not the thesis of a scholarly article comparable to her 1984 piece "After Long Silence: Tillie Olsen's 'Requa' "—an example of the sort of adulatory scholarship that impedes rather than enhances a straightforward understanding of Olsen's work. As for Pearlman and Werlock's promise to investigate the suspicious aspects of Olsen's silence, it went unkept. As Mark A. Bernheim noted in his review of their book, Pearlman and Werlock fell into the familiar trap of unreservedly praising their subject (236). Janet Goodwyn concurred: "In their introduction [Pearlman and Werlock] seek to discriminate between the critics, good and bad, who have created the climate of 'reverence' in which Olsen's work is read. However, from the very beginning of their study they fall victim to the critical difficulty of assimilating and moving beyond such 'reverence' " (744).

The reviewers I've cited—Bernheim, Goodwyn, Gelfant—would seem to welcome a reassessment of Olsen's career if one were possible. But production of such a reassessment is blocked by the reticence of scholars who rely on Olsen's cooperation to conduct their research, and who must answer to a larger community of protective scholars who hold Olsen's narrative as sacrosanct. Fishkin recounted in 1994 how, in the spring of 1990, several of her graduate students, both male and female, raised objections to Olsen's whiny tone and "the spirit of rhapsodic self-pity" that pervades her prose ("Reading" 34). "Two years earlier," she added, "I heard similar comments from a prominent feminist critic I had interviewed who did not wish to be cited by name" (39). In other words, such critical observations are voiced, but they rarely face, let alone pass, peer review except as anecdotal asides in essays that are otherwise sufficiently adulatory.

Typically, in *Protest and Possibility in the Writing of Tillie Olsen*, Mara Faulkner questioned the authenticity of Olsen's author legend. "Why has Olsen apparently not claimed the power of written language these past fifteen years?" she asked in 1993 (138). But Faulkner ultimately backed down, providing the obligatory honorifics of conventional Olsen scholarship. Perhaps Nora Ruth Roberts has come closest to questioning Olsen's story in an unfettered fashion in a study of Olsen, Meridel Le Sueur, and Josephine Herbst called *Three Radical Women Writers*. "None of the factors indicated in *Silences* or developed in the most useful biographical writings on Olsen seem sufficient to explain her rather enigmatic career," Roberts wrote in 1996 with no caveats or hand wringing over the implications of such a statement (75). "Clearly, she had early on been given the opportunities many young writers cried out for" (76).

But the following year, an issue of the journal *Frontiers* collected six articles about Olsen that suggest that the author's direct involvement still impedes inquiry into her work and career. The six essays were first given as talks at a joint meeting of the Western Literature Association and the Western History Association, with Olsen in attendance. The written manuscripts were then submitted to Olsen for a response prior to publication. According to Linda Ray Pratt, the six *Frontiers* articles "point to some of the new directions that scholars are pursuing" in Olsen scholarship (133), but none of the scholars was impolite enough to press Olsen on the bothersome aspects of her author legend. Upon reading the six articles, Olsen was overwhelmed with gratitude and reduced to tears; in her "Response," she expressed love, honor, and esteem for the six scholars (159). One can appreciate the emotional rewards gained by producing scholarship that venerates a grateful elderly woman. But it is every scholar's obligation to approach all authors, male or female, young or old, in a manner suitable for serious academic inquiry, and to read all varieties of texts, even deliberate silence—*especially* deliberate silence—with a clear eye and a willingness to hold the artist to minimum standards of coherence, plausibility, and basic logic.

CHAPTER TWO   Henry Roth's Second
High-Modernist Masterpiece

Following the republication of Henry Roth's 1934 novel *Call It Sleep* in 1960 and the popular success of the 1964 paperback edition, a saga grew around the book and its author that was itself a compelling narrative. But the story was not in every respect true to the facts. Certain elements could not be easily altered: Roth's Communist Party membership; his lapse into silence after the 1930s; his relocation from New York City to Maine and subsequent employment in such diverse fields as precision machine drilling, mental health care, and waterfowl farming; and the unusual reclamation of Roth's one early novel nearly three decades after its original publication. Other elements, however, could be constructed, omitted, or shaded in various ways, and it is precisely those processes that make Roth's second book, *Shifting Landscape* (1987), such an interesting study.

Shifting Landscape turns the silence of an unproductive author into a conventional and more accessible text by placing it conveniently between hard covers; it thereby provides the author with a collated narrative for a professional literary career that never took place. That this would be the purpose of *Shifting Landscape* is made overt in the book's opening pages, first by Roth in his foreword and then by editor Mario Materassi in his introduction to this compilation of everything Roth published before and after *Call It Sleep*, up to 1987. Roth stated that he gave his consent to this project only after he realized its purpose: "Nothing less really than to exhibit the continuity within the desolating discontinuity over all those barren years" (xiii). Materassi expanded on this: "The first objective of *Shifting Landscape* is, of course, to provide the reader with the totality of Henry Roth's publications. The second objective, as the title suggests, is to offer as detailed a picture as possible of the evolution of Roth's views on his dominant interests—namely, writing, literature, family, politics, and Judaism" (xvi). This evolution of views is normally made available to the public when an author publishes at regular intervals. But Roth's publication history was irregular, to say the least (a gap of fifty-three years between books, gaps of five and ten years between magazine articles), and some of the pieces Roth *had* published were inaccessible to even the most determined scholar. Little critical attention has been paid to some of these short works; the danger in that, Materassi warned, is that "having based our studies of *Call It Sleep* and its author upon an incomplete knowledge of his production, we have risked making inaccurate assumptions and, therefore, arriving at dubious conclusions" (xv).

Though the purpose of the book is clearly stated, there is ambiguity regarding who the progenitor of the text really was. Leslie Fiedler described the collection as "ghostedited to be sure, if not quite ghostwritten" ("Many Myths" 17). Roth generously concurred in his foreword: "The book is primarily Mario's, not mine" (xiv). It was Materassi who "assembled the fragments," Roth reported, though the fragments originated from Roth's pen.

If Materassi assumed greater responsibility on this project than is usual for an editor of a book by a living writer, a plausible explanation for this is offered in the text. The book, Roth said, is "a sketch of an ambivalent and often anguished period." He therefore credited Materassi with accomplishing something the novelist was unable to accomplish himself due to the disabling discontinuity that the book chronicles. Materassi did this, Roth said, by constructing "a connective tissue" (xiv), referring not only to passages from letters and interviews published over the previous twenty years but also to excerpts from taped conversations conducted by Materassi within the previous half decade, all of which separately frame Roth's thirty-one collected pieces. For his part, Materassi claimed that he chose to construct the book this way in order to let Roth "do it in his own words" (Dickstein, "Call It" 35) and said that the magazine pieces and the connective tissue together result in "an informal autobiographical discourse" (introduction xvi).

It would seem, though, that Roth, with basic editorial assistance, could have assembled a conventional collection himself, once his earliest and most obscure works had been tracked down. (Or he could reasonably have chosen to leave out the esoterica.) But the logic of *Shifting Landscape* requires the appearance of extensive editorial intervention. Roth could not be seen delivering, by himself, a creative reworking of "the widespread collapse of creativity" he suffered during the decades in question. Such a text would not make sense—not yet.

Evidence of independent achievement by the author would have become a distraction; the text as a whole would have less usefully aided our understanding of Roth's career after *Call It Sleep* was published if Roth had been seen doing the work himself. And providing a clear understanding of that career is the purpose of the Materassi/Roth collection. Rather than distracting the reader, the fragmented tapestry of Roth excerpts, cut and pasted by Materassi, serves as a structural reminder of the text's main agenda (demonstrating continuity in the discontinuity) and gives it added resonance.

The general critical response to *Shifting Landscape* was one of fascination and deep respect. As Leonard Michaels put it, Roth is "far more interesting in his meditations on failure and sterility" than most writers are when they talk about their productive and successful careers (19). One dissenting voice, though, was that of Elaine Kendall in the *Los Angeles Times*. Reporting that "this miscellany could have benefited from more rigorous editing," Kendall missed the point entirely that the collection was edited all too rigorously. Kendall charged Materassi with including much that is "trivial, mundane or so rudimentary that the effect of the whole is diminished" (12). But diminishment, of course, may have been the intended effect. Even more forceful in expressing her distaste for the project and its stated purpose was Donna Rifkind in the *New Criterion*. "I find it hard to understand how development can occur in a writing career that has not happened," she bluntly concluded (76).

Both Roth and Materassi were aware that *Shifting Landscape* was a grab bag of sorts. In his foreword, Roth reported that, at first, he saw no reason for publishing "a bunch of random pieces of various literary value, and some with no pretense at all" (xiii). Materassi admitted in his introduction to including "certain minor pieces" written for "a public not necessarily literary" in nature and meant to serve "an ad hoc purpose" (xviii). Though neither writer singled out any specific piece by title, both must have been referring to a do-it-yourself article on the slaughtering of waterfowl called "Equipment for Pennies," originally published in the trade journal *The Magazine for Ducks and Geese*, and two pieces of juvenilia: an assignment for Roth's freshman composition class at CCNY, and a critical piece on the playwright Lynn Riggs, which Roth described as "an undergraduate-level attempt at literary analysis." ("Don't blame me," Roth wrote in a 1986 letter to his editor and friend. "How did I know in 1929, when I wrote the 'critique,' that Mario Materassi would some day single-mindedly scour every obscure niche and cranny of the abode with feather and wooden spoon, in order to retrieve any crumb with the least leavening in it that chances to escape the fire?" [12].)

Also included are a story ("Many Mansions") long forgotten by Roth but "properly reinstated in the Roth canon" by Materassi, which Roth himself dismissed as "a bit of fluff" (73); an essay ("Prolog im Himmel") that Materassi described as "an apparently haphazard collage of snatches from a journal" (178); and a statement of purpose for a National Institute of Arts and Letters grant application.

Padding the book further is the connective tissue of interview and letter excerpts, which, grouped around each piece, sometimes fill twice as many pages as the text proper. The very first excerpt, preceding "Impressions of a Plumber," runs in part: "By the time I got [to City College], there were no longer any English courses open. The second half, I had a choice ahead of the incoming freshmen, so I took English One, which was a requirement—Composition One, or . . . what the hell was it called? I think it was Composition One" (3). And on and on the excerpts go.

And yet, in his introduction, Materassi insisted that he intended the book as a corrective, to draw critical attention away from what Roth had *failed* to do toward "what he had actually accomplished"—those instances when he broke his silence (xvi). But this is where the absurdity of this text seems most carefully underscored. It is a persistently self-denigrating work: it purports to reinstate unfairly neglected pieces of writing to the Roth canon, but it features those pieces in a format that makes them seem inadequate and deserving of neglect (the "connective tissue" implies the articles cannot stand on their own). It makes inflated claims for the essays and fiction, then calls them precious "bits of fluff" and "crumbs" behind their backs, so to speak.

This is not to suggest that *Shifting Landscape* fails its subject. This paradoxical text serves the author in at least four vital ways. In addition to composing a career narrative for a man who had not actually had a career as a professional writer, the book instructs us how to read *Call It Sleep* "correctly," as an exemplary work of high modernism. This in turn affects our reading of Roth's silence as well: it, too, is a deep, complex work apparently influenced by the Joyce of *Ulysses* and the Eliot of *The Waste Land*. And finally—notwithstanding Materassi's explicit claims to the contrary—the contents of *Shifting Landscape* attest to the fact that Roth had been an essentially "dead" author for decades, which is meant to prepare us for the newly productive author's triumphant resurrection through delayed publication of his multivolume "memoir-form novel," *Mercy of a Rude Stream,* which is excerpted here. Offered as evidence of Roth's neglected productivity, *Shifting Landscape* actually clarifies Roth's nearly complete immobilization, and yet it promises that the era of literary frustration has finally come to an end.

The practice of commodifying frustration and silence by assembling minor, fragmented, or incomplete works under an author's name took on urgency once theorists announced the demise of the author figure. "What difference does it make who is speaking?" Michel Foucault asked rhetorically at the conclusion of "What Is an Author?" (120). For the silent author, it makes all the difference in the world. Having no conventional works to offer for publication, a silent author who lacks a public identity fails to leave a trail of texts and ceases to exist.

Addressing the problem of how to define an author's oeuvre, Foucault wrote:

> When undertaking the publication of Nietzsche's works, for example, where should one stop? Surely everything must be published, but what is "everything"? Everything that Nietzsche himself published, certainly. And what about the rough drafts for his works? Obviously. The plans for his aphorisms? Yes. The deleted passages and the notes at the bottom of the page? Yes. What if, within a workbook filled with aphorisms, one finds a reference, the notation of a meeting or of an address, or a laundry list: Is it a work, or not? Why not? And so on, ad infinitum. How can one define a work amid the millions of traces left by someone after his death? A theory of the work does not exist. (103–4)

In the case of a silent author, those millions of traces—the laundry lists and marginalia—are all we have. It is imperative, in practice, that a theory of the work include them. And it is a professionally astute maneuver to collect those traces into a book if one is planning to end one's silence. Without this act of consolidation, the shaping of the author's years of confusing desuetude is out of the author's control to an uncomfortable degree.

There are dissenters, of course. Donna Rifkind viewed Roth's sad story as a tragedy with a villain. "That villain is perversity," she explained, "and it thrives in too many hangers-on of the literary world who pant for some literature to publish—who will go so far as to create an oeuvre for an author where one has never existed" (76). In her review of *Shifting Landscape*, Rifkind dumped buckets of scorn on Materassi for forcing Roth into "producing material about why he was unable to produce material," which, she correctly noted, comprises the bulk of the book. Treading inadvertently on Foucault's observations about the difficulty of defining what qualifies as an author's work, Rifkind continued: "[*Shifting Landscape*] is a book composed entirely of false starts, notes, scribbles, second-rate stories, transcribed interviews, endless explanations of and mediations on writer's block—everything, in short, except actual literary achievement. One would be moved to laugh at this bizarre enterprise were it not for the fact that the victim of this fraud, Henry Roth, is a figure worthy of respect, and his misfortunes are not funny" (75).

Foucault's methods on this matter were empirical. He stated that certain modes of discourse in our civilization are endowed with an author while other, lesser modes are deprived of it. "A private letter may well have a signer—it does not have an author," he claimed; "a contract may well have a guarantor—it does not have an author. An anonymous text posted on a wall probably has a writer—but not an author" (107–8). Rifkind, on the other hand, offered a prescriptive variant of the same point: trivial genres *should not* be misrepresented as significant works worthy of attribution. They *should not* have an author. One cannot disprove Rifkind's point exactly—it is an opinion. But Foucault's observation clearly does not hold in this case: all modes of discourse are afforded official sanction by the silent author Henry Roth; none is deprived of that privileged connection.

That Henry Roth's silence was read at all was largely beyond Roth's control. A truly silent writer—a writer who produces nothing his entire life—gains no recognition; therefore, he has no legend, and his silence is not a work of literature. For silence to be disseminated as a text that is read, studied, and discussed, it needs a notable beginning—in Roth's case, the publication of a masterwork, a classic novel. This was also the case for Ralph Ellison. But because *Call It Sleep* slipped out of the general literary consciousness, and out of print, for twenty-five years, Roth's masterwork needed reclamation before his silence could take shape as a literary text, whereas Ellison's literary silence commenced a few years after the publication of *Invisible Man*, when expectations for a second novel first began to go unmet. The reclamation of *Call It Sleep*, however, was not primarily Roth's doing—it was, in fact, a source of puzzlement to the author. "How was it that I should be singled out?" Roth asked in a taped interview from 1986 (*Shifting* 20). Reflecting on the fact that he had run with a crowd that included many brilliant 1920s and 1930s intellectuals more talented than himself (including Hart Crane, Léonie Adams, Mark Van Doren, and Margaret Mead), Roth concluded that it must have been by mere chance that he felt the vibration of the time more accurately than many others and tapped into it so successfully. For that reason, he figured, his novel resonated.

But what accounts for the emergence of Roth's silence as a text is the fact that his novel resonated with readers in the mid-1960s and vibrated with that time, not with its own. "It is hard to believe that so complete a withdrawal resulted from the sudden loss of so abundant and varied a talent," Marie Syrkin observed in 1961; "it may have been rather a loss of faith. This, however, is pure conjecture excused only by a nagging desire to understand a mystery of the creative life" (93). Three years before Roth's republished novel became a bestseller, his silence was already teasing and troubling readers and goading critics into offering conjectural explanations for his writer's block. It is not difficult to understand why Roth's story generated interest. His disappearance from the literary world seemed far fetched, even freakish. As the elderly Ira Stigman, the autobiographical narrator of Roth's late tetralogy, *Mercy of a Rude Stream,* succinctly puts it: "There should have followed novels written in the maturity gained by that first novel" (*Star Shines* 52). But none did. The newly rediscovered Roth was a one-novel writer unlikely ever to publish again, and he was all the more fascinating for that reason.

The readership for *Call It Sleep* grew in number from the hundreds to the hundreds of thousands within weeks of the 1964 release of the novel's Avon paperback edition, which went on to sell more than a million copies. Key to the reprint's unexpected and unprecedented success was an adulatory notice on the front page of the *New York Times Book Review,* in which Irving Howe expressed hope that the novel would "finally gain the public it deserved" ("Life" 1)—something close to a self-fulfilling prophecy. The 1960 Pageant Books hardcover edition of *Call It Sleep* formally launched the legend of Roth's unique silence among literary scholars, but Howe's 1964 review brought both the novel and that legend to a much wider audience and helped to make Roth something of a celebrity, as did Jane Howard's *Life* magazine feature "The Belated Success of Henry Roth," published on 8 January 1965, just as *Call It Sleep* was climbing the paperback bestseller list. As Steven G. Kellman put it, Roth "suddenly became famous for being unknown" (76). For his part, Roth admitted to having felt like Lazarus suddenly raised from the dead (*Shifting* 291).

From the mid-1960s on, Roth more actively contributed to the construction of his own singular legend as a silent writer. In letters and occasional works of short fiction, essays, memoirs, and interviews published over the next twenty years, Roth recalled his crippling frustration at not being able to follow *Call It Sleep* with a second book, and he expressed hope that he might one day do so. That Harold M. Ribalow in 1962 deemed Roth an author "satisfied to have produced his one novel" seems curious if not outright suspect now, in light of Roth's subsequent outpouring of anguish over his inability to continue producing publishable work ("Henry Roth" 14). But initially, Roth reacted to the renewed interest in *Call It Sleep* with reticence and barely concealed resentment at the disruption of his nonliterary life in Maine (*Shifting* 131–32). Roth's letters to Ribalow at the time underplayed the freakishness of his predicament, while emphasizing his contentedness and the imposition posed by celebrity. In subsequent writings and interviews published in the *New Yorker,* the *Atlantic, Commentary,* the *New York Times, Shenandoah,* and other journals, however, Roth expounded on his lapse into nonproductivity and its possible causes.

It is useful here to reflect again on Foucault's notion of the author function—the literary collective responsible for the reception of an author's texts—to review precisely who offered Henry Roth's silence to the public as a work of literature. Initially, at least, it seems to be less the work of Henry Roth, the flesh-and-blood man, than the collaborative effort of "Henry Roth," which comprised critics Alfred Kazin, Leslie Fiedler, and Walter B. Rideout, who in the 1950s placed *Call It Sleep* on the radar screen for the first time in over twenty years; Harold M. Ribalow and Charles Angoff, whose maneuvering behind the scene helped bring the novel back into print; publishers Chap Chafetz and Sid Solomon at Pageant Books, and Peter Mayer and Frank Taylor at Avon, who took on the project "mostly as a labor of love" (Lyons, *The Man* 29); reviewers and journalists such as Marie Syrkin, Irving Howe, and Jane Howard; and even Howe's editor at the *New York Times Book Review,* who made the unprecedented decision to run a review of a paperback reprint on page 1.

But Roth himself, beginning with the pieces "At Times in Flight: A Parable" (1959) and "The Dun Dakotas" (1960) and continuing through a series of essays and interviews over the following decades, contributed to the mature rendering of his legend as a silenced writer. Though Roth's Italian translator, Mario Materassi, edited the pieces in *Shifting Landscape* and shaped them into an intricate collage of contradictory texts and excerpts of texts, Roth provided nearly all the raw material. (If parallels emerge with Ezra Pound's reshaping of Eliot's *Waste Land* manuscript, so much the better.) *Shifting Landscape* hones Roth's biography and reconstructs his career narrative by emphasizing various social and personal causes of Roth's silence: the book includes passages in which the author attributed his writer's block to a single cause—his loss of a nurturing, homogenous Jewish milieu at age eight or his membership in the Communist Party—but at the same time it places those passages in a context that reshapes Roth's entire literary output sans *Call It Sleep* into a matrix of competing ideas and explanations. Roth offered a variety of hypotheses throughout his published articles and his letters—Materassi was not making these quotes up. But *Shifting Landscape* reshuffles these passages so as to dilute the strength of any single hypothesis. More so than in any individual essay or interview, the cacophony of ideas *is* the idea.

The irony here is that beginning in 1979—eight years before *Shifting Landscape* appeared, and six years before Materassi involved himself in the project—Roth began drafting a massive manuscript that would offer a different explanation for his disappearance from the literary scene. This work of thinly disguised fiction would overtly suggest and, by its sheer weight, implicitly confirm that the real reason Roth lapsed into silence sprang directly from the author's history of sexually abusing his sister, beginning when she was ten years old and he was twelve, and later his cousin, beginning when she was thirteen. The only way finally to break the silence, the elderly Roth suggested, was to come clean, at which point the pages would flow.

Roth seems to have allowed Materassi to compile a book that usefully shaped Roth's biography and legend, knowing full well that he, Roth, would eventually offer a much more significant series of books largely debunking his own prior statements and musings and, in the process, undermining Materassi's efforts to construct a definitive career narrative for the author. The final posthumous revision of Roth's legend would be the novelist's own, or so he must have thought. But as chapter 3 documents, the revised version of Roth's legend was soundly rejected by the literary community.

"Nineteen thirty-four began with a major event in publishing, the first American edition of Joyce's *Ulysses*," wrote A. Sydney Knowles Jr. in a 1965–66 essay in *Modern Fiction Studies,* one of the first scholarly articles on Roth to appear in the wake of *Call It Sleep*'s popular resurgence. "When *Call It Sleep* was published eleven months later," Knowles continued, "reviewers were struck by similarities between the novels" (396).

No, they were not. The vast majority of reviewers acknowledged no role for Joyce in Roth's writing—that would come later, with coaching from the author. Bonnie Lyons in 1984 summed up more accurately than Knowles the critical reception to the December 1934 publication of *Call It Sleep*. The novel received remarkably adulatory reviews, she reported, but particularly noteworthy was the wide variety of things the critics found to praise, including the novel's "realism, vision, use of language, characterization, and plot" (*Twentieth Century*

260). H. W. Boynton was impressed by the book's "dramatic balance" (7). Paul Wren singled out the powerful sense of detail (82). Even Joseph Gollomb in a negative review praised Roth's "sensitive ear for speech" and his gift for photographic verisimilitude (552). Roth's ability to enter the mind of a young child received almost unanimous praise.

So thoroughly have the aesthetic criteria of modernism come to dominate the reception of literature today that when we hear a novel praised for its dramatic balance and verisimilitude, its strong characters and expressive language, we often interpret that to mean the book is a successful work in the modernist tradition. But that does not seem to have been the intention of the majority of reviewers responding to *Call It Sleep* in the mid-1930s. They praised Roth not because he eschewed Dreiserian techniques or the conventions of Michael Gold's proletarian fiction for the higher calling of modernism; rather, they praised Roth because they believed he perfected those techniques and transcended those conventions through talent and craft.

It follows, then, that the renewal of interest in *Call It Sleep* in the late 1950s owed less to Roth's high-modernist influences than to the novel's stain of association with proletarian fiction. In *The Radical Novel in the United States* (1956), Walter B. Rideout grouped *Call It Sleep* with nine other books that he felt were excellent and durable literary achievements (287). His point seems to be that even a good novel can qualify as proletarian fiction, including a novel as good as *Call It Sleep*. (Modernism and proletarian fiction were understood to be mutually exclusive categories.) In an article that appeared in *American Jewish Archives* in 1959, Rideout gave a more detailed account of what makes Roth's novel noteworthy: it has "a complex and powerful symbolic structure"; the language is effortlessly precise; and, taken together, the book's strengths give the reader an accurate sense of a child's inner and outer world ("O Workers" 169). One could argue that the book's widely praised verisimilitude is owed in part to the Joycean stream-of-consciousness technique Roth sometimes employed. But this is not what Rideout chose to underscore as he prepared the reading public for the book's reappearance. Even the book's most Joycean section, the penultimate chapter in which young David Schearl is knocked unconscious by a jolt from the trolley line's third rail, was praised by Rideout for its revolutionary fervor. Rather than associate the diverse cacophony of voices that David overhears with high-modernist experimentation, Rideout emphasized the proletarian nature of individual snippets of dialogue, claiming those are what made the passage worthy of notice. In this manner the critical community of the late 1950s was predisposed to read *Call It Sleep* as a politically "radical" novel.

In "Henry Roth's Neglected Masterpiece," a 1960 essay announcing the imminent republication of *Call It Sleep,* Leslie Fiedler commenced the necessary campaign to disassociate Roth's work from didactic proletarian novels such as Edward Dahlberg's *Bottom Dogs* or Clara Weatherwax's *Marching! Marching!* There is little social consciousness manifest in Roth's book, Fiedler observed. "If there is a class struggle and a revolutionary movement, these are revealed only in an overheard scrap of soapbox oratory at the climax of the novel, where they seem singularly irrelevant to the passion and suffering of Roth's child hero who is living through that climax" (103). Once again, the novel's penultimate chapter—the orgy of ultramodern stylizations—was cited as evidence of the author's social commitment. For Rideout, the chapter was crowning proof of the entire work's proletarian credentials, whereas Fiedler merely conceded that this one section contains some incongruous, politically charged language. He refuted the novel's general classification as Marxist or revolutionary. Neither critic cited the influence of Joyce.

Fiedler's piece was the first among many to realign *Call It Sleep* with a Jewish tradition in American literature, rather than a proletarian tradition. "*Call It Sleep* was written by a deeply Jewish human being," stated Ribalow in his prefatory essay to the novel's Pageant reprint ("History" xxxiv), unaware that Roth during the years he was drafting the novel and for some decades afterward was an agnostic assimilationist with strongly anti-Semitic tendencies. Maxwell Geismar, in his introduction to the same edition, placed Henry Roth in the context of contemporary Jewish authors: Saul Bellow, Bernard Malamud, and Philip Roth. "*Call It Sleep* reminds you there is another missing element in the contemporary assimilated Jewish-American novel," he wrote (xxxvii).

In making his case for *Call It Sleep* as a realistic Jewish slum novel in need of reclamation, Geismar risked placing it in the proletarian category. He therefore pondered: "But is it really a 'radical novel,' and does it strictly deserve the honor of being called 'the most distinguished proletarian novel?' " Yes, he conceded, it does, but only in a limited sense. "In terms of literary history, the work which is 'the best' of any genre usually defies the genre altogether" (xxxviii). *Call It Sleep* therefore does not defy the category of proletarian novel by slipping into the rival category of high modernism, he argued. Rather, it defies the proletarian category by being better than any similar novel (xxxviii).

Meyer Levin in his "Personal Appreciation," the Pageant edition's third prefatory essay, compared *Call It Sleep* to James T. Farrell's *A World I Never Made,* with which it has many superficial resemblances, including the arrival in New York City of a Jewish child in the arms of his immigrant mother (xlvii). But

Levin acknowledged the Joycean influences of Roth's work, if only to explain them away and offer an apology. I quote the key passage at length:

> Roth must have taken some impetus from James Joyce, particularly for the last section of his book, in which David's stream-of-consciousness throughout his electrocution experience is polyphonally interwoven with the existence-experience of a variety of persons who witness and react to the accident. This tour-de-force is to me the only out-of-character note in the entire work, as it represents a change of point of view and of method, acceptable indeed as a device for heightening the tension of the climactic episode of the book, but distracting in that it carries the reader into the realms of literary appreciation whereas up until that point he is so completely identified with David's views and reactions that he is living, rather than reading of life. But in so important a work, the virtuoso effect of this section may well be disregarded. (xlviii)

Instead of valorizing the penultimate chapter and allowing the rest of the novel to bask in its experimental glory, Levin asked that we kindly overlook this section as a lapse in judgment. "The amazing achievement of *Call It Sleep*," Levin explained, "is the poetic spell maintained with complete intensity even while the book is written on a naturalistic basis" (xlviii). That is, the astonishing verisimilitude of the text may *seem* high modernist because it works so very well, but in fact it is naturalism of the highest order, and the slip into Joycean stream of consciousness near the end breaks the poetic, naturalistic spell, according to Levin.

With the exception of Henry Roth's own contribution to the interpretation of his novel—that *Call It Sleep* is a triumph of high modernism—the major interpretive avenues were in place by 1964: the book is an exceptionally skilled proletarian novel, the book is not a proletarian novel, the book is the missing link in Jewish-American literature, the book is a triumph of naturalism, the book was written by an author with a freakish biography. Irving Howe's review of *Call It Sleep* in the *New York Times Book Review*—the single most important document in the campaign to resurrect Henry Roth's literary career—merely reaffirmed points made by others. It is no surprise, then, that the following year when Jane Howard in her *Life* magazine profile on Roth observed that "critics have likened Roth to James Joyce, Nathanael West and James T. Farrell," she seemed innocent of the fact that this trinity of authors comprised an incoherent variety of writing styles and thematic concerns (75). The critical consensus on the nature of Roth's novel remained splintered in the mid-1960s, so much so that, within a twelve-month period, Knowles claimed that comparisons between *Call It Sleep* and *Ulysses* were inevitable, Sanford Pinsker credited the increase in critical interest in the book to the rising popularity of the Jewish novel ("Re-Awakening" 149), and Kenneth Ledbetter brought the matter full circle by—once again—making the case for *Call It Sleep* as a proletarian novel (129).

Into this shifting critical landscape stepped the newly celebrated author, who began to set things right, first and foremost, by conclusively shedding the proletarian label. Much later, as the publication of *Mercy of a Rude Stream* approached, Roth softened on this point. "I thought I was writing a proletarian novel," he admitted in 1993 (Michaels 20). But in his first extensive interview in a literary journal, Roth distanced himself from the stigmatized label. "After the publication of *Call It Sleep* a number of critics pointed out what they thought were its social implications," he stated. "My own feeling was that what I had written was far too private for me to have given much thought to specific social problems. My personal involvement had absorbed my entire consciousness, leaving no room to focus on anything else" (Bronsen 269). In subsequent interviews, Roth claimed that the book was certainly *not* a proletarian novel, and that he had never felt that it was (Lyons, *The Man* 166; Freedman, "Conversation" 152; Friedman 35).

Retroactive attempts to distance a 1930s novel by a leftist author from a proletarian interpretation were not unique to the repositioning of *Call It Sleep*. In the afterword to the Feminist Press's 1984 republication of *Rope of Gold*, Elinor Langer insisted that Josephine Herbst's book "is hardly the didactic novel its 'proletarian' reputation suggests" (444). What is special about Roth's case is that he went further than anyone else in supplying the correct interpretation of his own book.

Over and over in his interviews, Roth cited Eliot and Joyce as the writers who interested him most at the time he was writing *Call It Sleep*. *The Waste Land*, he claimed, had a "devastating effect" on him (Bronsen 270), and he reread it until he had it memorized. ("I would say that Eliot was the major influence on my life" [*Shifting* 191].) When he got hold of a smuggled copy of *Ulysses*, he spent ten days straight pouring over it. ("I think this was the second great influence on my life" [Lyons, "Interview" 53].) In published essays, as well, Roth acknowledged the debt he owed to his "great master, Joyce," and to T. S. Eliot (*Shifting* 189). And in "Itinerant Ithacan," a 1977 memoir that was later revised and absorbed into volume 3 of *Mercy of a Rude Stream*, we see Roth perusing *The Waste Land* "for the nth time" and intently reading that contraband copy of *Ulysses* (*Shifting* 197–98).

Roth never suggested that his modernist novel is at the same time a deceptively political or subversive text. Rather, he placed emphasis entirely on the book's "lyrical impulses." He explained: "The whole texture of the novel is like that of a long poem or metaphor" (Lyons, *The Man* 168)—a statement that flies directly in the face of those dicta on writing once issued by the Communist Party through its literary organs when Roth was writing *Call It Sleep*. In 1930, Michael Gold, as editor of the *New Masses,* scoffed at the notion of proletarian writers studying and exploiting the technical innovations of "bourgeois writers" (though, clearly, all did to some extent, even Gold). "There is no 'style,' " Gold wrote, "there is only clarity, force, truth in writing. If a man has something new to say, as all proletarian writers have, he will learn to say it clearly in time" (Cowley 246).

It is entirely likely that Roth was, as he himself claimed, "under the influence of the critics and writers of the late 20s: art for art's sake, apolitical, in fact antipolitical" (Lyons, *The Man* 161). I am not suggesting Roth invented these influences in retrospect. But he carefully emphasized in interviews and articles the influences that helped readers approach his novel the way he wanted them to. One can understand that Roth would emphasize his fascination with titanic achievements like *Ulysses* and *The Waste Land* (both of which he admitted he did not understand [*Shifting* 191]), rather than *Jews without Money*—a mere footnote in American literary history, but a work whose influence on *Call It Sleep* is more readily apparent.

Soon after Roth's 1969 interview with David Bronsen, in which the author began to make claims for his novel as a document of high-modernist complexity, critics fell in line, joining Knowles in acknowledging the "inevitable" comparisons of *Call It Sleep* to *Ulysses*. By the late 1980s and the 1990s, as Roth's subsequent books were published and reviewed, critics and scholars were insisting in near unison that Roth's early novel was a work of Joycean high modernism: Michael Haederle in 1994 noted that Roth "was deeply influenced by James Joyce's protean use of language in *Ulysses*" (E3); Gert Buelens in 1996 called *Call It Sleep* "one of the most Joycean of American novels" (142); and in 1999, Jeffrey Folks stated, "The style and technique of Joyce are stamped upon *Call It Sleep*" (review of *Mercy* 285).

In his 1994 review of *A Star Shines over Mt. Morris Park,* Robert Alter argued that *Call It Sleep* was "the most brilliant American adaptation of Joycean techniques outside the novels of Faulkner" ("Desolate Breach" 3)—a reaffirmation of his assessment six years previous that, together with *The Sound and the Fury, Call It Sleep* was "the fullest American assimilation of Joyce" ("Awakenings" 34). In that earlier piece, a review of *Shifting Landscape* in the *New Republic,* Alter set out to compare Roth's poetics in *Call It Sleep* to Joyce's. But saddled with a largely naturalistic work, Alter had to improvise: he insisted that Roth emulated not the Joyce of *Ulysses* but the earlier Joyce of *A Portrait of the Artist as a Young Man*, with which *Call It Sleep* shares a concern with the youthful development of a writer. That thematic connection, however, would not seem to justify Alter's later statements praising Roth's assimilation of Joycean *techniques*.

Brian McHale followed Alter's lead in attempting to establish the Joycean credentials of Roth's novel, but he took on the more difficult task of referencing *Ulysses*. His analytical methods were ingenious. "It is the poetics of roughly the first half of *Ulysses*"—what Joyce called his initial style—"that became normative for modernism," McHale wrote. The novel's "heterogeneous and nonnormative later chapters" containing its more transgressive poetics emerged only later as models for *post*modernist fiction. "Roth's practice in *Call It Sleep* largely corroborates this analysis," McHale stated. Mainly, then, "Roth's narrative poetics is oriented toward the normatively modernist first half of *Ulysses*. Only once does his text shift from the normative model to a poetics resembling that of *Ulysses*' second half. This shift has always been perceived, by readers of *Call It Sleep* as well as by Roth himself, as a transgression of the text's own norms, or (Roth's word for it) a 'rupture'" (87).

McHale provided the analytical basis for a wholesale shift in interpretive schematics for *Call It Sleep*. The vast bulk of the narrative, originally praised as naturalistic prose of the highest order, was now Joycean stream of consciousness modeled on the early chapters of *Ulysses*. The penultimate chapter of *Call It Sleep*, once singled out—favorably or unfavorably—as a modernist anachronism, was now a postmodernist rupture, but with its roots firmly in Joyce. And all this was in accordance with Roth's own retroactive analysis of the novel and often expressed in Roth's own words.

Of course, this sea change in the critical consensus toward Roth's first novel must be understood within the larger mood swings of literary fashion. Roth's book was caught in a larger groundswell of critical favoritism shown toward modernism. But it is important to remember that modernism was already the reigning critical orthodoxy in the 1940s and 1950s, when *Call It Sleep* went almost completely unnoticed. Furthermore, the 1980s were a time of canon busting and reformation in American academia—a time during which *Jews without Money* and other didactic works reappeared on college syllabi. At this time more than any other the proletarian elements of *Call It Sleep* might have received their due. Moreover, the emphases on multiculturalism and ethnicity studies in academic courses and journals would suggest that the time was ripe for scholars to pick up the fallen baton of Geismar, Ribalow, and other midcentury scholars who prized the novel first and foremost as a brilliant archival document of Jewish literary expression from a prior generation.

But instead the modernist credentials of *Call It Sleep* only solidified. Most revealing about Roth's efforts to recategorize his novel were the subsequent writings of persons who first commented on the novel at the time of its resurrection. Sanford Pinsker, who in 1966 saw *Call It Sleep* riding the crest of a wave of interest in the indigent Jewish past, credited Roth's complex novel in 1994 with unleashing "a lyrical stream of consciousness that put Freud and Joyce squarely on native American ground" ("Roth Redux" 20). Leslie Fiedler, who likewise did much to realign the novel away from the proletarian tradition toward the Jewish tradition in American literature, claimed in 1996: "I have always known that the two works which most influenced Roth . . . were James Joyce's *Ulysses* and T. S. Eliot's *The Waste Land*" ("Many Myths" 19).

Alfred Kazin, who admired the novel's naturalism in 1956, used his introduction to the 1991 Farrar, Straus and Giroux edition of *Call It Sleep* to insist on a completely different reading. "It is a work of high art, written out of the full resources of modernism," Kazin belatedly asserted (ix). "Anyone who recognizes Joyce's immense achievement in *Ulysses* will recognize his influence on Roth" (xiv). Kazin directly contradicted his contribution to the 1956 issue of *American Scholar* in which he compared Roth to Dreiser. "*Call It Sleep* is not a naturalistic novel," he now declared. "With this novel we are in the city-world not of *Sister Carrie* but of James Joyce's *Ulysses*." There are signs, in fact, of absolute desperation in Kazin's attempts to abandon his previous assessment and accept Roth's coaching: "Notice that Roth spells 'grey' in the British fashion, as did Joyce" (xiii).

"In retrospect," asserted Jeffrey Folks in 1999, "one can understand how the cultural and linguistic confusions of Roth's childhood could be adapted so well to the artistic purposes of modernist prose" (review of *Mercy* 285). But this understanding came only in retrospect. At the time of publication, it was generally believed that a *naturalist* sensibility could best depict the confusions of the immigrant experience. Even twenty to thirty years' hindsight was not enough to make clear to Pinsker, Fiedler, or Kazin in the 1950s and 1960s the useful adaptability of modernism to Roth's artistic purposes.

Much changed in the literary world between 1956 and 1991, but the most important development affecting the critical analysis of *Call It Sleep* was the introduction in the 1960s of Roth's own extensive instructions on who his influences were and how to categorize the work. It became a nearly mandatory act of respect toward the elderly, venerated novelist to accept the author's word on this matter as final.

Not surprisingly, then, Roth's obituary in the *New York Times* stated that Roth's 1934 novel was "unlike the proletarian fiction being produced at that time"; rather, it was "influenced by the work of James Joyce" (Nicholls 41). *Mercy of a Rude Stream,* in which the author openly rejected and discredited his earlier Joycean allegiances, strengthened the hold the modernist reading has on *Call It Sleep. Mercy of a Rude Stream* is not a work of high modernism, but in it the Roth-like narrator continues to assert that his first novel is steeped, all too deeply, in the techniques of Joyce and Eliot—the politically evasive maneuverings of modernism. What *Mercy of a Rude Stream* does attempt to completely revise, however, is our reading of the autobiographical narrator's second great work, his silence. In volume 2, *A Diving Rock on the Hudson,* Roth dropped the bombshell about his alter ego's sexual involvement with his young sister and in so doing drastically rewrote how his extended period of nonproductivity should be interpreted. Until the publication of volume 2 of *Mercy of a Rude Stream,* Roth's silence was understood to be a complex modernist text, like *Call It Sleep;* in 1995, it became merely a tawdry narrative of personal shame.

For decades prior to offering that significant revision, Roth claimed to be haunted by the question of why he stopped writing. "Understandably, the answers he has found are many," Materassi reported (*Shifting* 75). One explanation for Roth's silence, proffered by sympathetic critics, was that he had been unfairly denied recognition upon initial publication of his novel. This was one of the few solutions to the puzzle that Roth ruled out categorically. "I was given a large measure of acclaim, enough to encourage any writer," he told Bronsen (271). To John S. Friedman, he reported, "I was successful and disciplined and even a recognized literary talent" (34). In fact, Roth continued to research his fiction and write intensively for another five years after the appearance of *Call It Sleep,* publishing two stories in the *New Yorker* and signing a contract for his second novel, several chapters of which were submitted to Maxwell Perkins at Scribners, who was delighted to land the promising novelist. But the young Roth never completed the second novel or any other book-length manuscript. As the United States entered the Second World War, Roth began working as a precision tool grinder. He published no new fiction for sixteen years.

What accounts for Roth's failure to complete another book at this time? Thirty years later, when the delayed success of *Call It Sleep* first made him a celebrity, Roth offered the simplest of explanations: he lost artistic inspiration. "I wasn't sure of anything anymore," he explained to Jane Howard in 1965, "I no longer had a point of view." In direct contrast, he noted, the four years he spent writing *Call It Sleep* had found him "in a sort of mystical state. I had a sense about the unifying force of some power I neither knew nor had to bother to know" (Howard 76).

Roth spent the remaining thirty years of his life expanding on and reshaping that explanation, aiming to illuminate the root causes of his loss of inspiration. Key to that illumination is, again, the penultimate chapter in which young David Schearl, having jammed a metal milk ladle into the track's third rail, overhears fragments of working-class conversations. Using a kaleidoscopic effect, Roth emitted a chorale of street voices of various ethnic origins.

For some time, it was common to read this passage as signaling not merely the protagonist's acquisition of class consciousness but also his spiritual rebirth. It was viewed as a procreative act, or an act of mystical transcendence. (David inserts his metal tool into a crack in the earth, siring a multiplicity of voices.) But the contents of *Shifting Landscape* tell us otherwise. The electrical shock is not David's delivering epiphany; rather, it is the end of Roth's creative life. As Brian McHale suggested in his piece establishing Henry Roth's Joycean credentials, Roth viewed his narrative as ruptured and spilling over into apocalyptic chaos. Roth saw the form of the novel broken down along with the creative psyche of the novelist (*Shifting* 76). This "short-circuiting" was considered by Roth to be most prophetic. He wrote: "[T]he apocalyptic end of the novel may very well depict what the author consciously felt: in the novel the child lives on, but his identity seems to have no future. The same thing it would appear was true of the novelist: he lived on, but his identity disintegrated" (*Shifting* 299).

As Roth's autobiographical protagonist approaches puberty, his narrative ends explosively rather than continuing shamefully. Within a few years, the precociously incestuous child would be bullying his younger sister into frequent and prolonged bouts of frottage and, later, intercourse. This was not to be revealed, however, until the publication of volume 2 of *Mercy of a Rude Stream*, in 1995. For three decades prior to that, the author explained his disintegrated identity by other means.

At the age of eight Roth was taken from the Lower East Side, a homogenous environment that seemed to Roth, in retrospect at least, like a real community where he had "a sense of belonging to both a place and a people" (*Shifting* 230), and moved to Harlem, where his neighbors, mostly Irish and Italian, seemed to find Judaism repugnant; Roth himself came to be influenced by that opinion. "I lost connection with the Jewish world," he stated in an interview published in 1979 (Lyons, "Interview" 54). This "highly hostile environment" produced a shock from which he did not recover until many decades later, he claimed. Having announced his atheism the year after his bar mitzvah, he wrote, "[I]t became almost inevitable that *Call It Sleep,* based on a lost identity, would be all the novel I could genuinely write—all the creating I could do from that sense of identity—because at that point where my novel ends, I no longer belonged" (*Shifting* 299).

Readers of *Call It Sleep* will be puzzled by this explanation. They will recall that the Lower East Side represented in that text is anything but hospitable to the child protagonist. With the exception of David Schearl's mother and aunt, every person—child or adult, Jew or gentile—is hostile toward the protagonist. This, Roth explained, is because *Call It Sleep* violates the truth of what the Lower East Side was actually like back then: "In reality, I took the violent environment of Harlem—where we lived from 1914 to 1928—and projected it back onto the East Side" (Bronsen 267).

More puzzling is the statement's internal logic. Shouldn't the expatriated Roth have found it insurmountably difficult to write even that first novel? How is it that a man in his midtwenties, who has been harmfully separated from his own people since the age of eight, managed to write a brilliant modernist novel in this dislocated and alienated state? And why is it that he was then unable to continue writing afterward (still in the same dislocated and alienated state)? Roth didn't really answer these questions in *Shifting Landscape.* Once his story reached that point in his childhood where his family was about to leave the Lower East Side, a neighborhood that he later called "a Jewish mini-state" but that he depicted in the novel as a zone of anti-Semitic harassment, the narrative had to splinter apart, and he was unable to continue writing. This was the best explanation Roth could give at the time.

A more obvious and consistent explanation is that Roth stopped writing, or writing well, the moment the Communist Party got hold of him (he joined in 1933, the year he finished *Call It Sleep*), and that after the Moscow Trials (1937), the Nazi-Soviet Nonaggression Pact (1939), and other disillusionments in leftist politics had battered Roth's psyche, he went into creative remission, like a host of other leftist writers of his generation. But that explanation, by itself, does not serve Roth well (it associates his work with proletarian literature) and is too simplistic besides. Still, the party does not escape blame in *Shifting Landscape.* Roth at times was highly critical of the party's effect on his creativity ("it was sterile," "it was a disaster" [46]). Indeed, Roth lamented having ever been committed to the party. *Shifting Landscape* includes a public statement Roth made about the Moscow Trials, an essay called "Where My Sympathy Lies," published in the 2 March 1937 issue of the *New Masses*. The essay is, according to Materassi, "a candid avowal of [Roth's] deference to the Communist Party's official position on the subject" (*Shifting* 48); in it Roth stated that, although several things about the trials confused him, "enough and more than enough" evidence was revealed about the accused to settle the matter. "I believe them to be, as they themselves acknowledged, guilty" (50).

In an excerpt from a 1985 taped conversation that followed the piece, Roth stated: "That's the very example of, the perfect example of conversion, the definition of the very thing I would condemn utterly, today, after I had once completely committed myself to blind allegiance. It's something you have to live down, and it is something that (needless to repeat) continually haunts you" (51). But in spite of the harsh evaluation that Roth offered of the party and its influence on writers, party allegiance was not singled out as the most fundamental cause of his literary immobilization. That cause, as stated earlier, was the loss of his communal East Side identity, his separation from the Jewish ministate.

Actually, Roth offered numerous reasons for why he became immobilized after publishing *Call It Sleep*. As Leslie Fiedler observed, far from being silent during the six decades that followed *Call It Sleep*, Roth was "talking and writing compulsively" about his long bout of writer's block and the abortive attempts he made to end it ("Many Myths" 17). In *A Diving Rock on the Hudson*, Roth offered an odd, indirect denial of his compulsive efforts to construct an author legend. Reflecting on the meaning of frequent requests from journalists for interviews, the elderly Ira Stigman observes in third person, "They reflected a degree of public curiosity regarding the extraordinary hiatus of production that was the dominant feature of his literary career. They sought information from him and about him on which to base hypotheses as to the cause. He wasn't prepared to advance any" (37).

Roth, of course, advanced a plethora of hypotheses. "I've got a number of theories," he told William Freedman in 1972. "It seems I develop a new one just about every week" (*Shifting* 76). Roth claimed in *Shifting Landscape* that he lost sight of his aims in 1934; he lost his purpose; he lost momentum (99); he lost faith (xiv); he lacked persistence (53); he lacked motivation (59); he lost values and allegiances (44); he lost a sense of history (109); he received financial support from his lover Eda Lou Walton and "just fooled around" (44–45); the demands of editors cramped his expression (59); he failed to mature; he suffered a failure of imagination, a failure of will (44–45); he was too lazy (134) ("I am throwing out these ideas as possibilities" [50]); he suffered a neurotic depression (78), anxiety (78), an "approximate nervous breakdown" (60); he lost the urge, the impulse (75); he had bad timing (107); he was too self-involved (46); he yearned for the vile, perverse, and pornographic (169); he developed acute pain in his elbow when writing (92); there were too many diversions (44); writing was hard work and there were easier ways to make a living (59); and no project seemed pertinent enough or close enough to him personally to justify entering into a long-term writing commitment (257). Unlike the relatively straightforward reasons for immobilization that might be used in the career narrative of a proletarian writer (it was the party, it was the times), the primary theme in Roth's narrative, loss of community, gives rise to a surprising number of variations—"delicate problems," which he said are "all interwoven" (*Shifting* 44–45)—the same way that, in a Joyce novel, the psychological, generational, and folkloric elements combine and play off one another to construct a complex text. "I mean if it was all coherent, fused together into a whole," the Roth character in "Itinerant Ithacan" states of *The Waste Land,* "it almost would have been contradictory to what [Eliot] was trying to say" (*Shifting* 211).

"*Call It Sleep* is an elaborate, densely-wrought novel which demands the close scrutiny usually given to poetry," wrote Bonnie Lyons in the opening paragraph of her book-length study of Roth; "the organic symbolic structure, complex inter-weaving of motifs, wide variety of narrative techniques, and subtle exploitation of language and dialect all deserve careful critical attention" (*The Man* iii). The same could now be said of the author's silence, for Roth was not to be considered a proletarian writer or, worse, someone who couldn't cut it as a proletarian writer. Rather, he was to be ranked alongside Joyce and Eliot, who escaped the stigma of party involvement entirely and who were responsible for complexly structured, difficult texts. The correct reading of Roth's early novel and the correct reading of the barren years that followed its publication are closely related—they share many of the same themes and formalistic techniques. And our understanding of them is essential as preparation for Roth's third major text, the promised "memoir-form novel" *Mercy of a Rude Stream,* which would reconfirm the high-modernist credentials of *Call It Sleep* while gutting his silence of all mystery and complexity.

CHAPTER THREE

The Revised Edition
of Henry Roth's Silence

In his March 1963 *Midstream* essay "The Meaning of
Galut in America Today," Henry Roth suggested that the greatest boon Jews in
America could confer on humanity is neither becoming Zionists nor continuing
as Diaspora Jews but rather reorienting themselves toward ceasing to be Jews
altogether (*Shifting* 114). Two years later, he told a journalist he had no interest
in traveling to Israel, though he guessed he might like to see England and Ireland
("Joyce and Eliot are my favorites" [Howard 75]). But after the June 1967 Arab-
Israeli War, Roth's attitude toward Israel changed. "I felt at last that Jews had
redeemed themselves by self-sacrifice and sheer valor," he explained. "From that
point on, and there were many other reasons, I experienced a resurgence of my
long dormant literary vocation" (*Shifting* 176).

In 1971, Roth went public with his new allegiance in the *New York Times*.
In a brief essay, "No Longer at Home," he recounted how he had long ago lost
touch with his East Side neighborhood home, the Jewish ministate of his youth,
but added: "I'll tell you though, I have now adopted one, out of need, a symbolic home, one where symbols can lodge, whatever it is in actuality, whatever
wanderings and residual reservations I may have: Israel" (*Shifting* 168). Despite
reservations about Israel's connections to "American imperialism," Roth began
to speak of his "overpowering attachment to Israel" and call himself a staunch
supporter of the Jewish state and "a crusty pro-Israel author" (*Shifting* 186,
193–94).

During the same time that his allegiance to Israel was building, Roth claimed,
he began to write again consistently. In a 1971 letter, he referred to a play he was
working on (*Shifting* 179), and in a 1972 interview, he mentioned a continuum

journal that had become "something else" (182). In 1979, Roth commenced accumulating stacks of typescript pages that became a first draft of the multivolume novel sequence *Mercy of a Rude Stream,* a work he originally intended to publish posthumously because, he said, it would "offend everybody" (Kaganoff 68). As it turns out, the only person whom Roth took pains not to offend was his wife, Muriel, who saw none of the four thousand manuscript pages that accumulated before her death in 1990. In 1992, Roth changed his mind about posthumous publication and sold the books to St. Martin's Press. Volumes 1 and 2 appeared early in 1994 and 1995, respectively. Roth continued working on the remaining volumes until his death in October 1995. Volumes 3 and 4 appeared posthumously.

That Roth's literary rebirth and religious-ethnic reassociation are linked the author made very clear. "Israel is my chief concern now," he stated, "and any work of literary merit that I can achieve would be in her behalf, to muster sympathy and support for her struggle for survival and security" (*Shifting* 176). Still, the renewed links between Roth's art and his people need not obscure *Call It Sleep*'s important relationship to high modernism. "My conversion reminds me of Eliot's conversion," Roth remarked. "*The Waste Land* verges on the unintelligible. The only way [Eliot] retained coherence was by conversion. It gave him a center" (Friedman 38). Likewise, Roth's reunion with his people, he believed, "was something Joyce never allowed himself, refused to do; and so for him history remained a nightmare from which he couldn't wake. The result is *Finnegans Wake*"—a work Roth deplored as "the 'Black Hole' of English literature" (*Shifting* 258). *Call It Sleep* must stand as a youthful indulgence in irresponsible modernist pyrotechnics, Roth implied. But Roth's renewed vigor for writing, and his enthusiasm for Israel, demanded from his future works of fiction the violent negation of Joyce, with "his monstrous detachment and artistic autonomy" (*Shifting* 260).

In the interviews and essays from this period— approximately the mid-1960s to the 1987 publication of Roth's second book, *Shifting Landscape*—Roth instructed the literary community how to read his early masterpiece and composed the text of his prolonged silence, purportedly originating from the author's prior loss of homeland, his subservience to the Communist Party, plus myriad offshoots from those catastrophic developments. But Roth significantly revised this story in the mid-1990s when he published the anti-Joycean *Mercy of a Rude Stream.* In February 1994 he told Jonathan Rosen, "In *Call It Sleep* I invented a victim to cover over the true me."

But in *Mercy of a Rude Stream*, he explained, "I tried to reconcile myself with the louse I was. Who I detested. I loathed. And maybe get the reader to do it, too" (39). Rather than blame a tyrannical father, a smothering mother, or anti-Semitic neighborhood children for his suffering and weakness, Roth now blamed his own unsavory self.

This new take on Roth's autobiographical protagonist had implications for the narrative of the author's silence. Its cause now shifted: Roth had brought the silence on himself by violating the incest taboo with his sister, thus damaging his own psyche and making his postpubescent personal history off-limits as material for future literary works. The reason his silence *ended* was related to this explanation as well. Roth never stopped citing the 1967 war as a watershed in his personal life, but the immediate source of the author's literary rejuvenation was his decision to pull the rug out from under the innocent victim of *Call It Sleep* and show him as a victimizer. In the first volume of *Mercy of a Rude Stream*, the autobiographical narrator reveals that the details of his early violation of societal norms became less embarrassing or, at least, less "shamefully, crushingly important" with age, thereby permitting him finally to start confessing them in 1979. Twelve years after the Jews had "redeemed themselves by self-sacrifice and sheer valor," it was time for Roth to commence redeeming himself through an honest—and therefore brave and valorous—literary project. By confessing his own personal transgressions, Roth produced publishable, book-length fiction at last.

Beginning with *A Star Shines over Mt. Morris Park*, the four volumes of *Mercy of a Rude Stream* are narrated in alternating sections of differing typeface. The narrator dates the composition of the original narrative sections from 1979 to the mid-1980s, before he had use of computer technology to ease his task. The sections that interrupt the conventional narrative, printed in sans-serif type, are attributed to the years 1985 to 1995. They contain relentless editorializing about the elderly narrator's manuscript by an even more elderly second narrator obsessed with confirming the veracity of the material, and they take the form of a dialogue with the narrator's computer, which he names Ecclesias. In the books the sans-serif narrator looks on in horror as the original narrator goes public with his sordid history, but that sans-serif narrator also confirms the accuracy of the unpleasant details.

At no time during the drafting of *Mercy of a Rude Stream* did Roth reveal to the public the incestuous secret his late novels would hinge on. Even volume 1, published in 1994, only hints at what is to follow in subsequent volumes. The protagonist in *A Star Shines over Mt. Morris Park,* young Ira Stigman, encounters a number of unsavory characters as he passes through puberty: a stranger who engages Ira in conversation and later masturbates while grabbing the boy's buttocks (54–57); two neighborhood boys who suggest on separate occasions that Ira "pull off" with them (64, 283); and Mr. Lennard, Ira's Spanish teacher, who exacts a price when Ira requests an afternoon off from school: he unbuttons his own fly, then Ira's. Guilt ridden, Ira insists he is late for work. His angry teacher permits him to leave (240–44).

In all these instances, however, Ira remains the passive victim, much like David Schearl in *Call It Sleep.* In only one scene in volume 1 does Ira instigate sexual contact, and even then he does so while unconscious. With his father away visiting family, his mother invites her eleven-year-old son to sleep in her bed. He awakes in horror.

> He was playing bad against Mom's naked leg, lying on his side and pushing, rubbing, squeezing his stiff peg against Mom's thighs. She woke up.
> "I didn't mean it!" Ira wailed in his shame. "I was dreaming—"
> She laughed indulgently. "Go back to sleep." (104)

Ira, we are told, thereafter sleeps in his own bed. But the episode ignites in him the desire to feel the rubbing sensation again, perhaps with one of the neighborhood *shiksas.* We learn in later volumes that, in fact, Ira has a sister two years younger, and that the following year he initiates sexual contact with her—bullies her into it, actually. "[W]hat ruse, what provocative coaxing, what consummate opportunism, shifty suborning, did he resort to, stoop to, until the blistering green kitchen walls lilted with consent," he declares in volume 2 (*Diving Rock* 77). But for now, such material is concealed, though just barely. Ecclesias, whose dialogue is denoted with initial dashes, states:

> — I told you at the outset, when you deliberately omitted that most crucial element in your account, that you would not be able to avoid reckoning with it.
> You did, Ecclesias. Perhaps I wasn't ready for it.
> — And are you now?
> Yes. Face-to-face with it as a consequence of continuing. Which is something, you notice, Ecclesias, I managed to evade in the only novel I ever wrote: coming to grips with it.
> — It was adroit. You made a climax of evasion, an apocalypse out of your refusal to go on, an apocalyptic tour de force at the price of renouncing a literary future. As pyrotechnics, it was commendable, it found favor, at any rate. (*Star Shines* 85–86)

The sans-serif Ira concludes volume 1 by lamenting the contradictions, subterfuges, and ambiguities the narrator must resort to, but also dreading the unavoidable truth telling yet to come. "Had he been a nineteenth-century novelist," he states, "or in fact, a true novelist mirroring the society about him, then so much that pertained to himself he could have projected onto a fictive character, into a fable about others. But alas, trapped in this mode of his own devising"—he means the flagrantly autobiographical memoir form—"he had no alternative but to acknowledge the actuality" (283–84).

Early in volume 2, the sans-serif narrator, citing passages from the typescript his earlier self generated in 1979, explains that what was to follow—revelations about his "wickedness" and "corroding evil"—was the keystone to the entire project: "without it, the subsequent narrative tumbles to the ground" (*Diving Rock* 7). The damage caused to the artist by his own infractions was immeasurable: "I tore apart the ligatures, my psychic ligatures, sundered them irreversibly," the elderly Ira reports. "God, how one can ruin oneself, be ruined; it's inconceivable" (38–39).

The sans-serif narrator, in his role as editor, considers erasing the abomination from the earlier draft or evading the issue subtly, continuing to hide behind subterfuge, as in *Call It Sleep*. "No, it would never do," he concludes in resignation. "You've enough to do rendering a straightforward account, without trying to skate on your ear. You're not clever enough" (64). But he does ask Ecclesias if he has any advice. "Only that the unspoken and unspeakable must become spoken and speakable," the computer responds (128).

Finally, Roth recounts a Sunday morning in November 1922, late in Ira's sixteenth year. His father is working the breakfast shift at a restaurant, and his mother has stepped out to buy groceries. "Minnie. Okay?" Ira calls out, and on the opposing page the author inserts a corrected Stigman family tree, with fourteen-year-old Minnie Stigman assuming her rightful place as sister to Ira, daughter to Chaim and Leah. Their sexual involvement has been ongoing for four years, we infer, and Ira hardly has to coax her anymore. "She was ready as soon as he snapped the lock," the narrator states. Indeed, Minnie has adopted a repertoire of dirty phrases to egg her brother on: "Fuck me, fuck me good!" "Ah, ah, oooh wah, ooowah!" "Oooh, you're a good fucker" "Fuck me like a hoor." Ecclesias is dumbstruck by the graphic nature of the revelation as Ira presents it. "Oh, horror, horror," he manages to get out (*Diving Rock* 140–42).

Along with explicit depictions of sex, Roth included matter-of-fact dialogue of considerable verisimilitude between the two siblings.

"All right, let me in, will ye?"

"The rubber's all right?"

"Of course."

"O-o-h, o-oh, my poor brother, my poor dear brother. Oh, that's good."

"Yeah? Ah."

"Don't kiss me." (275)

When Ira imagines his parents taking a week-long vacation, leaving him and Minnie unchaperoned, "the prospect ma[kes] his temples bulge" (295). And though he admits this "act of glorious abomination" with his sister is craven, puerile, evil, brutal, wicked, and depraved, his greatest desire is to "pump that 'o-oh, my darling brother' out of her" (268, 172).

"This is confession with a capital C," Sanford Pinsker observed ("Torments" 21). Roth made a strenuous effort to align the biography of Ira Stigman in *Mercy of a Rude Stream* with the existing author legend of Henry Roth before wrenching it horribly with a shocking revelation that, were it true of the author as well, would usefully explain his decades of literary frustration in a new way—in a way that debunks much of the familiar legend he and others constructed during the three decades since *Call It Sleep* topped the bestseller lists. "Once Minnie was admitted to the story," his narrator insists, "everything was different, drastically different, nay, it would be nearer the truth to say flagrantly different, *self-revealing in approach, in treatment, in the contour of the narrative*" (*Diving Rock* 399, emphasis added). How much more adamantly can an author emphasize the autobiographical implications of his fiction? The sans-serif Ira becomes upset when he detects inaccuracies in the original 1979-to-1985 manuscripts, which he is editing. "No, your timing is wrong again," he scolds his younger self, "your timing and your sequence, your causality. Once again you can say, what difference will it make to another, your attributions and accuracy? This is a work of fiction. But the fact is, it makes a difference to me" (*Star Shines* 213).

"How long it had taken him to square with the truth," the narrator of *A Diving Rock on the Hudson* laments; "how long he had clung to subterfuge!" Lest anyone assume the Minnie story was a further indulgence in deflection, Roth had Ira yet again consider removing Minnie from the story and projecting the sordidness of her situation onto another character who would serve as a stand-in for the narrator's sister. But that, Ecclesias assures him, would leave "a lopsided tale" dangling in "some surrealist limbo" (287). The narrator has stuck long enough to the old explanation for his prolonged silence, feeling like "a juggler keeping aloft a number of incongruous objects, an orange, a skillet, a paintbrush" (405). It was time to negate the metaphor of a victimized child from his early masterpiece, which had "forged the shackles on the spirit of the artisan himself" (402). Only thus, the narrator reasons, could he win renewal of self—of which these many late volumes are proof.

In the prologue to volume 3, published posthumously in 1996, Roth wrote jubilantly of the aftermath to his confession one year earlier: "Liberated at last in the year 1995 from bondage imposed on himself more than seventy years ago, from bondage whose depiction he had begun, and would now endeavor to continue" (2). But the posthumous continuation of his story hit roadblocks imposed by a litigious sibling who objected to the depiction of Minnie Stigman in *A Diving Rock on the Hudson*. Under pressure from Rose Broder, Roth's surviving sister, St. Martin's Press removed portrayals of sexual relations between Minnie and Ira Stigman from the remaining volumes of *Mercy of a Rude Stream* (Pogrebin B9). The final two published volumes continue to acknowledge the incestuous relationship, but mostly in past tense. There remain scenes in which Ira confesses that he considered murdering his sister ("cure her for good" [*From Bondage* 109]), but scenes of graphic sex between brother and sister are gone.

Instead, the editors left intact coarse, even brutal passages in which Ira mounts his thirteen-year-old cousin, Stella (*From Bondage* 120, 266), with whom he had begun a sexual relationship near the end of volume 2. The published editions of *From Bondage* (volume 3) and *Requiem for Harlem* (volume 4) closely resemble the expurgated version of *Mercy of a Rude Stream* that Ira Stigman himself considers issuing but rejects in his painful pursuit of closure and renewal. Still, the full damage had been done in volume 2, which, paradoxically, meant the full benefits accrued: Roth rode the confessional trail to literary rebirth; he saw enough of his manuscript into print to guarantee a complete rewriting of his legend—a major revision of his text of multidecade silence. Or so he must have believed.

Roth's revised legend met resistance, however, from critics. The long-awaited end to Roth's monumental silence was clearly topic number one for reviewers of *Mercy of a Rude Stream* and the reason the works received such widespread attention on publication. It is therefore striking that, after the author admitted in volume 1 that he harbored a shameful secret that would explain his decades of anguish and promised to reveal and further address that secret in subsequent volumes, this admission was downplayed and often unreported in the novel's reviews.

Robert Alter in the *New York Times Book Review* made passing mention to the fact that Ira is "troubled by his own emergent sexuality and the aggressive sexuality of certain of the adults around him" (3), but Alter did not develop the point or anticipate that sexual guilt may play a role in the author's subsequent artistic breakdown and sixty-year silence. Instead, Alter wrote at length about "the rupture in identity" that was inflicted on Ira in his youth: the years of exile from his old Jewish neighborhood, a life of troubled assimilation, the rejection of his own ethnic origins (3). These were the themes Roth developed in his own career narrative over the previous three decades, themes that editor Materassi collated in *Shifting Landscape.* They were the narrative elements that reviewers across the board seemed most comfortable addressing because they were familiar and, therefore, called for no serious revision of Roth's existing legend, and because they placed the onus for Roth's personal disintegration on the outside world, not on the author himself.

Similarly, Morris Dickstein reported that the narrator's discussions with Ecclesias obsessively return to two concerns. But, oddly, neither of the concerns Dickstein mentioned was sexual. Rather, they were "the problem of remembering, of restoring the lost plenitude of the past, and the protracted anguish of [Stigman's] writing career, which he blames on the distorted development of his deeply conflicted personality" ("Henry Roth" 6). This novel, Dickstein observed, is "a diagnostic work," but Dickstein disregarded the preliminary diagnosis: that the virus of sexual shame caused the disease of silence.

Granted, the passages in which the sans-serif narrator and his computer converse seem strangely alarmist; though the interpolated voice of dread tips us off to the fact that an abomination resulted in the author's decades of deep despair, the novel gives only cryptic guidance as to what the unnamed abomination might be. (The absence of a sister from the Stigman family tree doesn't help.) But to the extent that Roth did prepare us for the bombshell, the warning went largely unreported. The peculiarly alarmist nature of the passages deflected rather than attracted attention.

It is not as if the subject were alluded to only tangentially. By book's end, the narrator grows tired of the subject and his own coy method of repeatedly holding back information. After Mr. Lennard's aborted molestation scene, the narrator asks himself, "Why did you let him do it? Why didn't you run out?" prompting Ecclesias to speak up:

— It was because you already felt guilty, wasn't that the chief reason?

Yes, because I might betray something even more heinous than Mr. Lennard's molestation.

— Isn't it time you cleared the air, exposed the clandestine burden? You can't go on indefinitely in this fashion, with an unaccountably eccentric orbit, like a visible astral body with an invisible satellite. Beside, the enigma is beginning to wear thin.

Very well, soon. (249)

But the revelation arrived too late to affect most reviewers of volume 1.

This was not the first time a strange, sexually themed passage had been politely overlooked by Roth scholars and critics. In "No Longer At Home," the 1971 *New York Times* piece discussing the reasons for his prolonged silence, Roth cited the loss of his "snug, orthodox" home on the homogenous East Side and his ill-advised attempts to write a conventional proletarian novel. But Roth devoted two paragraphs of this six-paragraph essay to his own sexual degeneracy, which he offered as an alternative explanation for his professional immobility and desuetude (*Shifting* 169–70). This passage, however, elicited no commensurate reaction from subsequent interviewers or from Materassi, who otherwise prodded Roth in a timely chronological manner throughout *Shifting Landscape* for comments on issues newly raised in his published works. Like a drunken man's loud, jarring declaration at a party, which those within earshot tacitly agree to ignore, eyes averted, Roth's sexual confession was passed over by his editor and the rest of the literary community, who were unable to place the outburst within Roth's existing biography.

"What are we to make of this?" asked Hillel Halkin in his 1994 *Commentary* piece "Henry Roth's Secret," which broke the silence on Roth's sexual self-disgust and examined the polite avoidance of the topic in the press. Roth may have left the enigma of his self-diagnosis intact at the end of *A Star Shines over Mt. Morris Park,* Halkin reasoned, but he provided enough information for us to make clear inferences about "Oedipal feelings, incestuous promptings, and homosexuality" (46).

Halkin derived the Oedipal theme from Roth's interviews and the family dynamic in scenes from both *Call It Sleep* and *A Star Shines over Mt. Morris Park,* specifically the numerous heated confrontations between father and son and the scene in the latter novel in which the adolescent Ira is invited into his mother's bed and experiences sexual arousal. Halkin was directed toward homosexuality as a probable cause of Roth's shame by the numerous passages in volume 1 of *Mercy of a Rude Stream* in which male acquaintances either attempt to molest the boy or entreat him to "pull off" with them, and by confessional statements Roth made about the degeneracy of the 1930s artistic milieu in a *Vanity Fair* article published three months before the Halkin essay (Rosen 40). The apparent bull's-eye Halkin scored—the attribution of Roth's anguish to "incestuous promptings"—may have originated from the "stiff peg" scene, but it also seemed to pick up on Roth's general allusions to a wound left festering for decades, and to the breaking of a taboo with catastrophic consequences. If not incest, what *could* Roth be alluding to so cryptically? (When an octogenarian admits to a journalist that, to his great shame, he had homosexual tendencies in his youth and allowed his female lover to cuckold him in an embarrassing menage à trois, but he refuses to say what's really been bothering him all these years, one can reasonably consider incest a possible cause of his wounded psyche.) Moreover, the autobiographical author leaves a gaping hole in both his novels, a conspicuously missing character: a younger sister.

What was most significant about Halkin's air-clearing article was not that, by scattering speculative buckshot widely enough, he hit on the shameful secret Roth planned to reveal the following year in volume 2. Rather, Halkin's prescience about Roth's imminent attempt to revise his career narrative made the piece noteworthy. More than any other critic writing at the time, Halkin detected significant movement by the author toward recasting the explanation for his long silence. Just as the party-membership explanation for Roth's writer's block was once subsumed under a larger narrative umbrella that recounted how Roth was torn from his homogenous Jewish neighborhood, both of these earlier accounts would now be further subsumed under the guilt-ridden explanation offered as an extenuation of Roth's incestuous involvement with his sister. After the full four-volume cycle of *Mercy of a Rude Stream* was published, Roth believed, one could no longer approach his writer's block in an honest manner without taking into account his incestuous past, any more than one could attempt to calculate the force of the tides without factoring in the moon. The confession would have been sensational regardless of how it was handled, but Roth's decision to devote volume 1 to building suspense for the ultimate revelation in volume 2, all the while steering journalists away from the truth in interviews, guaranteed an explosive reception to the material once it was released. Roth seems to have calculated the move for maximum impact, to fully demolish previous accounts of his uniquely troubled career and upend existing interpretations of his artistic struggles; but, if so, he underestimated the staying power of the high-modernist rendering of his silence offered in *Shifting Landscape*. Critics and scholars continued to avert their eyes from the embarrassing admission Roth offered and turned elsewhere for an explanation for his silence.

The rejection by scholars and critics of the autobiographical basis of this revision is, at the very least, inconsistent. The consensus in the literary world has long held that the material used by Roth in his fiction is drawn directly from his life. Mario Materassi, calling Roth a "fundamentally autobiographical author" ("Shifting Urbanscape" 30), concluded about *Call It Sleep:* "David's story follows quite closely Henry Roth's life up to the time of the family's move to Alphabet City in the Lower East Side" ("Shifting Urbanscape" 41). "Roth's autobiographical impulse is obvious not only in *Call It Sleep* but in his subsequent career as well," wrote Bonnie Lyons; "his short stories clearly relate to his own experience, and at least one of the reasons for Roth's failure to complete his second novel was the fact that its focus was *not* autobiographical" (*The Man* 117–18, emphasis in original). Roth, it seems, could concentrate on a subject for a length of time necessary to complete a significant work of literature only if the protagonist was clearly patterned after himself. "I apparently belong to that category of writers who has to write about the stages of his own development," he told Lyons (*The Man* 164).

Predictably, then, a majority of reviewers in 1994 emphasized the autobiographical nature of the material in *A Star Shines over Mt. Morris Park.* Indeed, Robert Alter specifically faulted Roth for *not* recasting more rigorously the material drawn from actual experience so as to form a more satisfying novelistic structure. The narrative merely comprises an unsatisfying string of autobiographical vignettes, Alter concluded. "Ira is Henry Roth in all but name" (3). This unshaped, repetitive, slack novel, in fact, was deemed more nakedly autobiographical than the expertly structured *Call It Sleep* by nearly everyone who reviewed it. The transparency of the fictional guise seemed especially evident in the passages in which Ira discusses his childhood with the computer Ecclesias— by general consensus, the weakest sections of the book. In particular, Zachary Leader observed, the moments of panic when the elderly narrator confesses that he may have misremembered a minor detail in an earlier section create the impression of "absolute fidelity to experience" (20). Even the inside cover of each volume chronicling Ira Stigman's youth displays group portraits of Henry Roth's family and friends. A reader of *Mercy of a Rude Stream* who was unable to identify the character "M" as Muriel Roth, or who failed to associate the narrator's early modernist masterpiece with Henry Roth's *Call It Sleep,* or who did not accept Ira Stigman as the young author, lacked "the basic tools to read the work," Hana Wirth-Nesher insisted ("Facing" 273).

In a 1994 feature article in the *Los Angeles Times,* Michael Haederle—like so many others—reported that the circumstances in Roth's life were very much like those recollected in volume 1 of *Mercy of a Rude Stream,* but he innocently included a significant detail in his description: "Like the Stigman family in his books, Roth's parents moved him and his sister to Harlem in the summer of

1914" (E3). Haederle neglected to point out a major discrepancy: no Stigman daughter makes the move to Harlem, whereas Rose Roth—later Rose Broder—did. This discrepancy is accounted for, and the text amended, in volume 2. At that point, Sanford Pinsker observed, "the thin line separating fiction from autobiography became problematic" ("Against the Current" 15). Reviews of volume 2 and subsequent volumes did not backpedal on the issue of the *generally* autobiographical nature of Roth's work, but reviewers often hedged on the specific issue of Ira Stigman's incestuous relationship with Minnie. The majority conceded that *on this one detail* the author disregarded his actual biography; *in these uncomfortable passages* they found him to be a wholly imaginative writer. "It would be a sad irony if, after overcoming his writer's block of so many decades—if because we live in an age obsessed with the facts behind the fiction—his novel was reduced to autobiography," Jonathan Rosen stated in 1998 (Pogrebin B9). The real irony, of course, is that Roth was *counting* on a public obsession with the facts behind his fiction to facilitate the explication of his career narrative in its definitive form, and Rosen, with every good intention, attempted to block that process. No one deemed it sad or ironic when volume 1 of *Mercy of a Rude Stream* was unquestioningly accepted as autobiographical. The author took pains to make it appear so, in fact. Yet when Roth went about the meticulous demolition of his previous career narrative in volume 2, most journalists chose to protect the author by taking the revelations as fiction and scolding colleagues who read them otherwise.

In his review of volume 2 in the *Times Literary Supplement,* Andrew Rosenheim cited numerous explicit scenes of incestuous sex in the novel only to dismiss them as "implausible" and "ludicrous." Yet Rosenheim concluded his review by praising the author's valuable and accurate memory: "Our curiosity of Roth's remarkable reappearance in print should now be replaced by admiration for his continuing and powerful account of a lost world" (20).

Objections to the revised author legend were often couched in artistic or aesthetic terms. Critics especially objected to the inclusion of postmodernist asides from the book's self-critical narrator. Stephen Amidon criticized the sans-serif passages for weakening the book's literary power (8). "These are embarrassingly self-indulgent and the work would be better without them," Sean French concurred (35). Though French recounted how Ira Stigman "very shockingly indeed" embarks on a sexual relationship, first with his sister and, later, with a young cousin, he did not tie together the work's two major plot elements: incest is confessed; the narrator comes unblocked. Instead, French reflected on the youthful Roth's inability to root himself in the American culture and language and how, in turn, "Roth became a doctrinaire Marxist, which cut him off decisively from the vivid, pungent particularity which was his authentic subject." Reviewing a book whose characters and milieu transparently approximate those of *Call It Sleep,* advanced a few years—a book described by its own self-reflexive narrator as a long-awaited follow-up to that first novel—French arrived at this stunning conclusion: "Perhaps the true successor to *Call It Sleep* was written by the more assimilated Saul Bellow with *The Adventures of Augie March* in 1953" (35). The impulse to deny a legitimate role for *Mercy of a Rude Stream* in extending or reworking Roth's author legend is overpowering.

Similarly, the scholarly material on Roth following the revelations of *A Diving Rock on the Hudson*—as opposed to the immediate reviews—mostly rejected the spectacular revised version of Roth's silence in lieu of the more open-ended, pluralistic reading from *Shifting Landscape.* Hana Wirth-Nesher, in a 1995 article on *Call It Sleep,* acknowledged that "the first two volumes of *Mercy of a Rude Stream* follow the development of the artist through his teenage and university years," and she observed that the crossing of boundaries becomes an obsession for Ira Stigman ("Call It" 395–96). Wirth-Nesher did not, however, elaborate on the incestuous content of the novels—or even utter the word incest—nor did she link sexual guilt to what she called "Roth's legendary writer's block, a sixty-year spell of silence" (391).

Some scholars made the case for placing Roth's air-clearing confession in the broader context of a long, contradictory, ever-evolving career narrative, thereby minimizing the jarring effect of Roth's bombshell. "So the Roth legend continues to grow," wrote Materassi of the publication of volumes 1 and 2. "It is a legend that over the course of half a century has accrued by the slow accumulation of disconnected fragments of a unique, decidedly odd existence in and out of the literary world and the public eye." Each chapter, Materassi noted, is isolated by long periods of silence; "each contradicts the previous one and in turn is contradicted by the one that follows. Phoenix-like, Henry Roth appears, disappears, reappears out of the ashes of his prior avatars" ("Shifting Urbanscape" 29). The implication is that, given enough time, Roth would have abandoned this "final" explanation as well. As Mark Shechner asked in his review of volume 2, "What other surprises, one wonders, does Henry Roth have up his sleeve" (14).

In an editor's afterword to *Requiem for Harlem,* the fourth volume of *Mercy of a Rude Stream,* Robert Weil of St. Martin's Press similarly noted how Roth's account of his own life story shifted frequently—and suspiciously—over time. Roth emphasized the deleterious effects of various roadblocks as it suited him, Weil implied. "Roth suggested in the last few years of his life that his sexual preoccupations and obsessions lay more at the root of his unwillingness to continue writing for more than forty years," Weil conceded, but the scenes in which Ira Stigman is depicted in as sexually compulsive and loathsome a manner as possible—which comprise the entire relationship between Ira and his sister—are best understood as "Nabokovian flights of fancy" that make a small contribution to the much larger, more lasting, but oddly amorphous Roth legend, Weil claimed (278–80).

What Weil and Materassi gave insufficient weight to is the fact that Roth's multivolume sequence of novels—which threatens to dwarf even his long silence in sheer weight and size—was originally intended by the author to be published posthumously, as a message from the grave offering conclusive testimony that Roth could not possibly alter or revise subsequently. The confession of incest, then, appears in the legend's final and most painfully honest form. Had Roth's wife not predeceased him—and had Roth therefore not seen the first two volumes of *Mercy of a Rude Stream* into print—his obituaries would have reported the *Shifting Landscape* version of his literary paralysis. Only some years later would the posthumous appearance of his late novels have dislodged the existing version of his legend.

As it turns out, the *Shifting Landscape* version is precisely what his obituaries reported anyway. Typically, Richard Severo stated in the *New York Times:* "In later life, Mr. Roth tended to link his failure to write to his dedicated belief in Marxism." As for *Mercy of a Rude Stream,* Severo stated simply that it "was supposed to pick up where *Call It Sleep* left off. It was not well received" (27). Only Stefan Kanfer's obituary of Roth in the *Los Angeles Times* reported up front that, at the end of his life, Roth offered a confession "as provocative as anything in the chapters of St. Augustine or Rousseau." But Kanfer suggested, counterintuitively, that readers who accepted Roth's analysis of his sexual wrongdoing at face value were mere prudes. "Those who cannot endure full frontal history argue that Roth's writer's block had one cause—the inability to confront this sexual transgression." In reality, Roth lost his identity "in the crossfire between the Soviet Union and the independent mind," Kanfer argued (10). Discomfort over the salacious subject matter is clearly an impediment to well-reasoned, unrestricted discussion of Roth's work. But Kanfer's putatively audacious, no-nonsense comments confirm rather than expose that discomfort.

Discomfort and politeness notwithstanding, the overriding factors accounting for the literary community's refusal to abandon Roth's standard explanation for his silence seem to be simple inertia, the critics' fascination with the original story, and a general desire to preserve for Roth the high esteem that story enjoys as a rich literary text. Roth's subsequent reworking of his frustration and paralysis may be more internally coherent and consistent with the known facts, but by the standards of modernist fiction, it is a mediocre work: too simple, too pat. It reads like the notes of a therapist chronicling a breakthrough by a patient. The resulting narrative is pedestrian, uninvigorating art, but it got the job done: Roth concluded his life a highly productive author. And it also provided a more honest account of the facts, according to Roth's autobiographical narrator. This seems to be Roth's final epiphany: that great art as defined by the modernists demands a disingenuous denial of the truth, yet one could achieve painful clarity through other artistic channels. If the literature generated in a state of self-awareness is of lower quality than the obfuscated texts of the great artists, Roth reasoned, so be it.

Literary critics, however, experienced no such epiphany. When Morris Dickstein insisted that all of Roth's self-indictments are exaggerated or "over-determined," and that "it would be a mistake to take 'incest' (or Joyce, or Communism, or the loss of continuity with the Lower East Side) as the key to whatever paralyzed Roth as a writer" ("No Longer" 7), he was typically directing us back to the preferred modernist reading of Roth's silence—to the rich multiplicity of causes, and to the Eliot-like slippage toward overload and fractured incoherence, toward the deliberate inability to settle on any true answer.

In an adulatory 1988 *New Yorker* article about Roth, Lis Harris reported that the elderly author did not intend to release his multi-volume novel sequence during his lifetime. "That being the case," she wrote, "there are compelling reasons to include here an attempt at an imaginary review" of the unpublished *Mercy of a Rude Stream*—to which Roth "seems entitled," she claimed. "This extraordinary book by one of the most original of twentieth-century American authors picks up where his earlier book ended," she hypothesized. "Without self-pity, it conveys the difficulties encountered by a spirit that was almost crushed by dreams of social promise which got left behind in the onrushing thrust of American society. Perhaps even more poignantly, it describes what the author has elsewhere called the 'terrible truncation' experienced by an immigrant trying to conform to the expectations of an alien culture" (92).

The irony, of course, is that the majority of reviewers in the mid-1990s wrote nearly the same imaginary review, for a series of books that bore only passing resemblance to the description therein. It was as if the critics examining the volumes of *Mercy of a Rude Stream* had dug up old copy from the same era as Harris's piece—1988, just after the release of *Shifting Landscape*—and published it, giving no account of the actual books under review. These were the notices to which Roth seemed entitled.

The literary community, which had spent the previous thirty years admiring the rediscovered author of *Call It Sleep,* discounted Roth's shocking confession even though it placed formerly ill-fitting pieces of his biographical puzzle snugly into place. Roth's shame, for example, explained his reticence in 1964 when his obscure life in rural Maine was disrupted by the success of his rediscovered novel. "Most authors would jump with avaricious joy at the thought of such long-delayed riches and fame," a perplexed Jane Howard noted in her January 1965 *Life* magazine article (75). But Roth's reaction was the opposite of joyous. He grumpily told a journalist that his initial response to "all this hullabaloo" was to slip into a depression. "I was being dislodged all over again," he complained (*Shifting* 132). A month earlier Roth was quoted saying, "All this publicity has had the tendency to kind of stir up what has been in abeyance for a long, long time" (*Shifting* 132). Exactly what was being held in abeyance, of course, would not be made known for another thirty years.

Moreover, scholars who downplay the significance of the incestuous confessions in *Mercy of a Rude Stream* and who dismiss the autobiographical implications forfeit use of a new lens through which to view *Call It Sleep,* a novel in which sex is otherwise inexplicably associated with bodily corruption and moral putrefaction to a hysterical degree. If the assumption is that the narrator's jarring confessions of incest in *Mercy of a Rude Stream,* like Quentin Compson's in *The Sound and the Fury,* must be a fabrication because actual incest is too horrible to speak of, that same reasoning points an accusing finger at the author's alarmist yet circumspect language in *Call It Sleep* and the erasure of a sister from his autobiographical narrative.

The peculiar intensity with which shame is associated with sex in Roth's early novel received notice upon the book's initial publication, most witheringly in the *New Masses* review, which lampooned the book's bizarre overemphasis on "the sex phobias of this six year-old Proust" (review of *Call It Sleep* 27). Less caustically, H. W. Boynton observed in the *New York Times* that "the book lays all possible stress on the nastiness of the human animal"—so obsessively, in fact, that it constructs a queasy "cult of the excremental" (7). Reviewers generally reacted to the coarse sexual nature of the book's street talk. More important, though, are two episodes of sexual childplay that horrify David, pollute his entire worldview, and send him into a panic.

In the book's opening section, "The Cellar," a neighbor girl entraps David into "playing bad." (" 'Put yuh han' in my knish,' she coaxed.") The scene takes place in a bedroom closet (53–54). Thereafter, David feels instinctive revulsion toward another dark, enclosed space: the tenement building's cellar, which he visualizes as a writhing, animalistic trap for children, crawling with rats and other misshapen things. Though the seduction scene with the neighbor girl is comic, the experience seriously damages the psyche of the boy, who comes to associate sexuality with abhorrent and loathsome images of violence, death, and physical decay. And the guilt he feels over his unwitting participation in the encounter is similarly lasting: weeks later when David gets lost in the streets of Brooklyn and winds up at a police station, he tells himself that the ostensibly friendly policemen know about his experience of playing bad and are planning to punish him for it. "They made believe they didn't know," the narrative voice states, "but they knew" (102).

The second episode occurs years later, in the novel's final section, "The Rail." David is pressured by his Catholic friend Leo to arrange a sexual tryst for Leo with David's step-cousin, Esther, in the cellar of his aunt's candy store. Faced once more with the reality of sex, David reverts to cowering form: he shows signs of panic when passing a basement door in the family's new building on the Lower East Side of Manhattan. His mother notices this and other peculiarities of his behavior. " 'Do you know, . . . you've been acting of late almost the way you did in Brownsville when you clung to my side like pitch. And how you feared that short flight of stairs! That can't be troubling you now?' " (330).

After the tryst between Leo and Esther takes place, David is attacked physically and verbally by his father with inappropriate fierceness for a nearly disinterested observer. (The deflowered girl is his wife's step-niece.) The confrontation might seem more fitting as a reaction to the narrator's far greater transgressions in *Mercy of a Rude Stream;* it reads like the scene Ira Stigman imagines he will one day face when his father discovers his appalling secret.

Bewildered comments about David Schearl's extreme reaction to sex are not limited to the novel's original reviewers. Leslie Fiedler commented at length in 1960 on the obsessive transformation of all experience in the novel into "equivocations based on a hated and feared sexuality" ("Henry Roth's" 104). For the young protagonist, the act by which he was generated is an "unmitigated horror," Fiedler wrote; David longs for "a purity he cannot find in his world, a fire, a flame to purify him from his iniquity as he has learned in *cheder* Isaiah was purified" (105).

Later that same year, in his introduction to the Pageant edition of *Call It Sleep,* Maxwell Geismar considered the raw, vulgar sex scene at the candy shop and asked significantly: "But why does David react to this, as to all the normal sexual adventures of childhood, only with a revulsion of panic-fear?" (xlii–xliii). From the vantage point of 1960, Geismar lacked a satisfying explanation. The same was true decades earlier for Alfred Hayes, who reviewed *Call It Sleep* favorably in a 1935 issue of the *Daily Worker* and similarly concluded: "If there is anything suspect in the book, it would be the layer of symbolism Roth has spread over the 'meaning' of David Schearl's childhood. The symbols do not impede the movement of the novel, but one is aware that they represent a meaning over and beyond the crisis in David's family life, and the life of the streets. One is forced to fish around and guess for 'ultimate' meanings" (5).

Today, with four volumes of *Mercy of a Rude Stream* in print, we have Roth's deathbed confession as clarification for otherwise puzzling elements of the novel; we need no longer fish around so cluelessly for ultimate meaning. David Schearl, the highly autobiographical child protagonist of *Call It Sleep,* is upset by sexual events and mere innuendo because the author who created him was a self-loathing wreck with a sexual past he found shameful to the point of debilitation. Roth re-created in the life of his alter ego his own perilous slide toward a ruinous sexual habit he later explicitly assigned to Ira Stigman in *Mercy of a Rude Stream,* burdening young David with foreknowledge of what was to come or, at the very least, with the appropriate dread.

The purity from fire and flame that David seeks in order to relieve the unmitigated horror he anticipates finally arrives in the twenty-two pages of disconnected street chatter emitted in the penultimate chapter. The novel moves toward this climax with a sense of inevitability. In this sexually charged chapter, images of evil, death, and uncleanliness from the book's earlier sections reappear. David's writhing metal milk dipper, thrust between the lips of the trolley track, strikes the electrified third rail, setting off sparks and causing the earth to tremble—all of which is conveyed in "an orgiastic explosion of poetic prose," as Knowles put it in his article from the mid-1960s. "Thus the two themes are united," Knowles explained; "the generative touch of the fiery coal upon the lips of Isaiah is equated with the generative act of sex. David's struggles with sexuality, as well as with his total environment, are reconciled in a moment that relates the act of sex to the creative energy of God" (398–99).

Knowles was not alone in reading the event as a generative and creative episode in the child's life. Indeed, Tom Samet reported in 1975 that, in the decade since the rediscovery of *Call It Sleep,* the novel had generated "a remarkable sort of critical orthodoxy," a "nearly unanimous agreement among critics" that the novel's closing episodes present a radical and potentially creative transfiguration in David Schearl. The terms Samet found mentioned most often in the Roth scholarship of the 1960s and 1970s were "redemption," "salvation," "vision," and "transcendence." But—twenty years before Roth dropped his bombshell in *A Diving Rock on the Hudson*—Samet astutely deemed David's moments of purported illumination to be episodes of betrayal that promised not redemption but shrinkage, retreat, death, and the silence that plagued the author over subsequent decades (570).

Samet's essay helped to reshape the critical orthodoxy on this point. Still, sixteen years later, Alfred Kazin, in his 1991 introduction to the Farrar, Straus and Giroux edition of *Call It Sleep*, cited the thrust ladle that spurts underground flames in the novel's apocalyptic ending and concluded that David has succeeded in bringing light to the rat-infested cellar of his mind. "David has won the essential first victory," Kazin wrote. "He is on his way to becoming the artist who will write this book" (xx).

Prior to 1995, then, the ending of *Call It Sleep* elicited competing interpretations with varying implications for Roth as an artist. Like Stephen Dedalus at the end of Joyce's first novel, the protagonist could be viewed emerging from the electrocution chapter as a true artist, hardened by the ritualistic trials of childhood and about to commence writing the novel we hold in our hands. Or, with Roth's decades of frustration foremost in mind, a reader could interpret the violent shock the child receives and his subsequent passivity as a sign of the author's loss of creative power. Much depended on one's attitudes toward sex, or what one knew of the author's attitudes toward sex. At its polar extremes, sex can be viewed as a natural, procreative act blessed by God or as a sinful transgression that damages the guilt-ridden psyche of the participants and, for an artist, blocks future creative efforts.

Though Roth spent decades emphasizing the high-modernist credentials of his novel, on this one point he made an exception, advocating the *non*-Joycean interpretation of the book's penultimate chapter. In a March 1972 interview with William Freedman, published in 1975, Roth made his case while suggesting there are implications for an entire generation of leftist writers:

R[oth]: It seems to me [the] final image of the novel was in a way prophetic.

F[reedman]: You mean the electrocution? In what sense?

R: Well, it's the short-circuiting. The short-circuit that occurs there seems to be the short-circuit that hit us all. I was short-circuited and I wasn't the only one. We were all somehow cut short.

F: That strikes me as a little odd. In the context of the novel the short-circuit, the electrocution at the end seems to me not an image of termination, but of beginning, an image of creativity, sexual and mystical at the same time. The sexual symbolism seems to me unmistakable in that scene. It's a procreative act and at the same time an act of almost mystical transcendence.

R: What I'm saying may not be in the novel itself, but in retrospect, as I look back on it now in light of everything that happened, the short-circuiting seems to me the most important thing about it. It seems prophetic. ("Conversation" 154)

In further retrospect, this exchange is exceedingly ironic due to the participants' mismatched knowledge of the author's sexual history and its implications for *Call It Sleep*. The interviewer naturally found the case against a procreative reading of the sexually charged chapter "a little odd." He had no idea that sex, for David Schearl as for the author, spells the end of artistic productivity, whereas Roth, aware of the peculiarly inverted function of sex in this case but unwilling to explain the cause of that dysfunction, remained equivocal ("What I'm saying may not be in the novel itself").

Seven months later, in an interview published in 1973, Roth explained further the ending and its meanings to Bonnie Lyons, referring to himself in third person: "The meaning it has for the novelist is a short circuit. It seems too far-fetched that he should have already intuitively realized that his own career was going to suffer this kind of short circuit. And yet how well the fable speaks of the rest of the man's history—it did become the metaphor of himself. But how did one know at the time what was going to follow—now there's really something worth pondering" (*The Man* 170). How could this autobiographical novelist predict with such accuracy the approaching impasse in his writing? By simply noticing that his protagonist was about to hit puberty, which spelled an end to the novelist's useable autobiographical material unless or until he addressed his sordid involvements with his younger sister and his cousin. "You are the painter who painted himself into the corner of childhood," Ecclesias sums it up for Ira in *A Star Shines over Mt. Morris Park* (135). The only other solution, an attempt to write a nonautobiographical novel, proved unworkable as well. In his 1977 essay "Kaddish," Roth recounted—again in third person—how progress on his follow-up to *Call It Sleep* stalled: "The very narrative he was engaged in writing, with wholesome stalwart proletarian as hero, became sicklied over with eroticism, veered toward the pornographic. Jesus. He had a vested interest in the sordid, the squalid, the depraved. He became immobilized" (*Shifting* 188). Significantly, an interest in the sordid, squalid, and depraved is precisely what kept the narrative of *Call It Sleep* moving, as long as the protagonist was safely prepubescent. It was the attempt to transfer these concerns to an adult character, who could act on his sexual interests and be held responsible, that triggered Roth's writer's block.

In 1978, Roth explained his original conception for *Call It Sleep:* the book was to have included the author's entire autobiographical trajectory up to that point, from ghetto child to fledgling Greenwich Village artist. But, Roth stated, in the end he decided to leave David at childhood (Sollors 158). By so doing, Leslie Fiedler noted in 1960, Roth stopped "safely short of the point where 'playing bad' becomes an act that can lead to deflowering or pregnancy." Fiedler pondered the autobiographical significance of this retreat from adult sexuality. "To have written such a book and no other," he concluded, "is to betray some deep trouble" ("Henry Roth's" 105).

It is no surprise, then, that Fiedler was among the few scholars who significantly altered their reading of *Call It Sleep* upon publication of *Mercy of a Rude Stream*. "David seems finally a textbook case of the 'Oedipus Complex,'" Fiedler wrote in "The Many Myths of Henry Roth," published in 1996 (25). About David's final act of thrusting the milk ladle into a dark gap in the earth, Fiedler commented, "Surely, this parody of Phallic penetration and the nearly fatal orgasm which ensues represent both his infringement of the ultimate taboo"—that is, incest with his mother—"and his self-punishment for it" (26). Fiedler did not introduce the revelation of brother-sister incest into his analysis. (The volume in which Fiedler's essay appeared went to press shortly after Roth's death in October 1995. It is unclear if Fiedler had access to volume 2 of *Mercy of a Rude Stream*, published in February of that year, or only volume 1, published in early 1994, prior to drafting the piece.) But Fiedler made use of the preliminary atmosphere of sexual panic and foreboding found in *A Star Shines over Mt. Morris Park* for his revised analysis of *Call It Sleep*, particularly of its ending. This Oedipal reading, which connects the breaking of a sexual taboo directly to Roth's great silence, seemed obvious to Fiedler in 1995, but he admitted: "[I]t has taken me nearly fifty years of reading Roth's novel to perceive it" (28). It also took coaching from Henry Roth himself. Still, Fiedler is among the minority of scholars who appear to have accepted as conclusive Roth's final gloss on his own silence.

In May 1998, Robert Weil, Roth's editor at St. Martin's Press, released to the press a letter that seemed to confirm the incest in Roth's life. Written by Roth's sister and dated 3 July 1994, it was a response to a warning Roth sent her that volume 2 of *Mercy of a Rude Stream*, due for publication the following year, would expose their sexual history in raw detail. "How can you do this to me?" Rose Broder responded before imploring her brother to remove the sexual passages from his manuscript. Broder did not, however, accuse Roth of fabricating the alarming material. Rather, she reasoned with him that making public the incestuous "revelation" would besmirch her and hurt his image "as a man, brother and writer" (Pogrebin B12).

In the London *Times,* whose reviews of *Mercy of a Rude Stream* downplayed the significance of Roth's confession, James Bone announced in his 23 May 1998 "New York" column: "An incestuous relationship between a New York novelist and his sister may hold the key to this century's most famous case of writer's block" (15). Coming more than three years after publication of *A Diving Rock on the Hudson,* this was hardly news. But it suggests that critics who have held tightly to Roth's early, preliminary explanations for his artistic frustration may in the end acquiesce to a revised explanation confirmed by outside documentation. The effect of Broder's letter, however, remains inconclusive. In 1999, Jeffrey Folks maintained that Roth had misinterpreted his own troubled biography. "If Roth believed that in *Mercy of a Rude Stream* he had 'solved' his writer's block," Folks declared, "he is mistaken" ("Henry Roth's National" 291). Roth's hiatus from writing, according to Folks, could best be understood as "symptomatic of a condition of subservience" to an adopted national culture (279). Roth's own suggestion that his writer's block originated in his memory of incest risks trivializing the real issue, Folks insisted (291). Still, Folks was willing to retain such "private markers" if they were put to good use. "I would assert that Ira's memory of incest symbolically expresses the cultural bondage toward which Roth felt a paralyzing ambivalence," Folks wrote (292).

My own conclusion is that Roth's final account of his silence has much to recommend it. The cause-and-effect narrative is plausible. It accounts for the sexual panic in *Call It Sleep.* It provides a continuation of Roth's ghetto-childhood narrative into adulthood. And it undammed Roth's writing at an age when most authors see their productivity decline or stop. But working against its acceptance is the fact that Roth's revision guts a previously complex text of its richness, reducing the status of Roth's silence from high-modernist masterpiece to tacky personal anecdote. By retaining the multifaceted version of Roth's silence from *Shifting Landscape,* scholars preserve its elevated stature and give themselves easier access to the text via theoretical approaches currently popular in the discipline. (Folks applied the vocabulary and analysis of postcolonial studies.) Perhaps the intrusion of extraliterary fact into the narrative will ultimately swing the consensus toward Roth's revised version. If so, that intrusion is entirely unnecessary. To disregard a four-thousand-page *mea culpa* from an infamously blocked writer is to ignore the obvious.

CHAPTER FOUR

Augmenting the Salinger Oeuvre
by Any Means

In February 1977, *Esquire* magazine ran an unsigned short story with the Salingeresque title "From Rupert—With No Promises." Its appearance triggered widespread speculation that J. D. Salinger authored the work, thereby ending twelve years of nonpublication. Reports surfaced within weeks, however, that *Esquire*'s fiction editor, Gordon Lish, wrote the piece himself. "My feeling," Lish later explained, "was that if Salinger was not going to write stories, someone had to write them for him" (Alexander 248).

Efforts to pad Salinger's oeuvre without the knowledge or cooperation of the author extend beyond his fiction. In 1982, an aspiring writer named Steven Kunes submitted to *People* magazine the transcript of a purported interview with the author (the two never actually spoke). Before the interview could run, however, Salinger filed suit against Kunes in U.S. District Court. Salinger had received reports of counterfeit letters on falsified letterhead distributed by Kunes buttressing claims of authenticity for the interview. In his signed affidavit, Salinger objected not only to the illegality of the forgeries but also to their quality, which he found "dreadfully conceived and written" (Williams C2). Salinger, a native New Yorker then as now resident in Cornish, New Hampshire, hypothesized in the affidavit about his recurring victimhood. "I publish my fiction seldom," he wrote. "I have tried, all my professional life, to live and work in privacy. It may be precisely because I live and work as quietly and as remotely as I do, that I have from time to time been the mark for opportunists" (Williams C1).

Salinger's hypothesis about his predicament is sound. It is precisely because he publishes seldom—since 1965, never—and remains remote and inaccessible that bootleggers, forgers, critics, and editors have had a financial incentive to supplant the void left by the author's withdrawal and feel compelled to extend his aborted career narrative. Salinger's aversion to publicity ultimately gives rise to the journalistic stakeout, usually of Salinger's home or the local post office; the ambush photograph; harassing questions shouted at the fleeing author; the forged story, letter, or interview; and attempts to excerpt, paraphrase, or otherwise bring to light extant documents penned by Salinger, particularly letters dating from his apprenticeship as a professional author. At the very least, these badgering efforts ultimately succeed in eliciting public statements in the form of legal affidavits and depositions. The journalists and biographers cannot fail, then: either they concoct secondary texts for and about Salinger, or they force the author to supply them himself in his attempt to frustrate their designs.

In most of these cases, the pursuers have no qualms about their methods. According to a 1988 article in *Newsday*, Frank Devine, editor of the *New York Post*, regarded as "nonsense" the notion that Salinger had a right to be left alone. When Salinger swung his fist ineffectually at a *Post* photographer who blocked the author's car in a New Hampshire parking lot, Devine complained that the "subject"—Salinger—was "interfering with the photographer doing his job" (Collins 10). Lish was likewise unrepentant about his Rupert story. "I did not see that fiction as a hoax," he later wrote, "so much as an attractive plausibility" ("Fool" 409). Most famously, Ian Hamilton believed he was on secure ethical and legal footing when he included long excerpts from unpublished Salinger letters in a proposed biography of the author in 1986. But the courts ruled differently, blocking the book's publication and demanding the removal even of paraphrasings of those excerpted passages. (Two years later, Random House published a curious work by Hamilton, *In Search of J. D. Salinger*, the focus of which was its author's quest for and failure to deliver a satisfying biography.)

The singularity of Salinger's authorship and its trappings routinely trips up critics and other writers who apply conventional expectations of productivity and public interaction to all famous living authors. In 1981, Thomas LeClair grouped Salinger, Don DeLillo, Thomas Pynchon, and William Gaddis together as a clique of relatively homogeneous, publicity-shy authors. "For them," he wrote, "talking, with its instantaneousness and simplification, is the exact opposite of writing fiction" (50). What all four authors fear, he claimed, is the inevitable process by which bad language—literary gossip, celebrity chatter, discussion of advances and other forms of remuneration—drives out good language. "The invisibility necessary for Salinger and DeLillo to write is also one way they, along with Pynchon and Gaddis, preserve the integrity, the strange discreteness, of their novels," LeClair observed (51). But Salinger's case was unlike the others': he no longer published new work. A former author, he simply avoided listening to chatter and refused to generate his own. In 1970, Salinger repaid with interest a seventy-five-thousand-dollar advance from Little, Brown for a proposed fifth book; in 1974, he told a *New York Times* reporter that he derived great satisfaction from writing only for himself (Fosburgh 1); and since then, he has published no new fiction and removed himself from the arenas of public discourse. His four extant books, to which his publishers retain rights, remain in print.

J. D. Salinger's author persona, therefore, is ultimately unlike any other, with the near exception of Harper Lee's (see the conclusion). Katherine Anne Porter, Ralph Ellison, and Truman Capote each went a decade or considerably longer without publishing a book of fiction, but each also wrote book reviews and other essays or sat for interviews, therein commenting on their progress drafting, respectively, *Ship of Fools,* a follow-up to *Invisible Man,* and the ultimately uncompleted *Answered Prayers.* DeLillo, Pynchon, and Gaddis may have shunned publicity and therefore been subjected to incidents of journalistic ambush or subterfuge similar to those Salinger has suffered, but they spoke to the reading public through their major works of the 1970s, 1980s, and 1990s. And whereas countless unknown or failed writers neither publish books nor generate secondary texts, these authors have not gone missing in any specific sense. Salinger's notoriety as the author of *The Catcher in the Rye, Nine Stories, Franny and Zooey,* and *Raise High the Roof Beam, Carpenters and Seymour: An Introduction* guarantees that the critical establishment will speculate on his whereabouts and the condition of his unnervingly static oeuvre.

There are numerous authors whose string of published works ended abruptly—Flannery O'Connor, Nathanael West, and F. Scott Fitzgerald come immediately to mind—but a perfectly reasonable explanation exists in these cases: they died. Jerome David Salinger, born 1 January 1919, is by all reports alive and healthy; the condition of J. D. Salinger the author, however, is a source of contention, mainly between Salinger himself and the literary community, which insists on the author's existence beyond his textual demise and concerns itself with filling what Lish calls "Salinger's gigantically perfect silence" ("Fool" 415). If Jerome David Salinger is not going to produce more texts, the literary community reasons, then someone has to produce some for him, which at the very least means attributing to him volumes of strategically shaped silence. Lish's offhand remark attempting to justify his faux-Salinger story is indicative of the pervasive attitude toward Salinger; Lish's methods for expanding Salinger's stunted canon were simply more proactive than that of the majority of journalists, critics, and scholars who have treated Salinger's extended period of nonpublication as text ripe for critical interpretation—that is, as a deliberate (and cunning) extension of his authorship. As a strategy for filling the Salinger void, this is only somewhat less manipulative than the puckish or illegal methods employed by Lish and Steven Kunes. The critical establishment, denied access for decades to whatever pages Salinger is actually accumulating in his desk drawer, simply will not permit Salinger to depart the active literary scene. Rather than disappear, he is reconfigured as a prolific, nearly conventional author inundating the marketplace with silence.

"For the past two decades I have elected, for personal reasons, to leave the public spotlight entirely," Salinger stated in court documents supporting his 1986 suit filed to block publication of Hamilton's biography. "I have shunned all publicity for over twenty years and I have not published any material during that time. I have become, in every sense of the word, a private citizen" (Alexander 280). When the 1987 ruling of the United States Court of Appeals for the Second Circuit came down in Salinger's favor, it was widely feared in publishing circles that the decision would curb First Amendment rights and have a chilling effect on future scholarship. But Salinger's lawyers insisted there was nothing ominous about the ruling. They maintained that an author, too, has First Amendment rights, including "a right *not* to speak" (Margolick 44).

Most members of the literary community who analyze Salinger's fiction have rejected that assertion, at least implicitly. Their working assumption is that Salinger, a professional author for more than two decades, cannot revert to private-citizen status. He remains a public figure issuing texts, even if he does not actually publish or otherwise address the public directly or willingly. As such he clearly has no right *not* to speak. He is helpless, in fact, to block their close textual analyses of the nonexistent works through which they believe he communicates.

"I am sometimes made to wonder where it is Salinger's mind has kept itself going to—now that we no longer have even the coded record the fellow used to mark down for us of the turnings of its travel," Lish wrote in 1986 as a prelude to indulging in idle speculation. "But there I go again," he admitted in the same essay, "guessing about Salinger with nothing to go on to back me up" ("Fool" 408). This literary guessing game elicits the participation of numerous scholars, who focus their analyses on the few public statements Salinger *has* made, in an effort to decode the subsequent workings of the uncommunicative author's mind.

In his 1999 biography of Salinger, Paul Alexander picked over the brief author's notes included on the inside flaps of Salinger's final two books to try to unlock the puzzle of his withdrawal and attribute to the author a careful, premeditated design to his silence. In the second author's note, from 1963, Salinger explained that his decision to collect "Raise High the Roof Beam, Carpenters" and "Seymour: An Introduction" in a single volume was made "in something of a hurry" to avoid close chronological contact with new material in his series of works on the Glass family: "There is only my word for it, granted, but I have several new stories coming along—waxing, dilating—each in its own way, but I suspect the less said about them, in mixed company, the better" (Alsen 238). Because only one subsequent work, "Hapworth 16, 1924," appeared in print, Alexander attributed deceitful intent to Salinger in these notes, the textual and biographical evidence of which he parsed with single-minded humorlessness. ("What exactly did he mean by 'mixed company'?" [225].) Alexander was suspicious of nearly every phrase Salinger penned; the majority he deemed deceptive or disingenuous.

Alexander was building a case supporting the accusation that Salinger's reclusion is elaborately designed to initiate a dialogue with the audience and fuel the publicity machine, the workings of which the conniving recluse in truth welcomes rather than resents. It is the same accusation that Ian Hamilton, smarting from his failed legal wrangling with Salinger in the mid-1980s, made in the quasi biography Random House ultimately issued. In fact, a dialogue of sorts *has* been initiated and maintained, not by Salinger, but by journalists, critics, scholars, biographers, and readers who believe Salinger is speaking to them.

In 1975, C. David Heymann published an article in the *Village Voice* about his efforts to find out more about Salinger by trekking to New Hampshire. "My approach was from the side," he reported of his arrival at Salinger's Swiss chalet–style home. "The door appeared to be locked; a large curtained picture window to the left of the door was dark. I knocked and called hello. My voice trembled. I was scared" (35).

Salinger does not make an appearance at this point in Heymann's narrative, but his dog does; it barks when Heymann raps on the door. "It was a miserable whine, empty-sounding and hollow, and it shattered the perfect silence," wrote Heymann. "I waited and listened." Finally, Heymann turned to leave, but the whining continued. "As I walked back down the slippery hill to my car I could still hear the dog baying in the background. I could hear it as I backed the car out of the driveway and into the road. It echoed among the hills as I drove down the road away from the house and toward the town. It stayed with me all the way into town. It was, I reflected, an unpleasant, forbidding sound" (35).

This strikes me as an inordinately detailed and nuanced account of a guard dog doing what guard dogs are supposed to do: bark at intruders. It suggests that nonresponses from Salinger to contact initiated by outsiders are imbued with undue importance and meaning, even assigned a mood ("unpleasant, forbidding") and a tone ("hollow," "empty-sounding," "miserable"). Reports such as this demonstrate that, upon significant reflection, we can gain some understanding of the life that the author J. D. Salinger leads. For one thing, it is sad. And it must therefore follow that his silence calls out to us from that unhappy place.

Ron Rosenbaum made the pilgrimage to Cornish for *Esquire* magazine. In a 1997 article, he reflected on his visit from the vantage point of Salinger's driveway, where he claimed the author's mailbox beckoned to him. "It's not a passive silence," he commented on the wall of inaccessibility and reclusion Salinger has built around himself, and his refusal to publish; "it's a palpable, provocative silence" that speaks to the reader and exerts power over him. "Something draws us to it, makes us interrogate it, test it," Rosenbaum explained. "[W]hen a writer won't break his silence, we think of ways to break into it" (50).

Apparently Salinger's mailbox beckons to innumerable others; how else to explain the 2002 collection *Letters to J. D. Salinger,* edited by Chris Kubica and Will Hochman and published by the University of Wisconsin Press? Hochman explains in his postscript that the volume "shows readers 'talking' critically and creatively" to an author whose response is fully muted, and whose status as a publishing author has lapsed (243). A majority of the correspondents in the book are professional writers, editors, and academics (including Tom Robbins, George Plimpton, and Sanford Pinsker) solicited by Kubica. "Would you consider publishing a letter to Salinger," he asked them, "in a collection of such letters for all of us to read and to save it, in effect, from Salinger's nearest landfill?" (xvii). Some seventy-eight solicited contributors were willing to do just that, knowing that the exchange was not with a human writer but with a Foucauldian author function largely of their own design, but who was no less legitimate for being so. Novelist Jessica Treadway praised the author for the revelatory truth of *Nine Stories* (44). Poet and fiction writer David Huddle apologized for writing in a style too closely imitative of Salinger's (37). The editors also opened up the exchange to unsolicited e-mailers, who submitted their letters via Kubica's Web site. Among the seventy-one such items selected is a letter from David Miller questioning the rightness of the project itself: "I think to attempt to write or visit J. D. Salinger betrays what Salinger has stood for, for the past 50 years" (200). But the vast majority of correspondents played along with the conceit of directly addressing J. D. Salinger and offered thanks, praise, or puzzlement at his disappearance.

With Salinger's ultimate status as an author uncertain, readers reject his withdrawal from the public sphere and its attendant duties, like reading fan mail. In this light, *Letters to J. D. Salinger* can be viewed as an attempt to return the missing author to his rightful place as an accessible figure who welcomes adulation and responds to querying from the reading public. In a related fashion, Warren French has twice reworked his book-length study of Salinger. First published in 1963, *J. D. Salinger* was issued in revised form in 1976 to incorporate, one might have thought, analysis of a new work of Salinger fiction, "Hapworth 16, 1924," which appeared in 1965. But in fact the revisions largely addressed Salinger's withdrawal from public life and his eleven-year silence. In *J. D. Salinger, Revisited* (1988), French returned again to the same unchanged canon of Salinger works, with no purpose other than to acknowledge—to "revisit"—the expanding silence the author was emitting, and to speculate on its sources and meaning, as if Salinger were an author whose list of published works continued to expand.

Of course, not all critics engage in a hermeneutics of Salinger's silence. "I have no idea why Salinger has not in recent years graced us with more stories," wrote Robert Coles in a 1973 "Reconsideration" of Salinger in the *New Republic*. "It is no one's business, really" (32). In his contribution to *Letters to J. D. Salinger*, Andy Selsberg concurred: "You don't have to publish. You don't have to read the letters or reviews. You don't have to explain. We've got what we need. Don't say another word" (Kubica and Hochman 40). But the fact that Selsberg's comments are written in second person, directly addressing an author whose disappearance he condones, suggests just how strong is the tendency to confront the author's silence and reclusion and analyze them, either as acts of manipulation or, in the words of Dipti R. Pattaniak, as "a conscious intellectual and spiritual stance worthy of sober critical attention" (114).

In the early 1960s, novelist Herbert Gold and a coeditor were preparing an anthology of American short stories and requested permission to reprint one of Salinger's. "You wrote a short note to deny us the privilege," Gold stated in his contribution to *Letters to J. D. Salinger*. Though he has since lost the actual note, its mysterious concluding sentence remains fixed in Gold's memory. "It read: 'I have my reasons' " (Kubica and Hochman 33).

Salinger's reasons for refusing anthologization of previously published work are open to speculation. The same is true of his reasons for exiting the literary world altogether a few years later. "It's because he can't stand any criticism," Salinger's sister, Dorris, told her niece (Margaret Salinger 428). According to novelist Tom Wolfe, Salinger "seems to be a classic burnt-out case" who has exhausted his "small, precious talent" (60). In the same vein, British novelist Emma Forrest suggested in a 2001 collection of essays focused on this very topic that the author, unlike Philip Roth, may not have been "good enough" to sustain a career that would build toward ever-greater accolades and popular success and therefore retreated to avoid failure (61). Joel Stein, in the same volume, emphasized Salinger's discomfort at receiving attention, which sounds more like a rephrasing of the question of why the author withdrew than an attempt at an answer (171).

Much speculation of this sort conflates Salinger the nonpublishing author with Salinger the recluse, who, according to Jonathan Yardley, defends his privacy "with a tenacity that at times has spilled over into something more like lunacy" (c1). The apparently irrational extent to which Salinger protects his privacy has given rise to the most extreme and intrusive hypotheses for his silence, such as one offered in Alexander's biography: that Salinger had "a penchant for young women that he did not want to reveal to the public" (312–13). More often, though, Salinger's "lunacy" generates less offensive if no less fanciful explanations for his retreat from the world. Two of the many suggested by Hamilton are, one, that Salinger, a fledgling actor in his adolescence, is now sinking his teeth into the role of a lifetime, that of a reclusive artist (*In Search* 22); and, two, that the author—an egotistical, ill-tempered, unforgiving man—wants so badly to be canonized that he has invented a Salinger-like character named Seymour Glass, "a saint who writes beautiful poetry" (Salinger writes prose), "who has a breakdown in the war" (as did Salinger), "who marries the wrong woman" (Salinger's short-lived marriage to a war bride seemed doomed from the start), "who commits suicide" (Salinger has not killed himself, but has made himself semiposthumous by not publishing or even addressing the public for four decades) (*In Search* 150).

The religious aspect of Hamilton's second hypothesis moves the focus of the discussion away from biographical or psychological speculation toward at least a fleeting consideration of the content of Salinger's works, something I do at greater length later in this chapter. The characters populating Salinger's later novellas—members of the Glass family—are heavily schooled in, and at times obsessed with, spiritual matters, particularly those addressed by Vedanta Hinduism, Zen Buddhism, and Eastern Orthodox Christianity. Supported by the biographical information available about Salinger, the widespread assumption has been that the author himself began seriously to focus on such matters in the 1950s, which might explain his professional self-removal a decade later. "The holy man, the initiate, withdraws not only from the temptations of worldly action; he withdraws from speech," George Steiner explained (*Language* 13). James Lundquist, reasoning that Zen Buddhism exploits the virtues of logical nonsense in the form of riddles rather than conventional logic (33), thought this applicable to Salinger's career: What could be more nonsensical than a diligent author who chooses not to publish? And even Ron Rosenbaum, contemplating the compelling void one confronts from the bottom of Salinger's driveway, described the eerie nonresponse as "the deliberate silence that represents some kind of spiritual renunciation" (53).

Lost on none of the scholars interpreting the author's silence is the apparent irony that the more Salinger insists on anonymity, the more famous he becomes; the lengthier and more remarkable his period of nonpublication grows, the louder his text of silence speaks. For some, including his two biographers, it is only a short leap from making such observations to voicing the accusation—neither provable nor disprovable—that Salinger knowingly designed his career this way, to elicit greater acclaim and remuneration.

Observations about Salinger's inescapable celebrity status began early, while the author was still publishing. He had from the start avoided the usual trappings of literary publicity, refusing to sit for interviews, demanding that his photograph be removed from the cover flap of his novel, insisting that his publisher, Little, Brown, send out no review copies of the book, and departing New York City, America's literary epicenter, for rural New Hampshire in January 1953, the year his second book, *Nine Stories,* was published. At first, critics responded to the talented author's personal quirks with fond bewilderment or outright admiration. But by 1960, David Leitch had decided that Salinger's desire for anonymity was "almost an affectation" (70). That same year, Harvey Swados observed that Salinger had so sedulously avoided publicity that he had "aroused the liveliest curiosity about himself" (12). In Don DeLillo's 1991 novel *Mao II,* a Salingeresque character explains this phenomenon in terms of a fickle creator: "When a writer doesn't show his face, he becomes a local symptom of God's famous reluctance to appear" (36).

In *Before the Great Silence,* Maurice Maeterlinck spoke similarly of how familiar but unavailable persons—specifically, the dead—assume a fixed identity in our minds that supercedes the living and approaches the sublime power of the divine. "When I think of my mother, my father, my two brothers, or five or six friends of mine who are dead, they still exist, they live as distinctly as when they were alive" (84). In fact, he claimed, they are more clearly recognizable than when they were living. "They no longer change," he reported. "They have lost all their little defects, and are always smiling, as though they had returned from the most beautiful country" (85). In contrast: "The majority of the living weary us, or are strangers to us. We truly know and love only the dead" (195). Salinger's inaccessibility may likewise do more than merely pique the public's curiosity. It may permit them to perfect their mental image of the author and attribute a similar perfection to his recent work—the sublime silence of nonpublication— whose power is unlike that of any conventional book. "So long as a man is alive one does not know what he is or what he will do," Maeterlinck added. "We have unwavering confidence only in the dead" (195). Similarly, public confidence in J. D. Salinger may outstrip public confidence in any publishing author, the quality of whose prose may suddenly dip, whose personality may shift alarmingly, or who may begin to repeat himself to an annoying extent. Ironically, should a posthumous Salinger publish new works, public confidence may be shaken. But a living Salinger committed to silence and privacy is, for these purposes, safely and vividly dead.

Thomas LeClair warned that, in addition to the obvious paradoxes of reclusion ("The less a writer is visible, the more he is pursued"), there is a deeper danger that "the condition necessary for writing can become the novelist's subject: purification, obsession, silence" (52). But, professionally speaking, where is the danger in that? As Warren French concluded about Salinger in 1988, "His long silence has not affected his reputation" (*Revisited* 122). Similarly, Daniel M. Stashower observed in 1983 that Salinger's isolation "has done nothing to damage but rather has strengthened the claim of some literary critics that Salinger is one of the more important American writers in the postwar era" (375).

Because Salinger's silence and reclusion have been perceived as solidifying his professional reputation, some writers detect cunning deliberation in the author's behavior. As early as 1967, Howard M. Harper Jr. described the relationship between Salinger and his critics as "something of a cat-and-mouse game, the roles interchanging with each installment of the Glass saga" (95). Not everyone who views Salinger's behavior as calculating has been censorious. Som P. Ranchan congratulated Salinger for infusing his manipulation of the literary world with exemplary Hindu symbolism and mythology. "It is my conviction that Salinger is a mischievous mystic who has played an interesting game with critics," Ranchan wrote. "In this metaphysical game he has used primarily the Vedantic frameworks inlaid with Zen and shakta values" (v). But Salinger's two biographers, Ian Hamilton and Paul Alexander, made clear their intention was to expose not a playful mystic but a greedy fraud.

Even before Salinger sued to block publication of his book, Hamilton found the author's behavior inconsistent, his comments about not wanting to be contacted "flirtatious" and "teasing" (Field 63). An angry letter Salinger wrote berating Hamilton for contacting Salinger's sister and son was rejected as "somewhat too composed, too pleased with its own polish for me to accept it as a direct cry from the heart." Hamilton showed the letter to a friend in the literary business, who assured him it was really a come-on; he suggested that Salinger's helpless statement "I can't stop you" should best be translated as "Please go ahead" (*In Search* 7), which is precisely what Hamilton did, only to face litigation, after which the gloves came off. In his revised manuscript, Hamilton did not limit himself to the standard ironic observations—"He was famous for not wanting to be famous" (4)—but plainly and paradoxically accused the author of cheapening his talent by not selling his new works. "He said he wanted neither fame nor money and by this means he'd contrived to get extra supplies of both—much more of both, in fact, than might have come his way if he'd stayed in the marketplace along with everybody else" (8).

Salinger's suit against Hamilton and his publisher, Random House, was set in motion when an advance copy of the galley proofs got into the hands of Salinger's agent (Margolick 45). Eleven years later, Renaissance Books prudently released Paul Alexander's biography with little advance publicity and, in a Salingeresque twist, sent out no review copies (Quinn 26). Subjected to no revenge-inducing legal hassles, Alexander was still suspicious of his subject's true designs. "[S]imply because he turned into a recluse does not mean he didn't want fame," Alexander reasoned. "In fact, one could argue that by taking the position he did—and keeping it—he ensured he *would* remain famous for being a recluse" (26). The manner in which Salinger handled supposedly unwanted publicity seemed to Alexander a bit too contrived to get attention, just as it had to Hamilton. "The whole act," as he called it, "felt as if it were being put on by a master showman, a genius spin doctor, a public-relations wizard hawking a story the public couldn't get enough of" (302). And the author's ultimate motivation for this elaborate performance was again assumed to be pecuniary. When Salinger sought to block inclusion of his unpublished letters in Hamilton's original biography manuscript, Alexander asserted, he was concerned not so much about his copyright as his trademark: "[P]art of what Salinger was protecting by filing his lawsuit against Hamilton was the image he had created over the years, an image that promoted sales of books" (284).

Neither biographer offered statistical evidence to support his claims, nor could he: even if one tabulated actual worldwide sales of Salinger's four books, how would one then estimate, for the purpose of comparison, the hypothetical annual sales of a nonreclusive, actively publishing author who goes on television to hawk his books and sells film rights to Hollywood? Serious analysis is beside the point: this is an argument based on conjecture. It is an attempt to shape a compelling author persona where none exists outside reader expectations. Just as a dearth of published works prompted critics to produce some on the author's behalf, an absent author elicited a replacement figure, whose gaze remains fixed on the reader, and who is very self-aware. "He's a media animal," assumed one contributor to *Letters to J. D. Salinger*. "He's creating an icon, and he's smart enough to know it" (Kubica and Hochman 223).

The issue of public-relations savvy surfaces whenever Salinger is mentioned in the media. In 1998, Joyce Maynard published *At Home in the World*, a memoir that chronicled in embarrassing detail her nine-month relationship with Salinger. The following year, she placed at auction fourteen personal letters written by Salinger just before and during the affair. Included in the cache, which Sotheby's sold for $156,500, was the initial letter, dated 25 April 1972, written in response to Maynard's *New York Times Magazine* essay "An 18-Year-Old Looks Back on Life" (Smith B1). "No one forced J. D. Salinger in the spring of 1972 to initiate an epistolary relationship with an 18-year-old college freshman," wrote Joyce Carol Oates in a 1999 *New York Times* op-ed piece, published amid a flurry of bad press against Maynard, who was labeled a "leech" and a "highly skilled predator" the next day in the same newspaper (Dowd A23). "[N]o one forced the 53-year-old writer, at the height of his perhaps sufflated fame, to seduce her through words, and to invite her to live with him in rural New Hampshire" (Oates, "Words" A23). Brooke Allen, writing in the *National Review*, concurred. Salinger "should have had the good sense, if not the good taste, to keep his mitts off of impressionable young girls," she wrote. Allen took special note of the fact that the pair were ludicrously mismatched: in stark contrast to Salinger, Maynard is an exhibitionistic writer "who spills her guts in public about everything from her sexual dysfunctions to her breast implants" (34).

Both Allen and Oates questioned the judgment of an author whose chief fear is unwanted publicity, but if one approaches the incident from the inverted perspective of Hamilton and Alexander, the affair makes perfect sense. No longer is Salinger a lonely middle-aged recluse trading on his celebrity status to elicit the company of a young woman, ultimately causing his own downfall through inadvertent exposure. Instead, the author is a manipulative genius who introduces an uninhibited writer into his inner circle precisely so that, twenty-seven years later, she will raise a storm of controversy by violating his privacy, thereby extending the Salinger myth and selling yet more copies of his extant books.

But available evidence fails to support the accusation that Salinger is engaging in an elaborate publicity stunt. Every few years, Salinger approaches one of the fans or journalists who stake out his home and asks politely to be left alone. He returned a call to a *New York Times* correspondent in 1973 to voice his displeasure at the recent appearance of the pirated edition of his early stories. In 1980, in response to a pleading letter with accompanying photographs, he drove to town to meet an attractive young woman named Betty Eppes but fled once it became apparent she was conducting a formal interview for publication. He filed the 1981 suit against forger Steven Kunes and won. He filed the 1986 suit against Ian Hamilton for copyright infringement and won. And in 1997, he contracted with Orchises Press to publish in book form his final *New Yorker* story, "Hapworth 16, 1924," but publication was indefinitely suspended.

In every case but the last, someone other than Salinger initiated contact, but that means nothing if one assumes the author deliberately lured the intruders into his world. What determines if Salinger's behavior over the past four decades constitutes a public-relations coup or a largely successful attempt at self-seclusion is, I believe, the reader's understanding of suspended authorship. If a writer, by ceasing to publish, likewise ceases to exist as a public entity, then Jerome David Salinger has merely disappeared into the private world of his own free will. Attempts to break into that world are therefore affronts to his privacy. But if an author is doomed to fulfill his natural life span, publicly and against his will, then Salinger is still a writer concerned primarily about his career. That is, he remains a publicity hound taking pains not to lose his readership or access to their money.

Theories claiming that J. D. Salinger has deliberately attempted to remain viable as a public figure through silence do not hold up well under scrutiny. When the case of *J. D. Salinger v. Random House Inc. and Ian Hamilton* got extensive newspaper coverage in 1987, Andrew Delbanco wrote, "J. D. Salinger is back in public view because he has made another effort to keep himself out of it" (27). The implication of Delbanco's comment is that the unfettered appearance of Hamilton's original biography, with page after page of excerpts from Salinger's personal letters, would not have put Salinger back in public view, whereas the lawsuit to block the book's publication did. Hamilton agreed with Delbanco's analysis, summing up the media fallout from the lawsuit thus: "Salinger was getting more feature-length attention in the press than would surely have resulted from the unimpeded publication of my 'writing life' "—that is, of his original manuscript (*In Search* 209). Yet Hamilton's research methodology, which he outlined in the opening chapter of his book, suggests who is actually guilty of manipulation in this case.

Hamilton explained that he initiated his research on the book in 1984 by writing a letter to Salinger to request an interview and to assure the author that he, Hamilton, was a serious critic and biographer not to be confused with the fans and magazine reporters who had been approaching him for decades. "All this was entirely disingenuous," Hamilton admitted.

> I knew very well that Salinger had been approached in this manner maybe a hundred times before, with no success. . . . I had not, then, expected a response to my approach. On the contrary, I had written just the sort of letter that Salinger—as I imagined him—would heartily despise. At this stage, *not* getting a reply was the essential prologue to my plot. . . . The idea, or one of the ideas, was to see what would happen if orthodox biographical procedures were to be applied to a subject who actively set himself to resist, or even to forestall them. . . . It would be a biography, yes, but it would also be a semispoof in which the biographer would play a leading, sometimes comic, role. (*In Search* 3–4)

What Hamilton outlined, of course, was the biographer's equivalent of a perjury trap, set for an absent, inaccessible author, and designed to elicit a response in keeping with *how Hamilton imagined him.* When a writer abdicates his role as author, he loses most of the control that he—or his work, his publisher, his agent, his publicist—would normally exert over the shaping of his public persona, which falls instead into the hands of critics and readers who, ironically in some cases, insist the abdication never took place.

It is difficult if not impossible to refute conclusively a hypothesis as speculative and steeped in conspiracy as that emanating from Salinger biographers and critics. But it seems to me that Salinger's efforts to curb exposure of his personal life have largely succeeded, not deliberately backfired. The case involving novelist W. P. Kinsella is illustrative. His 1982 novel *Shoeless Joe* includes a character named J. D. Salinger whom the protagonist kidnaps, but the film adaptation of the novel does not. In *Letters to J. D. Salinger,* Kinsella wrote to the author, "When my book appeared my publisher's lawyers received a grumbling letter from your attorneys saying that you were outraged and offended to be portrayed as a character in my book, and that you would be very unhappy if the work were transferred to other media. Hollywood didn't have the balls to use you as a character in the movie *Field of Dreams,* opting instead for a generic black reclusive author that you couldn't claim was a thinly disguised you" (Kubica and Hochman 111). A hit feature film, of course, affords exponentially greater exposure than does a novel by a midlevel author; Salinger's efforts to remove himself from the narrative and thereby avoid additional publicity worked precisely as intended.

Even Ian Hamilton subsequently voiced reservations about his project and its guiding premise. "I was perhaps over-disposed to be skeptical about Salinger's reclusiveness," he admitted in a reflective essay published two years after his Salinger book finally appeared. "I didn't really believe that he wanted to be left alone. It didn't fit with what he'd written" (*Keepers* 19). What Salinger has written—or rather what he has *authored* (as opposed to copyrighted letters, which he refuses to publish)—should probably be treated as the only reliable source material on J. D. Salinger the silent author. That sounds like a tautology, but I believe it is worth stating in this case. Since 1965, Salinger's few public utterances have comprised either curt responses to would-be journalists or statements issued to block others from publishing his work. A reliable reading of the author's silence must originate from an examination of his published fiction, which constitutes the only statements offered by Salinger to the public voluntarily and unprovoked.

The advantages to such a reading are numerous. Most important, one is thereby directed away from reading the author's post-1965 period of nonpublication as a text that speaks ominously of his frustration, sadness, trickery, insanity, peacefulness, arrogance, spirituality, or whatever attribute one wishes to project onto the pliable, unresponsive private citizen named Salinger. Such a reading still gives consideration to the author's silence and places it in context, but the silence itself would remain merely what it is: not a text, but an absence of texts—a full suspension of the author's voice.

Such a reading would build on the work of Mark Silverberg, who examined Ian Hamilton's failed attempt to "find Salinger" within the text of silence and concluded that such an effort uncovers not the mysterious author but rather "the impossibility of ever accurately locating Salinger," at least among the "potent rhetorical entities" that surface from disparate sources unregulated by a central authority. "Rather than a biography," Silverberg wrote, "Hamilton's work is best seen as anti-biography which subverts the efficacy of the whole genre and opens a void similar to the ones opened by Barthes and Foucault in their discussions of the disappearance of the Author" (223). Hamilton's account, Silverberg concluded, suggests that an objective reading of Salinger of the kind Hamilton attempted is impossible because "the author's name has become tightly entwined not only with his works, but also with a whole network of accounts, assumptions, stories and beliefs from which the name can never be completely disentangled" (228). My goal is precisely to disentangle that confusing network.

In "Literature and Biography," Boris Tomaševskij expressed disdainful resignation toward the author legend one found threaded through most authors' oeuvres. Had he and Salinger been contemporaries, Tomaševskij might have been especially irritated by Salinger's fiction, which according to the critical consensus is marred by the author's overt interference in the narrative. James Lundquist wrote in 1979 that Salinger had a tendency "to talk *through* his characters rather than making them seem as if they are speaking *for* themselves" (116). In 1958, Paul Levine summed up recent Salinger works, including "Franny," "Raise High the Roof Beam, Carpenters," and "Zooey": "The stories hold the reader's attention not through the revelation of character but through the revelation of author" (114). Salinger himself, in the dust-cover notes for *Franny and Zooey,* described Seymour's brother, the fictional fiction writer Buddy Glass, as his "alter-ego and collaborator" (Alsen 237); for his part, Buddy claims credit for authoring not only the novellas he narrates or introduces but also such Salinger works as "Teddy," "A Perfect Day for Bananafish," and *The Catcher in the Rye.*

The British novelist David Lodge noted that Salinger's fiction has "a disorienting effect on the reader" because Buddy Glass cites criticism of his fiction and rumors about his private life that are nearly identical to those provoked by Salinger himself (241). John Wenke classified the effect as one of displacement: the fictional conceit that a real-life Buddy Glass is the actual author furthers Salinger's disappearing act, he claimed (66). My reading is the opposite: the effect is not a displacement of Salinger by the narrator, but rather a displacement of the character Buddy by the author. In the end, there is no Buddy Glass left in the narratives; there is only Salinger.

There may in fact be no Glass family members left at all. In "Seymour: An Introduction," Buddy admits that the Seymour described in "A Perfect Day for Bananafish," the earliest Glass story, "was not Seymour at all but, oddly, someone with a striking resemblance to—alley oop, I'm afraid—myself" (*Raise High* 113). The absurdly long and sophisticated letter that comprises the majority of "Hapworth 16, 1924," ostensibly composed by a hyperprecocious seven-year-old

Seymour, seems similarly to be the imaginative work of an intrusively adult Buddy, who claims to be reproducing the original document word for word. And the long conversations and private moments recorded among Franny, Zooey, mother Bessie, and even Franny's boyfriend, Lane, in *Franny and Zooey* are reconstructed by a narrator, Buddy Glass, who was nowhere near at the time. It would seem that Salinger, by his own admission, is Buddy, and that Buddy in turn is omniscient, embodying or at least speaking for everyone. Mary McCarthy came to a similar conclusion in her blistering attack on *Franny and Zooey* in 1962. "[W]ho are these wonder kids but Salinger himself, splitting and multiplying like the original amoeba?" she asked of the seven Glass siblings. "In Hemingway's work there was hardly anybody but Hemingway in a series of disguises, but at least here was only one Papa per book. To be confronted with the seven faces of Salinger, all wise and lovable and simple, is to gaze into a terrifying narcissus pool" (39).

All of this is merely to say that there is a strong justification for ascribing to the author the concerns and prejudices of the major characters. By presenting Buddy Glass as alter ego and collaborator, Salinger has directed us to do just that. Holden Caulfield and the Glass children are judgmental of outsiders, impatient with social niceties, and scornful of gratuitous displays of talent. The author persona that emerges from these works is likewise uncomfortable with society as it normally functions and has a similar ambivalence toward the sharing of creative works with the public.

Moreover, obvious connections can be drawn between the author's aborted career and his characters' specific observations about silence and artistic reticence. In *The Catcher in the Rye,* Holden imagines pretending to be "a poor deaf mute bastard" in order to avoid having "goddam stupid useless conversations with anybody" (198). He is offended by the adulation heaped on Ernie, "a big fat colored guy that plays the piano" in a Greenwich Village club (80). "I swear to God, if I were a piano player or an actor or something and all those dopes thought I was terrific, I'd hate it," Holden states. "I wouldn't even want them to *clap* for me. People always clap for the wrong things. If I were a piano player, I'd play it in the goddam closet" (84).

Four years later, in "Franny," the reluctance of the title character, a promising actress, to flaunt her artistic gifts must be read in the context of newly explicit religious concerns apparently shared by both author and character. One problem with such a reading, however, is that "Salinger's Big Religious Package," to use Stanley Edgar Hyman's dismissive phrase, is a wide-ranging mixture so varied as to make most critical analyses meaningless. "Zooey" alone, Hyman noted, includes references to "the Upinishads, the Diamond Sutra, Meister Eckhart, Dr. Suzuki on *satori,* saints, *arhats, bodhisvattas, jivanmuktas,* Jesus, Gautama, Lao-tse, Shankaracharya, Hui-neng, Sri Ramakrishna, the Four Great Vows of Buddhism, God's grace, the Jesus Prayer, *japam,* Chuang-tzu, Epictetus, and the Bible" (126), all intended to put Franny's spiritual crisis in context or, coming from Zooey's mouth, lift her malaise, which in fact they appear to do by story's end. In "Seymour: An Introduction," Buddy explains that the family's roots in Eastern philosophy, including Zen Buddhism, are "planted in the New and Old Testament, Advaita Vedanta, and classical Taoism" (208), thereby narrowing the field of references somewhat but preserving a range of influences on Salinger's characters and of potential sources for their epiphanies.

Placing Salinger's silence in meaningful context amid such a diffuse smorgasbord of religious influences requires that one adopt a vaguely Orientalist analysis of the kind presented by Yasunari Kawabata in his Nobel Prize acceptance speech, in which he spoke of a generically Eastern tradition that seeks enlightenment through "a discarding of words" (55). "Here we have the emptiness, the nothingness, of the Orient," he stated in 1968, before Edward Said made such pronouncements professionally precarious. "My own works have been discarded as works of emptiness, but it is not to be taken for the nihilism of the West. The spiritual foundation would seem quite different" (41). When a Zen disciple sits silent, motionless, with his eyes closed, for long hours, he enters an impassive state free from thoughts, ideas, or words. "He departs from the self and enters the realm of nothingness. This is not the nothingness or the emptiness of the West," Kawabata repeated, further delineating a simple Oriental-Occidental dichotomy. "It is rather the reverse, a universe of the spirit in which everything communicates freely with everything, transcending bounds, limitless" (56).

To lend coherence to Salinger's silence, then, it is convenient to attribute to him a point of view that similarly differentiates cleanly between East and West, and which favors the East. This is easily justified, considering the obsessions of his characters. Seymour, we are told, "was drawn, first, to Chinese poetry, and then, as deeply, to Japanese poetry, and to both in ways that he was drawn to no other poetry in the world" (*Raise High* 117). Buddy is similarly enthralled: "I haven't the gall to try to say what makes the Chinese or Japanese poet the marvel and the joy he is" (*Raise High* 119). This exclusive pairing of Japanese and Chinese literature assumes a natural kinship that does not in fact exist. But a kinship can be synthesized if one views both cultures as equally non-Western, assumes that artists in both have been influenced by a stew of mystical religious movements similar to that which the Glass siblings have studied, and attributes to both traditions a special sense of enlightenment rooted in a silence that is outside the realm of Western experience. Scholars have assumed that, in Eastern religions and mystical variants of Christianity, Salinger found answers to his quest for balancing spiritual and secular pursuits as well as life and art. His withdrawal from the publishing world can be made to fit this view. "Ultimately his 'silence' becomes the culminating gesture when his life becomes the message," Pattaniak explained, "a testament of the values his art hitherto professed" (115–16).

But, in fact, his art hitherto professed values that suggested the gifted artist must *not* disappear into a culminating gesture of silence. Rather, the artist owes it to the public to create and share that creation with a mass audience, Salinger's fiction implied. This is the fundamental complication inherent in any analysis of Salinger's post-1965 career in light of themes presented in his published work, particularly "Zooey."

In the 1953 story "De Daumier-Smith's Blue Period," Salinger offered a narrative in which a supremely gifted artist, Sister Irma, is nearly drawn into the corrupt world of public adulation by the narrator, an art instructor employed at a correspondence school. But administrators at the convent where Sister Irma works as an elementary school art teacher cut off contact between pupil and instructor, perhaps because the narrator's praise of her art is excessive (and, therefore, inappropriately personal and potentially amorous); perhaps because the administrators fear Irma's talents, if developed, might lure her away from her path of spiritual enlightenment; or perhaps because they fear her talents, if developed, might afford her professional alternatives and cost them their drawing instructor. Their motives are unclear. One is tempted to extract from the story a lesson about Salinger's disavowal of the corrupting forces of fame, but the extent to which this story can be said to parallel Salinger's own biography is limited. Irma is an innocent, not a famous artist who abandons a thriving career. She does not disavow fame; rather, others make that gesture on her behalf. And, presumably, she does not slip into reclusion. Rather, she continues to instruct her "kittys"—the beloved pupils at her school—as she always has (*Nine Stories* 148). In her peculiar case, forfeiting a successful artistic career prolongs the intimate and meaningful relationship she enjoys with humanity.

But the case of Franny Glass is very different. In *Franny and Zooey,* Franny is determined to cut herself off, first from the theater audience, but also more broadly from the mass of people whom she finds detestable for their mundane aspirations and egotistical pursuits. Most urgent is her fear that she, too, will be seduced by the glitter of conventional success. "I'm not afraid to compete," she tells her boyfriend, Lane. "It's just the opposite. Don't you see that? I'm afraid I *will* compete—that's what scares me" (*Franny* 30).

"Zooey" is the final chapter of what Eberhard Alsen termed Salinger's "composite novel" about the Glass family, which comprises three short stories and five novellas, all but one originally published in the *New Yorker*. (They are, in order of publication: "A Perfect Day for Bananafish," "Uncle Wiggly in Connecticut," "Down at the Dinghy," "Franny," "Raise High the Roof Beam, Carpenters," "Zooey," "Seymour: An Introduction," and "Hapworth 16, 1924.") Though "Seymour: An Introduction" and "Hapworth 16, 1924" appeared later, "Zooey" provides the thematic climax to the sequence. It delivers the ultimate and most fully formed statement readers can unhesitatingly attribute to the author legend constructed in Salinger's published works. As Alsen reasoned, "It is the only Glass story that contains explicit criticism of Seymour's religious ideas, but it also explains that the core of his later teachings is valid, even though Seymour was unable to practice what he preached and even though he killed himself in despair" (220). Indeed, by the end of the novella, Zooey uses Seymour's battle-tested ideas to lift Franny out of her religious crisis and place her on the path to a more charitable acceptance of her university colleagues and a more generous and open relationship with theater patrons.

What is so despairing in these works of fiction is the completeness of Franny's abhorrence, not only of successful artists, but of all persons thriving in the conventional world: her pretentious English-major boyfriend, Lane; his friends, "who look like everybody else, and talk and dress and act like everybody else" (*Franny* 24); the poets on her university faculty, who "write poems that get published and anthologized all over the place" but who are not real poets (18); her talented but somehow inadequate fellow actors. "It's *everybody*," she confesses to Lane (26). "I'm sick of everybody that wants to *get* somewhere, do something distinguished and all, be somebody interesting. It's disgusting—it is, it *is*. I don't care what anybody says" (29–30). And, apparently, one cannot escape from the bind of conventional expectations: "[I]f you go bohemian or something crazy like that, you're conforming just as much as everybody else," she laments, "only in a different way" (26). Her "solution," if it can be called that, is to drop out of theater, skip her college classes, and finally curl up on her parents' couch, attempting to put herself into a religious trance by endlessly repeating "the Jesus Prayer." That is to say, she chooses to withdraw from society, end her artistic relationship with the public, and lose herself in a mystical religious experience—precisely what Salinger is widely judged to have done.

Into the fray steps Zooey, called home by their mother to help Franny out of her incapacitated state. He tells her that, as a successful television actor himself, he can relate to her frustration: working on bad movie scripts has given him an ulcer. And participating in better-than-average projects is actually worse, as it only gives rise to widespread backslapping and "an orgy of mutual appreciation" over the courage and integrity involved (135). But, he insists, an artist must persist at his craft, regardless of the egos it encourages, even one's own. To do otherwise is merely to enter into a "little snotty crusade" against everybody (161) and usurp from our betters—Buddha, Christ—the prerogative to judge which behavior is or is not deplorably egotistical. "As a matter of simple logic," he adds, "there's no difference at all, that *I* can see, between the man who's greedy for material treasure—or even intellectual treasure—and the man who's greedy for spiritual treasure," clearly implying that, like the double bind of bohemian nonconformity, the spiritual pursuits of a reclusive nonartist offer no escape from the trap of egotism (148).

To bring his point home, Zooey repeats the instructions their eldest brother, Seymour, now deceased, gave them both when they were panelists on a children's radio quiz show. Seymour once insisted that Zooey had to shine his shoes before leaving for the studios, which made Zooey furious.

> The studio audience were all morons, the announcer was a moron, the sponsors were morons, and I just damn well wasn't going to shine my shoes for them, I told Seymour. . . . He said to shine them for the Fat Lady. I didn't know what the hell he was talking about, but he had a very Seymour look on his face, and so I did it. He never did tell me who the Fat Lady was, but I shined my shoes for the Fat Lady every time I ever went on the air again. (200)

Franny, as Zooey no doubt guessed, had received the same imperative from their brother to convince her to perform to her full potential, since "the Fat Lady," of course, is convenient shorthand for everyone in the audience, or in their lives. "That includes your Professor Tupper, buddy," Zooey tells Franny, referring to one of her annoying university instructors. "And all his goddam cousins by the dozen" (201). Moreover, he tells her, Seymour's Fat Lady is actually Christ, and as such every artist owes her (him) their finest effort. This realization is apparently what prompted Seymour himself to serve as a panelist on the show years earlier, painful though it must have been for the boy genius. In "Raise High the Roof Beam, Carpenters," the matron of honor deplores the exhibitionism of the absent groom's childhood, but Buddy corrects her, insisting Seymour was never an exhibitionist. "He went down to the broadcast every Wednesday night as though he were going to his own funeral," he reports. "He didn't even talk to you, for God's sake, the whole way down on the bus or subway" (59–60). But he went.

Such is the clear imperative Zooey gives Franny: she must still perform—she owes it to the Fat Lady, to the public, to Christ, to the God who dispenses talent. And, by the indications of the final paragraph of "Zooey," she will do precisely that. Having received the lecture from her brother, the heretofore insomniac and frazzled Franny takes off her footwear and slips peacefully into bed: "For some minutes, before she fell into a deep, dreamless sleep, she just lay quiet, smiling at the ceiling" (202).

The ending of "Zooey" was criticized for its simplistic resolution to Franny's crisis and its condescension toward the very Fat Lady it means to valorize. "It is rather like the end of a Russian movie," wrote Alfred Chester in 1963; "the heart-broken girl unexpectedly hears a speech by a commissar and is made miraculously whole" (472). Even David Samuels in a retrospective appreciation of *Franny and Zooey* conceded, "There are probably higher peaks of wisdom to climb" than the Fat-Lady-is-Christ idea (133). But this was how Salinger chose to resolve the thematic concerns of the entire Glass-family cycle, as it stands so far. Clearly, that resolution is at odds with the author's withdrawal from his audience.

"An artist's only concern is to shoot for some kind of perfection, and *on his own terms,* not anyone else's," Zooey assures Franny (199, emphasis in original). Yet Salinger seems to have proceeded after 1965 on terms other than his own, as spelled out in his fiction. Of course, new Salinger works may appear late in the author's life or posthumously, revising the artist's terms. But until they do, Salinger's silence stands in opposition to the message of his published fiction. The author himself has violated the spirit of his own works.

An alternative approach to analyzing Salinger would be to consider not the *content* but the *form* of the author's published works, particularly his later novellas, and recognize the logical relationship that their form has to the author's subsequent silence. Illuminating this form-centered analysis are two early essays by Susan Sontag. In 1967, in "The Aesthetics of Silence," Sontag described the aggressive attempts of modernist authors to direct attention away from the content of their works and to alienate their readership by adopting a difficult, disruptive writing style, the frustrating effect of which approximated the stony unresponsiveness of willful silence. Three years earlier, in the essay "Against Interpretation," Sontag insisted on the necessity of literary critics' discarding standard Platonic methods of hermeneutics in art—based currently on the influential doctrines of Marx and Freud—and replacing them with a method she termed "an erotics of art" (14), which would no longer bracket observable phenomena, including art objects, as *manifest content* that must be probed and ultimately discarded in order to arrive at the "true meaning" of events, books, paintings (7). Literary interpretation, she noted dismissively, was not merely "the revenge of intellect upon art" (7) or "the compliment that mediocrity pays to genius" (8–9); in most modern instances, she declared, it amounted to "the philistine refusal to leave the work of art alone" (8).

It would normally behoove a literary scholar to defend his right to interpretation, but in this case I sympathize with Sontag's point, since Salinger's silence, having been categorized as an art object, has ever since been picked at, interrogated, tamed, and otherwise *interpreted* in ways that are clearly opportunistic and even foolish. Readers and critics cannot leave it alone. "Our task is not to find the maximum content in a work of art," Sontag instructed, "much less to squeeze more content out of the work than is already there" (14). Rather, more attention must be paid to form, she wrote; equally valuable would be acts of criticism that supply "a really accurate, sharp, loving description of the appearance of a work of art" (13).

Truly accurate criticism in the case of Salinger's silence would be quite brief. Form? It has none. Description? It does not exist and, therefore, is impossible to describe. But because most criticism is steeped in interpretation, even of nonexistent works, critical texts on Salinger's "late period" often prove to be quite lengthy and involved. Without mentioning Salinger by name, Sontag suggested that artists often respond to such elaborate interpretive gestures through deliberate means of subversion. "In fact, a great deal of today's art may be understood as motivated by a flight from interpretation," she claimed. To avoid interpretation, art becomes difficult, abstract, parodistic, decorative. "Or it may become non-art" (10).

The ultimate non-art, silence, was the focus of Sontag's concern in "The Aesthetics of Silence," in which she cited a perennial discontent with language that she claimed arises in every major civilization "whenever thought reaches a certain high, *excruciating* order of complexity and spiritual seriousness" (*Styles* 21, emphasis in original). She cited early signs of discontent in modern Western civilization among the Romantic poets, but saw the high modernists as practitioners of a more fully developed disdain for language. In their great works, she detected a craving for knowledge beyond words, the substitution of chance for intention, a penchant for antiart, and an active pursuit of silence through the only means necessary, words. The exemplary modern artist rarely carries the pursuit to the final simplification of literal silence: "More typically, he continues speaking, but in a manner that his audience can't hear" (7). That is, he produces a nearly unintelligible book like *Finnegans Wake,* which goes unread. He constructs an elaborate, wordy void.

According to Sontag, the pursuit of silence is an arrogant gesture, both because in practice it results in abrupt, disjointed, arbitrary works that alienate the common reader, and because it implies superiority of thought. To be consumed by a craving for silence—for "the cloud of unknowing" beyond knowledge and conventional speech—suggests that "the artist has had the wit to ask more questions than other people, and that he possesses stronger nerves and higher standards of excellence." This arrogant gesture can be executed successfully only by a select few, Sontag claimed, for it requires an established reputation. "An exemplary decision of this sort can be made only after the artist has demonstrated that he possesses genius and [has] exercised that genius authoritatively" (7).

Salinger clearly belonged to this elite group before he ceased to publish. "Few other authors, major or minor, have had such immediate response from critics, who have almost caressingly touched upon special qualities in Salinger," asserted Carl F. Strauch in 1963 (39). "No serious history of post–World War II American fiction can be written without awarding him a place in the first rank, and even, perhaps, the preeminent position," wrote James E. Miller Jr. two years later (45). Even hostile critics have acknowledged the author's preeminence. In her unfavorable 1961 review of *Franny and Zooey,* Joan Didion wrote, "Among the reasonably literate young and young at heart, he is surely the most read and reread writer in America today, exerting a power over his readers which is in some ways extra-literary" (233). Didion's assertion clouds the fact that the "young at heart" comprised nearly the entire scholarly community. "Who is to inherit the mantle of Papa Hemingway?" Mary McCarthy asked in her sour dismissal of *Franny and Zooey.* "Who if not J. D. Salinger?" (35). And yet, as Walter Clemons subsequently observed, "Salinger no sooner won an ardent following than he began to abuse its loyalty" (73). Or as Elizabeth N. Kurian phrased it in her respectful monograph on the existential dilemma in Salinger's fiction, "His later stories are so asymmetrical, tolerant of chance and digression, that they warrant the name of antiform" (145).

Like James Joyce, Gertrude Stein, Samuel Beckett, and William S. Burroughs—Sontag's examples of modernist authors pursuing silence—Salinger employed circular, repetitive speech in his works. David Castronovo has suggested that Salinger's very first book, *The Catcher in the Rye,* was "anti-literary in a new way: its pages are filled with babbling rather than talk that builds to a climax" (180). But most commentators detect a full embrace of digression in "Seymour: An Introduction" (1959), with "Franny" and "Raise High the Roof Beam, Carpenters" (both 1955) marked as transitional stories not nearly as compact or concise as the works composing *Nine Stories,* and "Zooey" (1957) showing further progress toward the silence of indecipherability.

In 1963, Ihab Hassan compared "Zooey" to "Raise High the Roof Beams, Carpenters" and found it longer and more diffuse, its language "brilliantly shattered into letters, invocations of the audience, memoirs, footnotes, asides, quotations on beaverboard, telephone conversations, and, of course, endless dialogue" (10). Not merely its language but also its form was a departure: in their 1958 consideration of Salinger's fiction, Frederick L. Gwynn and Joseph L. Blotner complained that "Zooey" comprised eight undesignated sections, only two or three of which are integral to the plot, and of those none is in "happy proportion to one another or to the whole" (48). "Zooey," then, took a giant step away from what Hassan called "a critic's idea of a well-made fiction" and "a reader's ideal of a racy story" (5). From this point on, Salinger's work became unmistakably experimental, warranting the label antiform and characterized by what Bruce Bawer deemed a "nearly pathological logorrhea," the effect of which was "to keep the rest of us out of the lives of this family that he has created for himself by erecting an all but insurmountable lexical fence around them" (177).

And yet, following an initially ambivalent critical response to "Zooey" in 1957, *Franny and Zooey* was a spectacular popular success when published in book form in 1961. The Salinger Myth proliferated as a result, and the author's position among the first rank of American postwar authors was strengthened. "With the passage of time and the intervention of newer, more difficult works," Sontag explained of such aggressive moves into unintelligibility and inaudibility, "the artist's transgression becomes ingratiating, eventually legitimate" (*Styles* 7). Thus a puzzling work like *Ulysses,* two decades on, becomes a coherent masterpiece compared to *Finnegans Wake.* "The ugly and discordant and senseless become 'beautiful,' " Sontag asserted (8). In fact, the history of art, viewed from this perspective, is nothing but a sequence of successful transgressions, she claimed.

Thus the stakes were inevitably raised, and works subsequent to "Zooey" had to be much more aggressively hostile to the reader if Salinger was to disappear into silence, even while the earlier trail of off-putting fiction gained legitimacy as a result. "Seymour: An Introduction" (1959) appeared to be just such a work; its narrator even admitted tearing up some fifty previous stories "simply because they had that old Chekhov-baiting noise Somerset Maugham calls a Beginning, a Middle, and an End" (212). Whereas "Zooey" had been described by Maxwell Geismar as "an interminable, an appallingly bad story" ("Wise" 96) and dismissed by Gwynn and Blotner as the "dullest 'short story' ever to appear in the *New Yorker*" (48), "Seymour: An Introduction" elicited much harsher condemnation. "Hopelessly prolix," wrote Irving Howe (*Celebrations* 95); "static" and "anti-social" was John P. McIntyre's verdict (25); "turgid," "boring," and "preposterous" pronounced Stanley Edgar Hyman (126); George Steiner called it "a piece of shapeless self-indulgence" ("Salinger" 116).

The following quote from the novella's opening pages gives ample sense of the narrator's modus operandi. In this case, it is not misleading that the quote begins midparagraph and midthought, since throughout the piece paragraphs extend for pages, and lines of thought are routinely jumbled. Buddy Glass is addressing the reader:

> In this *entre-nous* spirit, then, old confident, before we join the others, the grounded everywhere, including, I'm sure, the middle-aged hot-rodders who insist on zooming us to the moon, the Dharma Bums, the makers of cigarette filters for thinking men, the Beat and Sloppy and the Petulant, the chosen cultists, all the lofty experts who know so well what we should or shouldn't do with our poor little sex organs, all the bearded, proud, unlettered young men and unskilled guitarists and Zen-killers and incorporated aesthetic Teddy boys who look down their thoroughly unenlightened noses at this splendid planet where (please don't shut me up) Kilroy, Christ, and Shakespeare all stopped—before we join these others, I privately say to you, old friend (unto you, really, I'm afraid), please accept from me this unpretentious bouquet of very early-blooming parentheses: (((()))). (97–98)

Six years later, in "Hapworth 16, 1924," Salinger resumed writing in this digressive manner, adding to the unusual effect by attributing the language to the epistolary pen of a seven-year-old child. ("I am relishing this leisurely communication!" young Seymour writes [33].) The piece was, in the words of Bernice and Sanford Goldstein, "universally despaired" ("Ego" 159). Indeed, the general critical dismissal of the novella was at least as harsh as that of "Seymour: An Introduction." Deeming the work "virtually unreadable" and "[p]ossibly the least structured and most tedious piece of fiction ever produced by an important writer," John Wenke lamented that " 'Hapworth' seems *designed* to bore, to tax patience, as if Salinger might be trying to torment his readers away from ever wanting the next new thing from him" (67, 108, emphasis in original). Terry Teachout deemed it "dreadful" ("Salinger" 64); Max F. Schulz found it even "more inchoate in structure" than "Seymour" (129). Most commentators since have dismissed it in terms similar to Wenke's: Paul Alexander called it "barely publishable" (230); Kerry McSweeney chose the adjectives "interminable" and "unreadable" ("Salinger" 61); and Bruce Bawer wrote it was "bizarre" and "virtually unreadable" (180).

By Sontag's estimation, then, Salinger succeeded. Without actually lapsing into literal silence—not yet—he made each successive work categorically less accessible and nearly as uncommunicative as silence owing to its turgid language and arbitrary structure. Buddy Glass could have gone on and on beyond the stories' conclusions, Wenke observed, or he could have ended his narratives thirty or fifty pages earlier than he did (105). It made no difference for the purposes of conventional storytelling. And the narrator was as aware of the problem as anyone. "I'm going on too long about this, I know," Buddy concedes about his disquisition on Seymour's sporting prowess, "but I really can't stop now" (*Raise High* 198).

And yet, as Sontag also predicted, over time some in the literary community acclimated, even warmed, to the final Glass-family works. In a 2001 *New York Review of Books* article, Janet Malcolm wrote, "Today 'Zooey' does not seem too long, and is arguably Salinger's masterpiece. . . . It remains brilliant and is in no essential sense dated. It is the contemporary criticism that has dated" (16). The "extraordinary rage" generated by critics against the Glasses, Malcolm concluded, merely points us toward the author's stylistic innovations.

In hindsight, these works are now deemed reader friendly in comparison to actual silence. James Lundquist in his 1979 monograph *J. D. Salinger* recategorized the late novellas, not as turgid and diffuse, but as "complex," "experimental," and "increasingly post-modern" (2). "Salinger does not impose any arbitrary pattern on his work, because he believes the work will grow its own shape and meaning if the writer follows his inspiration," reasoned Elizabeth N. Kurian (145–46). Bernice and Sanford Goldstein repositioned "Seymour: An Introduction" as "one of Salinger's most ambitious stories" and asserted that the prose style of "Hapworth 16, 1924" was "thoroughly intentional" for the purpose of presenting young Seymour's struggle to deepen his level of spiritual awareness ("Seymour" 249; "Ego" 166–67). And Eberhard Alsen, examining the Glass stories together as a single text, found their design coherent and organic. "Despite its fragmentary plot and despite the radical differences between the form of the early and the later stories," Alsen wrote, "Buddy's composite novel has a special kind of unity" (235).

Alsen's attribution of unity, however, carried unintentional irony. He asserted that, Buddy Glass's own demurrals notwithstanding, "Seymour" has a coherent structure. "Spacing and typography reveal a division into six major sections," Alsen observed:

I Buddy's credo
II Seymour as God-lover
III Seymour as artist-seer
IV Seymour as entertainer
V Seymour as Buddy's mentor
VI Physical description of Seymour (64)

The final section is further divided into eight subsections, Alsen noted with apparent seriousness:

1. Seymour's hair jumping in the barbershop
2. Seymour's hair and teeth
3. Seymour's height, smile, and ears
4. Seymour's eyes, nose, and chin
5. Seymour's hands, voice, and skin
6. Seymour's clothes
7. Seymour as athlete and gamesman
8. Seymour as Buddy's Davega bicycle (65)

While this may technically qualify as a structural design for a story, it is not a design that can generate a satisfying narrative. As John Wenke observed, "Buddy can render an *attempt* to present a face—he catalogs Seymour's hair, smile, ears, eyes, nose, and skin—but no one face emerges. The attempt must fail" (105, emphasis in original). Or as David Seed concluded, the difficulties and ultimate failures of narrative *become* the subject of "Seymour: An Introduction" (157). Such subject matter may give the story its metafictional bona fides, but when manifested in the narrative itself the subject of unsuccessful or inept storytelling does not captivate a readership. Rather, the reader is compelled to head for the exit, as instructed, or trudge through, observing firsthand the qualities of failed narrative. In the first case, the story lapses into silence—it goes unread; in the second, the author is challenged to top himself next time with a more outrageous attempt to dispel his readership. The most outrageous attempt possible, of course, is literal silence.

"'Seymour: An Introduction' represents a fictional extreme beyond which Salinger cannot go," claimed David Seed (158). Susan Sontag wrote, "Since the artist can't embrace silence literally and remain an artist, what the rhetoric of silence indicates is a determination to pursue his activity more deviously than before" (*Styles* 12). My contention is that both Seed and Sontag were wrong.

Salinger *could* literally embrace silence and remain an artist. He went beyond the extreme of "Seymour" to nonpublication and reclusion, yet many in the literary community persisted in reading and interpreting the text he "produced" and accused him of crass manipulation. "Don't you think it's a little bit pretentious to make such a big deal out of not publishing any more?" wrote the unsolicited e-mailer Dan Paton to the author in *Letters to J. D. Salinger,* neglecting to clarify what exactly he meant by the "big deal" Salinger was making. "You can't make yourself unfamous," he taunted. "Cough it up. Either publish everything you've got left in you or hurry up and die" (Kubica and Hochman 219).

It is a harsh sentiment, but one widely shared. "[T]he piece of prose his admirers anticipate most eagerly is his obituary," Craig Stolz posited about Salinger (13), who reportedly continues to work on new fiction, in solitude, but who has not signaled what his ultimate intent is for the manuscripts. Recent tell-all memoirs published by both Joyce Maynard and the author's daughter, Margaret Salinger, were hostile toward the author on many topics, but on this they were in agreement with him: Salinger continues to write. But does he intend to publish, even posthumously? In 1973, Lucey Fosburgh asked Salinger if he expected to publish new work soon.

> There was a pause.
> "I really don't know how soon," he said. There was another pause, and then Mr. Salinger began to talk rapidly about how much he was writing, long hours, every day, and he said he was under contract to no one for another book.
> "I don't necessarily intend to publish posthumously," he said, "but I do like to write for myself." (69)

It is an ambiguous phrasing. He may intend to publish, but not necessarily posthumously; or he may not necessarily intend to publish at all, even posthumously. In any case, Salinger's silence in its current incarnation will end, with his death, timely publication, or death followed by publication. And with that will almost certainly come a shift in the interpretation of his decades-long silence, regardless of the author's best efforts. "Make sure you burn it all," warned novelist Stewart O'Nan in *Letters to J. D. Salinger.* "Maybe the house, too. That might sound nuts, but trust me" (Kubica and Hochman 50). Prior experience suggests such drastic efforts would prove futile. Whatever gap Salinger leaves behind, whatever absence of primary or secondary texts remains, it will necessarily be filled by those in the literary community for whom the term "silent author" is no mere oxymoron but a strict impossibility.

CHAPTER FIVE **Subsequent Thresholds to**
Invisible Man

"[I]n principle, every context serves as a paratext," asserted Gérard Genette in *Paratexts: Thresholds of Interpretation* (1987), his consideration of cover art, title pages, blurb selections, author's prefaces, editor's introductions, and other forms of textual packaging and commentary (8). "Everything a writer says or writes about his life, about the world around him, about the works of others, may have paratextual relevance" (346). Ralph Ellison wrote and spoke extensively about his life, the world around him, the works of others, and about his own great novel from 1952, *Invisible Man,* and its presumed successor, the multivolume quagmire from which *Juneteenth* was posthumously extracted. In collaboration with a literary establishment eager to comment on his mounting pages of unpublishable fiction, Ellison assembled an enormous yet loose paratextual apparatus of "silence" that carefully situated his existing masterpiece.

Among the material loosely attached to *Invisible Man* are passages in which Ralph Ellison's professional and creative frustration sours his mood. "[I]f I ever complete my endless you-know-what you'll get a chance to see what different things we make of a common reality," Ellison wrote in a letter to friend Alfred Murray. " 'You-know-what' indeed. It is a rock around my neck; a dream, a nasty compulsive dream which I no longer write but now am acting out" (Ellison and Murray 8).

Ellison composed this epistolary lament on 24 January 1950; the "you-know-what" in question is therefore not the uncompleted second novel but rather the manuscript of *Invisible Man,* itself a seven-year project of excruciating endurance for the unproven author. My point is that such despairing comments, though prevalent among the documentary evidence from Ellison's prefamous years, did not emerge in time to provide an initial paratextual threshold to *Invisible Man*. Ellison's masterpiece met the literary world largely unsullied by inordinate expectations. In Genette's terms, the novel appeared without an "original assumptive authorial preface," two routine objectives of which are "to get the book read and to get the book read properly" (197). To the author's good fortune, the novel got read anyway, and to a surprising degree it got read properly—or at least very favorably—by members of the literary establishment whose appraisal mattered most to its permanent stature. Subsequent readings and rereadings, however, necessitated guidance by the author, particularly throughout the politically turbulent years of the 1960s and 1970s, when the disapprobation of black academics and writers threatened Ellison's professional status, and the career vacuum created by the stalled second novel further complicated the task of sustaining the reputation of an instantly canonized work and its increasingly controversial author.

When *Invisible Man* appeared in the spring of 1952, the critical reception was exceptionally laudatory for a first novel. "The reviews—at least those that counted—were excellent" is how Ellison's biographer, Lawrence Jackson, summarized the initial notices (435). Orville Prescott opened his piece in the *New York Times* by claiming that *Invisible Man* was "the most impressive work of fiction by an American Negro" that he had ever read (25). Saul Bellow wrote in *Commentary* about his friend's book: "[I]t is an immensely moving novel and it has greatness" (608). "Few writers have made a more commanding first appearance," Anthony West declared in the *New Yorker* (96).

As a result of so much positive attention, the novel sold well, reaching number eight on the *New York Times* bestseller list. The book was getting read, but precisely *how* it was read is of considerable importance. A number of reviewers favorably compared Ellison to rival black novelist Richard Wright; or they placed the book in a category entirely separate from black fiction. "*Invisible Man* is shorn of the racial and political cliches that have encumbered the 'Negro novel,'" George Mayberry wrote in the *New Republic* (19). "[I]t is not a 'protest' novel, in any sense, but one which questions," observed Milton S. Byam (716). Delmore Schwartz framed his comments similarly in *Partisan Review*. "*Invisible Man* is not merely a story about being a Negro, and not a protest novel," he wrote. "It is truly about being a human being, any human being and all human beings." Ellison's insistence that the hero's plight is universal, Schwartz claimed, is precisely what redeems the book "when the tendency to melodrama, to declamation, to screaming, and to apocalyptic hallucination is on the verge of going too far" (359).

Such was the qualified nature of many of the most adulatory notices, which conceded that the work was verbose, hyperbolic, pretentious, at times incoherent and crude, overearnest, and "rather thickly endowed with symbols" (Chase 682). Irving Howe summed up matters for most reviewers: "These faults mar *Invisible Man* but do not destroy it." Indeed, Howe asserted in the *Nation* that Ellison's book was "one of the few remarkable first novels we have had in years" ("Negro" 454).

It is significant that the critical community, even while singling Ellison out for praise because his book transcended the category "Negro novel," aimed their most cutting remarks at the author's stylistic innovations, which are in large part what made his book's artistic transcendence possible. A corrective was in order: under the author's guidance, the literary community would later conclude that Ellison was doing something highly innovative here. He was applying the techniques of high modernism to the traditional slave-narrative myth of a black man escaping north, which Richard Wright had recently updated in *Black Boy* while still focusing on the inescapably "black" nature of the degrading experience. Moreover, Ellison, a trained musician, integrated aspects of symphonic composition, jazz improvisation, and blues vernacular into his literary work, which made the result all the more startling. One could be forgiven for finding the result at times verbose, hyperbolic, crude, or pretentious. It was designed as a potpourri of extreme and discordant elements, yet it was structured to succeed, like *The Waste Land*, as a coherent, unified masterwork. The difficulty in executing such a complex vision is precisely what Ellison's subsequent essays and interviews insisted on. In fact, this was his excuse for not completing a second novel: to repeat such a task proved inordinately difficult.

For a time, Ellison avoided accounting for the delay of the second book. "I am a writer who writes very slowly," he finally conceded in "The Novel as a Function of American Democracy," a 1967 essay collected nineteen years later in *Going to the Territory* (308). He did not elaborate, but he was forced to address the issue elsewhere. "I hope that this new book will be good," he told an interviewer in 1972. "I've published some sections which I like very much, but the problem is to make a total functioning whole. If I make it function, it should be an interesting book" (*Conversations* 234). By so stating, the author implicitly reaffirmed his previous instructions to interpret *Invisible Man* as a sophisticated assemblage of disparate stylistic and thematic elements that miraculously coalesced. Thus, even when accounting for the gap created by his missing second novel, sometimes called "the Hickman project" in reference to the title character of excerpted portions, Ellison directed the public's attention back to his first book.

Some reviewers understood early on which qualities would set *Invisible Man* apart and guarantee its longevity. Among the most prescient critics was Harvey Curtis Webster, who praised the novel's "multiplicity of scenes, techniques, and ideas; the layers under layers of meaning; its complicated and skillful use of symbols" (22). For Webster, too much of a good thing was just fine, and a plurality of scholars have since agreed. "It is easy to see why the first reviewers gave such unqualified praise to *Invisible Man*," Robert Langbaum wrote already in a retrospective voice in the fall of 1952. "It packs an impressive wallop. It offers, with honesty and power, the only issue around which the social passions of the '30s can still rally, the negro problem—but dressed up, less honestly I think, with the literary *chic* of the '50s" (62–63). That literary chic proved more than ephemeral. But, in general, Langbaum's analysis was incisive: at a time of growing disillusionment with Communism and of "de-commitment in our literature," to use Langbaum's wording (58), the author of *Invisible Man* combined unorthodox political rhetoric and stylistic innovation in an invigorating/infuriating manner. Ultimately, the effect was impressive to some, vexing to others. "This was the quality the reviewers liked so much," Langbaum concluded about those who were impressed; "they were delighted to find a negro novel with universal application" (59). But Langbaum himself had qualms about the book. "To read it is an experience all right," he observed, "though not, upon reflection, entirely a legitimate one" (63).

Other reviewers—those who did not count at first—were blunter in their negative appraisal. In a June 1952 review in *Freedom*, the novelist John O. Killens denounced *Invisible Man* and its menagerie of misfit black characters, whom he listed as "Uncle Toms, pimps, sex perverts, guilt-ridden traitors." As Harold Cruse explained fifteen years later, Killens was simply adhering to the covenant of socialist realism by asserting "the inviolable range of social theme for the Negro writer," which Ellison was violating. "The Negro people need Ralph Ellison's *Invisible Man* like we need a hole in the head or a stab in the back," Killens asserted (Cruse 235), launching an early salvo in what would become a decadeslong battle between Ellison and foes within the black intellectual community who objected, first, to the novelist's attacks on 1930s radical politics and, later, to his lack of enthusiasm for 1960s race consciousness. When mainstream critics such as William Barrett deemed *Invisible Man* "the first considerable step forward in Negro literature," it likely inflamed resentment toward Ellison among literary artists who believed they had moved African American literature forward long before Ellison arrived on the scene (100). Likewise, Wright Morris's observation in the *New York Review of Books* that Ellison had shown a cool mastery of "the black man's rage" (5) hardly satisfied black writers who were convinced that their rage should not be mastered but rather should be inflamed by unbridled passion.

Ellison faced an increasingly divided critical establishment in the wake of his novel's success. And it was in this context that Ellison guided the book's reception as new generations picked it up, and prior readers wondered about a successor novel.

In *Paratexts,* Gérard Genette timidly defined a text as "a more or less long sequence of verbal statements that are more or less endowed with significance" (1). Such a text, he noted, rarely appears unaccompanied.

For the thirtieth-anniversary edition of *Invisible Man,* Ellison appended an author's introduction to the novel itself. "What, if anything, is there that a novelist can say about his work that wouldn't be better left to the critics?" Ellison asked at the beginning of the piece, with no apparent irony (vii). This attached paratextual element, however, is not my primary interest here. Rather, my greatest concern is for the unattached, "epitextual" publications that issued from the author during the forty-two years of purported silence that followed the publication of *Invisible Man,* particularly Ellison's two major unattached paratextual works: the essay collection *Shadow and Act,* published twelve years after *Invisible Man* in 1964, and a second collection, *Going to the Territory,* which appeared an additional twenty-two years later in 1986. More successfully and thoroughly than Ellison's thirtieth-anniversary introduction to the novel, these two books instructed the public how to read *Invisible Man.* And more conspicuously than his numerous interviews or published novel excerpts or individual essays, Ellison's essay collections additionally served as disappointing successors to his first novel.

Genette wrote at length about a paratext's temporal situation relative to the main text. Most paratextual elements appear concurrent with the text; Genette called these "original" paratexts (5). But he also noted two relevant moments after initial publication when an author might issue significant paratexts, and he called such works the "later preface" and the "delayed preface" (174–75). Typically, a later preface comes on the heels of an original edition, taking advantage of the work's lingering buzz, or on the occasion of a second edition; a delayed preface might accompany the republication of a work long out of print or appear on any retrospectively themed occasion in the twilight of an author's career.

Despite complications inherent in doing so, I will assign the labels "later preface" and "delayed preface" to *Shadow and Act* and *Going to the Territory*, respectively. Because these books are epitextual works, the term "preface" is not entirely appropriate: the collections are not "preludial" or prefatory to any specific edition of *Invisible Man*, since they are bound under separate covers. In that sense, they might more accurately be called "later epitexts" and "delayed epitexts," but I will use the terms "later preface" and "delayed preface" to emphasize how these works function in a manner nearly identical to that of more conventionally attached paratexts.

Moreover, *Invisible Man* has never gone out of print. Its buzz is perennial. But the two collections nonetheless seem to fit quite neatly into Genette's temporal categories. *Shadow and Act* appeared twelve years after *Invisible Man,* when the book's reputation could still be called ascendant (it has since reached a plateau) and before nervousness about the Hickman project's completion began to dominate critical discourse about Ellison's career. On the other hand, *Going to the Territory* followed the original work by thirty-four years, preceding the author's death by less than a decade. It is clearly a reflective work from the author's middle-to-late career, gazing back toward his early success. It is quite clearly delayed paratext, as Genette defined that term.

A second quality that Genette examined at length—the purpose or function or "illocutionary force" of the paratext (10)—further suggests that Ellison's two essay collections should be read as paratexts to *Invisible Man.* "A paratextual element can communicate a piece of sheer *information,*" Genette wrote; or it can make known "an *intention,* or an *interpretation* by the author and/or the publisher: this is the chief function of most prefaces" (10–11, emphases in original). Like any paratext—a book cover, say, or a copyright page—Ellison's essay collections provide information: simple facts about the origins of the writing of *Invisible Man* and testimonies about the veracity and appropriateness of the fictional material as applied to a black narrator of Ellison's generation. Indeed, in the introduction to *Shadow and Act,* Ellison claimed that the basic significance of the pieces collected therein is "autobiographical" (xviii). But more significant is the interpretation of Ellison's novel offered by the collections. The importance of *Invisible Man,* its novelty, the manner in which it respects yet transcends literary tradition, its overall unity—all of these themes are developed throughout Ellison's major paratexual works.

That Ellison, under pressure to deliver a second novel, gave special attention to the shape and ordering of his two essay collections is uncontestable. This gained posthumous confirmation in 2000 when Ellison's literary executor, John F. Callahan, approached Ellison's widow to discuss the Modern Library edition of the author's *Collected Essays*, which was to include part or all of the two existing collections. Fanny Ellison was adamant that the two remain intact. "Ralph worked too hard on the form and sequence of the essays in *Shadow and Act* and *Going to the Territory*," she told Callahan; "those books must not be touched. They should be part of the *Collected Essays*, but don't touch the form and sequence" (DeSantis 604). The integrity of *Invisible Man*'s two most important paratextual apparatuses is thus protected and will remain so even if the individual collections go out of print.

R. W. B. Lewis, in a typical review of *Shadow and Act*, noted that Ellison's second book contains "a fairly exact summary of the themes of *Invisible Man*" (20). In his introduction to the collection, Ellison helpfully explained that the essays address three major concerns: "literature and folklore," "Negro musical expression—especially jazz and blues," and "the complex relationship between the Negro American subculture and North American culture as a whole" (xviii). The essays concerned with the first two themes ultimately comment on the third, which is the most pertinent and inflammatory. The complex relationship between black and mainstream American cultures—a relationship Ellison insisted is inextricably entwined—is subject matter Ellison drew on to instruct readers how to interpret *Invisible Man*, and to launch his aggressive defense against hostile black (and sometimes Jewish) intellectuals who would come to misunderstand or denigrate his work.

In a 1958 interview included in *Shadow and Act*, Ellison was queried about attempts by black Americans to adopt "white values" in place of "Negro values." Ellison took umbrage at the question, refuting its guiding assumption that there is an element of choice in the matter. "[T]he values of my own people are neither 'white' nor 'black,'" he insisted, "they are American. Nor can I see how they could be otherwise, since we are a people who are involved in the texture of the American experience" (270). This passage allowed Ellison to perform two key tasks: he guided friendly readers to a deeper appreciation of *Invisible Man* even while he further infuriated (or just possibly disarmed) hostile readers. The author's admirers could better understand the predicament of the narrator in *Invisible Man* once they were clearly instructed by Ellison that his protagonist is more than just a black person limited by racist parameters. His existential dilemma has tragic resonance and universal application. All Americans have contributed to the shaping of their society, both to its vibrancy and its defects, Ellison claimed. And though black Americans face special deprivations, all Americans suffer the negative consequences of their malformed society. If the harrowing journey and bleak outlook of Ellison's unnamed narrator imply that the importance of *Invisible Man* extends beyond the realms of mere protest fiction or African American writing, it would seem natural that the book's author turned to Stephen Crane, Mark Twain, and other mainstream artists for inspiration and guidance, which Ellison explicitly and plausibly asserted that he did. Ellison's admirers must therefore place his book, if it is deemed so worthy, on the shelf of mainstream American classics.

At the same time, with the ample fuel found in *Shadow and Act,* Ellison's detractors could stoke their resentment of the author, who seemed to go out of his way to alienate foes. This is true of the famous passage from the 1964 essay "The World and the Jug" in which Ellison drew distinctions between relatives, whom one is stuck with regardless of one's wishes, and ancestors, whom he classified as an artist's chosen influences. His intent was to distance himself from, say, Richard Wright (an unchosen relative) and embrace Ernest Hemingway (an ancestor by choice). "Langston Hughes, whose work I knew in grade school and whom I knew before I knew Wright, was a 'relative,' " Ellison continued; "Eliot, whom I was to meet only many years later, and Malraux and Dostoievsky and Faulkner, were 'ancestors'—if you please or don't please!" (140).

Many did not please. Among them was Irving Howe, whose 1963 attack on Ellison, "Black Boys and Native Sons," set Ellison off in "The World and the Jug." Elsewhere in *Shadow and Act,* the author made conciliatory gestures of a sort, if not to Howe then to black intellectuals who were predisposed to object to his work. "If general American values influence us; we in turn influence them," he observed about the strength of black culture (271). Indeed, he tweaked southern whites for their dependence on blacks, asserting that they could not "walk, talk, sing, conceive of laws or justice, think of sex, love, the family or freedom without responding to the presence of Negroes" (116). But much more pointedly, Ellison made statements that were bound to irritate black intellectuals, and not just in essays directly concerned with the relationship between the black subculture and the white mainstream. "I use folklore in my work not because I am Negro," he wrote in a 1958 exchange with Stanley Edgar Hyman, "but because writers like Eliot and Joyce made me conscious of the literary value of my folk inheritance" (58). Likewise, jazz and spirituals, the constituent elements of American Negro music, "have been and are still being subjected to a constant process of assimilation," he noted. Both are shaped by white culture. As a result, he concluded, "jazz is a national art form" (268).

To readers committed to the black separatist movement, these remarks were offensive. Even more blunt and off-putting was a 1962 review of the book *Bird: The Legend of Charlie Parker* in which Ellison ridiculed the deceased saxophonist for his "grim comedy of racial manners," by which he means the calculated surliness Parker displayed on stage while rejecting the traditional black entertainer's role—"a heritage from the minstrel tradition"—exemplified by Louis Armstrong (*Shadow* 225). In an ironic twist, the arrogant contortions of jazzmen like Parker alienated those artists from their Negro roots, wrote Ellison. "Bird was indeed a 'white' hero," he asserted. "His greatest significance was for the educated white middle-class youth" who, Ellison claimed, applauded rudeness as a sign of hip revolt against the status quo (228). In this manner Ellison was able not only to spar with detractors but also to assert his own racial bona fides. If only Parker and others had recognized what Ellison recognized—that the give-and-take of American society crosses racial frontiers, that blackness infuses the mainstream, that white culture shapes black culture—then they too would be as comfortable in their own skin as the author was. They, too, would be legitimately black.

Jacqueline Covo, assessing the impact of *Shadow and Act* on the intellectual community ten years after its publication, observed that the public commentary on Ellison in the late 1960s consisted largely, though not uniformly, of white acclaim and black denunciation (28). Still, nearly every reviewer seemed to recognize the collection as a legitimate paratext to *Invisible Man*—as a threshold by which to reenter the novel. In fact, reviews of the book from 1964 anticipate Gérard Genette's 1987 treatise on paratexts to an astonishing degree, particularly on the matter of the later preface, which, Genette noted, inevitably responds to a book's earliest readers (240). Granville Hicks, like many other white critics, took the appearance of a second Ellison book as an opportunity to pick up *Invisible Man* again and reconfirm his admiration. "A re-reading at this date strengthens my belief that it is one of the major novels of the postwar period," he wrote ("Prose" 59). Richard Kostelanetz echoed Hicks: "With each passing year, with each rereading, *Invisible Man* confirms its place among the half-dozen best novels of the post-war years" (172). Roger Sale made his paratextual use of the essay collection more explicit: "First readings [of *Invisible Man*] tend to be baffled, admiring, and at least a little unconvinced because the book is so fiercely American and literary in its need to be 'original,' " Sale explained. "But it gets better with each rereading" (124). It gets better in part because Ellison made the effort to ease our bafflement by explaining precisely how the book is fiercely American, literary, and original. His most concentrated effort, *Shadow and Act*, instigated the mid-1960s rush to reconsider his masterpiece. "*Invisible Man* is one of the really distinguished modern American novels," Sale concluded, "that much becomes clearer all the time" (124). It was not merely the passage of time that made the novel's distinguishing characteristics clearer; paratextual guidance helped.

Eventually, Ellison scholars acknowledged the author's success at guiding and at times "correcting" the public's reading of his novel. Darryl Pinckney observed in his review of the posthumous *Collected Essays* that "Ellison had almost as much to say about *Invisible Man* as his critics did" (54–55). Michael Anderson, reviewing Lawrence Jackson's biography in 2002, concluded, "Probably no other writer has so successfully fashioned his critical image as Ellison" (7). Anderson explicitly concurred with Kerry McSweeney (*Invisible* 10), who implied in 1988 that the vast majority of scholars examine *Invisible Man* through the framework provided by Ellison himself.

All along, Ellison's fiercest detractors within the black intelligentsia were just as heavily influenced by the novel's paratext. If they seemed unimpressed by Ellison's fiction and resentful of his professional success, that was due in part to the explicatory statements Ellison made in *Shadow and Act* and elsewhere. Black authors who were antagonistic toward Ellison did not misinterpret what the author had to say; they simply rebuked him for saying it. "I wasn't, and am not, primarily concerned with injustice, but with art," Ellison told the *Paris Review* in a 1955 interview reprinted in *Shadow and Act* (169). "I have no desire to manipulate power. I want to write imaginative books," he repeated in 1960 (*Conversations* 63). "I can only ask that my fiction be judged as art; if it fails, it fails aesthetically, not because I did or did not fight some ideological battle," he wrote four years later (*Shadow* 136–37), insisting with dogged futility that other black writers and critics discard the ideological criteria to which they were committed. Most refused.

Some mainstream critics were oblivious to the hostility Ellison would face from black intellectuals, or they anticipated black resistance for precisely the wrong reasons. "Not all Negroes are going to care for *Invisible Man*," predicted the anonymous *Time* magazine reviewer in 1952. "Ellison . . . obviously thinks little of Negroes who educate themselves beyond the point of sympathy for their underprivileged brethren" (review of *Invisible Man* 112). As it turned out, many blacks resented Ellison because he put on airs and, in their opinion, turned his back on the underprivileged. As late as 1965, Robert Penn Warren asserted about Ellison in a review of *Shadow and Act:* "No one has made more unrelenting statements of the dehumanizing pressures that have been put upon the Negro" (96). This observation, it should be noted, was elicited by a book in which the author emphatically states that chattel slavery was not a system of absolute repression (*Shadow* 254). Taken together, Ellison's statements about the dehumanizing pressures on blacks were anything but unrelenting: they were balanced and shaded, while always emphasizing the toughness of those who survived mistreatment (*Shadow* 254). This helps to account for the divergent critical estimations of *Invisible Man* and its author. White critics were directed by the novel's later paratexts to appreciate the complexity and nuance of a work with universal literary credentials, which at the same time addressed the suffering of the author's own people. Black critics were directed by the same material to balk at the uncommitted, whitewashed pronouncements of a snobby aesthete.

What was included in Ellison's essay collections is highly instructive; equally instructive is what was left out. Interviews pressing the author to account for his delayed second novel failed to make the cut. Early works of hard-hitting "Negro fiction" such as the story "Slick Gonna Learn" were never collected during Ellison's lifetime. And from among the more than seventy-five essays and reviews he published from 1937 to 1994, Ellison passed over those that did not serve his intended design for the collections. Predictably, these included more than thirty articles he wrote for *New Masses* and other leftist publications in the 1930s and 1940s, but it also applied to some later works. "Tell It Like It Is," an essay written in Italy in 1956, was withheld from publication entirely until after *Shadow and Act* appeared in 1964. A bitter, outraged response to news from home that southern congressmen were defying the Supreme Court's desegregation rulings, "Tell It Like It Is" was just the sort of rebuke to white authority that might have helped to reshape the author's image to the liking of critics who demanded overt political commitment from black authors. Ellison finally published the piece in a September 1965 issue of the *Nation,* once the main damage from *Shadow and Act* had been done; he subsequently left it out of *Going to the Territory.*

In 1964, Leroi Jones declared: "The black man *cannot* become an American (unless we get a different set of *rules*) because he is black" (Walling 124, emphases in the original). Jones and other intellectuals for more than a decade thereafter attacked Ellison with regularity in the major black journals. In a skeptical *Negro Digest* review of *Shadow and Act,* Hoyt W. Fuller took offense at Ellison's literary association with William Faulkner, whom he deemed a violent racist (51). Don L. Lee asserted in 1968: "Black art is created from black forces within the body"; but Ellison, he lamented, had lost those corporeal forces (44). Ernest Kaiser called Ellison an Uncle Tom (95), an epithet widely adopted by black undergraduate students who confronted Ellison when he came to speak on their college campuses. "Ellison coldly and objectively writes about the Black people's plight and tragedy but never calls for a fight for freedom," Kaiser continued (97). "Does he have any humanity at all?"

Addison Gayle Jr., writing under the name Eka Igi, published a poem about Ellison in a 1971 issue of *Black World* that he snidely subtitled "Commemorating the Non-Completion of His Second Novel"; in it, he taunted the blocked novelist for being "a writer beyond words" (97). But Ellison had the last laugh. Much like Ned Rorem and other composers who simply rode out the twelve-tone fad in symphonic music, Ellison continued to issue his unfashionable, unorthodox literary pronouncements until the orthodoxy wheel for black intellectuals came round full circle. Darryl Pinckney, in his review of Ellison's *Collected Essays* in the *New York Review of Books,* assessed Ellison's professional status thus: "[H]e lived long enough to witness the elevation of *Invisible Man* to a sort of Ur-text of blackness" (52).

In a 1999 reassessment of the Howe-Ellison squabble, Seth Forman efficiently summed up the shift in academia away from racial essentialism, now widely condemned as conservative and masculinist, toward notions of pluralism and individual exceptionalism. By instigating this change, prominent black academics and critics—Henry Louis Gates Jr., Houston Baker Jr., bell hooks, Angela Davis, Paul Gilroy, among others—gave Ellison's longstanding insistence on the autonomy of the black artist new validity. "Subscribing to postmodern notions of identity in which the self is continually and voluntarily created and recreated, the black critics insist that the color line can be redefined, crossed-over, and shifted," Forman explained, "and [they] set for themselves the project of reconstructing a literary canon that 'recenters' black texts" (588). Ellison had long insisted that one could not *avoid* crossing the color line; at the author's insistence, *Invisible Man* has always been at the very center of the literary canon. Thus, even among black critics, literary fashion finally caught up with Ellison's overt positioning of his novel, which had served him well with mainstream critics all along.

This sea change among black intellectuals was underway before Ellison issued his "delayed preface" to *Invisible Man,* the 1986 collection *Going to the Territory.* His third book was therefore widely criticized as a superfluous reissue of the second. "Ellison turns out to have a few favorite hobby-horses which he mounts again and again," George Sim Johnston observed of *Going to the Territory* (72). The latest essay collection, wrote John Edgar Wideman, "bears a disquieting resemblance to *Shadow and Act.*" Still, Wideman acknowledged the book's paratextual function: "Great writers are always teaching us how to read them. One measure of greatness is how much we need the lessons" (15). In other words: a sublime, complex, ambiguous novel like *Invisible Man* requires explication and positioning, which the author has provided here. "This new collection of essays repeats many of the themes enunciated in *Shadow and Act*," Cushing Strout explained, "because Ellison's fundamental views about the novel, America, and Negro identity have been remarkably constant over the past thirty-five years." Like Wideman, Strout accepted the paratextual function of the collection as a delayed preface to Ellison's novel: "*Going to the Territory*, like *Shadow and Act*, is valuable for orienting readers towards a better understanding of the subtleties in *Invisible Man*" (811).

According to Gérard Genette, delayed prefaces allow authors to confront posterity by offering "a more 'mellow' consideration, which often has some testamentary or, as Musil said, pre-posthumous accent" (175). "The delayed preface to one work may also be the last preface to the entire oeuvre, and (with a little luck) the last word," Genette explained (260). "The theme most strongly distinguishing the retrospective . . . discourse of the delayed preface is doubtless the theme of 'I have not changed,' of emotional permanence and intellectual continuity" (256).

Again, Genette's schematics describe Ellison's paratextual offerings perfectly. Thirty-four years after *Invisible Man* and twenty-two years after *Shadow and Act*, the septuagenarian author chose to restate his pet themes in *Going to the Territory* as he headed into the final years of his life. In Ellison's case, the delayed preface to one novel would by necessity be the last preface to his full oeuvre, since *Invisible Man* is widely viewed as constituting the author's entire literary output. Everything else that followed merely testifies to the fact that this frustrated author gave us one masterpiece early in his career and subsequently issued four decades of silence. On two occasions, Ellison's silence was placed between hard covers and sold to the public, with the purpose of solidifying the reputation of the prior masterpiece, but on the latter occasion, the book's implicit message threatened to drown out the literary explication: I am not a true successor to *Invisible Man*, Ellison's third book informed the public, and don't expect one.

"Reviews were polite but disappointed," Brent Staples concluded of the reception to *Going to the Territory* (6). "The critics spoke of the book in whispers, like neighbors pitying an invalid child. Where was that novel that had been rumored since *Invisible Man*? Why did [the author] give so many interviews and, even though he found writing hellishly difficult, contribute so many minor pieces to obscure journals?"

Where was that novel? Uncompleted, of course, and thus it would remain. The author's dozens of essays and interviews since 1952 clearly explained why. Ellison was an ambitious novelist who insisted that any attempt he made to assemble disparate stylistic and thematic elements must succeed as a satisfying and coherent whole, or it would never see publication (in his lifetime). Miraculously, he had succeeded once at this Herculean task. The second major attempt was taking longer than expected and, God forbid, might ultimately run aground.

But why did the author give so many interviews and devote precious time to minor essays? To explain his masterpiece and, particularly at a time when the author's reputation was being assaulted by fellow black writers, to clarify what a singular accomplishment the novel is. Considering the troubles he had shaping his fiction after 1952, Ellison did well to salvage an impressive reputation. And no doubt he died confident that his legacy would remain intact.

In his introduction to *Juneteenth*, John F. Callahan wrote: "Ellison left no instructions about his work except the wish, expressed to Mrs. Ellison and to me, that his books and papers be housed at the national library, the Library of Congress" (xxii). Yet since 1994, numerous posthumous works by Ralph Ellison have appeared: a book of short fiction, the *Collected Essays*, a volume of letters, a book of interviews, and a reader's edition of *Juneteenth*. Due to follow are an annotated scholarly edition of *Juneteenth*, a more complete volume of letters, and early works of fiction that the author left uncompleted. Still, none of the posthumous editions has had much effect on the author's reputation, nor does it appear that any ever could. "*Juneteenth* is a lavish disappointment, a false sunset," wrote James Wood, insisting that the book could not even properly be called a novel (38). Rather, Wood explained, *Juneteenth* was "a commercial echo, bounced by publisher and executor off the resonance of that earlier great book [*Invisible Man*], and not approved or overseen by the author." Such was the exonerating stance typically taken toward the Hickman project once Callahan revealed that the manuscript was nowhere near completion at the time of Ellison's death and had in fact spiraled further out of the author's control the longer he worked on it (DeSantis 609). "This book should not unduly influence the author's reputation," declared Elizabeth Bukowski of *Juneteenth* in an article titled "The Author's Gone, So Whose Book Is It, Anyway?" Fortuitously, the consensus ruled that *Juneteenth* was *not* Ellison's book; his reputation would therefore stand solely on his masterpiece and its subsequent paratexts.

"*Invisible Man* holds such an honored place in African-American literature that Ralph Ellison didn't have to write anything else to break bread with the remembered dead," Darryl Pinckney asserted in a review of Ellison's *Collected Essays* in which, at times at least, the critic ignored the existence of the essays under review—the "anything else" that Ellison did write (52). The works Ellison published subsequent to *Invisible Man,* including the essay collections, are easy to dismiss because they are read as mere free-floating appendages to a previous novel. Yet that makes them essential to the author's purposes. "Ellison's craft adapts the techniques of high modernism to the moral imperative of an integrated American consciousness," Alan Nadel wrote in 2001 (399). That typical assessment comes straight out of Ellison's paratextual silence.

Conclusion

To mark the thirty-fifth anniversary of the publication of Harper Lee's only novel, *To Kill a Mockingbird* (1960), HarperCollins asked the author to write a prefatory essay. "Please spare *Mockingbird* an Introduction," Lee wrote in response. "*Mockingbird* still says what it has to say; it has managed to survive the years without preamble" (Lee n.p.). I am able to quote from Lee's letter because Lee's publisher printed the seven-sentence reply as a foreword to the book's thirty-fifth anniversary edition. Committed to extracting a delayed preface from the reticent author, HarperCollins issued what it could get its hands on. And, once again, a silent author was made to speak.

"A genuine emptiness, a pure silence is not feasible—either conceptually or in fact," Susan Sontag once observed. "Silence remains, inescapably, a form of speech (in many instances, of complaint or indictment) and an element in a dialogue" (*Styles* 10).

So universal is the view that silence is just one more form of communication that, through a breakdown in logic, the inverse is sometimes held to be true as well: clear utterances—Tillie Olsen's speeches, her complaints, her indictments—get valorized as silence. J. D. Salinger and Tillie Olsen are an illuminating pair: one has chosen to stop publishing and made no statements to the media for decades yet is accused of engaging in a lucrative dialogue with his readership; the other has published several books and toured universities solely to establish herself as an author denied access to the public. In short, the recluse was branded a cynic while the cynic reconfigured herself as a victim. Both were exploiting—or exploited by—the paradoxical trap of silence described by Sontag.

This was perhaps inescapable, due to the dominant position of the author in twentieth-century American literary culture. "We might never have existed," Maurice Maeterlinck wrote of the human individual, "but from the moment we do exist we are irrevocably immortal" (*Before* 198–99). The same is usually true of an acclaimed or popular author: once established in the media or in academia as a creative figure of genius, the author cannot end his or her existence through textual withdrawal. Expectations of further productivity and a sustained career narrative force the author to continue an ersatz dialogue with the public, if only through silence or near silence.

"The silence of a great writer needs to be listened to. If he has proved his genius, then his silence is an utterance, and one of no less moment than his speech," wrote John Middleton Murray in 1924 while reviewing *Billy Budd, Sailor* for the *Times Literary Supplement* (33). Herman Melville's professional revival in the 1920s took place amid growing interest in the biographical narrative attached to all celebrated authors. Like Murray, other twentieth-century scholars who rediscovered Melville's work were compelled to interpret the meaning of the author's unproductive decades. Melville's genius justified such consideration, they felt.

But will a silent author revived fifty or seventy years in the future receive the same treatment? Much depends on whether the "author" is a natural force instinctively embraced by the public or a construct that owes its existence to copyright legislation and publicity machines in the industrialized West. Phrased another way: Is the author becoming a mere relic from the Romantic era now that "most work in the entertainment industry is corporate rather than individual," as Mark Rose put it (viii)? Or will the author figure remain a recognizable part of collaborative, high-tech creative efforts?

Ever since the U.S. Copyright Act was amended in 1865 to include photographs among protected works, copyright legislation has had an ambiguous effect on the status of the author in our economy and society. Emendation of the U.S. copyright law to include foreign writers in 1891 plus the ever-expanding length of copyright protection helped to solidify the category of the professional author. But, over time, legislation taking into account a wide range of new techniques for capturing printed matter, visual images, and recorded sounds has expanded copyright protection to include episodes of television series, motion pictures, computer games, and other digitized products whose creators work in teams and whose "author" or copyright holder is an inorganic corporate entity. "Television as we know it is in several senses authorless," wrote Thomas Streeter in 1994. And yet, he continued, "In spite of its relatively authorless character, commercial television could not be what it is without copyright law, a legal institution that rests solidly on the principle of authorship as individual creation of unique works" (303–4).

Walter Benjamin, in his famous 1936 essay "The Work of Art in the Age of Mechanical Reproduction," traced the history of technological development in art and suggested that new technologies would "brush aside a number of outmoded concepts, such as creativity and genius, eternal value and mystery" (218). And, indeed, the manner by which entertainment products are now produced often obscures the contribution of the individual, whose recognized existence provided the impetus for our early beliefs in creativity and genius. A system of collaborative production would therefore seem to move us away from a literary environment that reads the silence of an unproductive writer like any other text. In this new creative environment, a blocked genius—now reconfigured as an unproductive colleague at the office—might elicit the condemnation, impatient ridicule, or sympathetic concern of collaborators, but he or she will not command the public profile required of a silent author. Nor will the copyrighted entity that replaces the author—the film studio or computer-game manufacturer—seize the public's imagination the way an author does, should that entity cease production or file for bankruptcy. In short, the days of the silent author may be numbered.

Copyright protection in the United States was originally limited to a fourteen-year term, renewable for an additional fourteen years if the author was still living. The U.S. Congress successively lengthened the term in 1831, 1909, 1978, and 1998, presumably for the benefit of professional authors. But copyright protection at present covers the life of the author plus seventy years. Thus, legislation meant to bolster the human author in his or her battle against encroachment by the public domain has long since exceeded its target. Estates and other corporate entities with inhuman life spans are now the prime beneficiaries.

Morton L. Janklow, a prominent literary agent, spoke as recently as 1981 about archaic methods still practiced at that time in the publishing world. "There are a lot of attitudes and techniques being held on to in this business that are not very relevant anymore," he pronounced. "We live in a world that is market-oriented" (Whiteside 57). In the decades since, copyright legislation and marketing practices within the publishing industry have grown more "relevant." They have adjusted to the realities of conglomerate ownership and the resulting multimedia packaging of literary property.

Screenplays, as we know, get handed from one script doctor to another; and though movie scripts are often credited to a single writer, they are copyrighted by the film studio. Nor do novelizations or other literary commodities spilling out of the multimedia package do much to elevate the public profile of an individual author. It is the popularity of movie actors or trademarked characters— superheroes, cartoon animals, computer-game vixens—that generate the sales of these product packages. Whereas the commercialization of American writing in the 1890s boosted the fame of Stephen Crane, Booth Tarkington, and other authors, the current hypercommercialization of the publishing industry now shrouds the individual author behind a veil of corporate profitability.

Of course, there will always be novelists who manage to resist the gravitational pull of Hollywood and its satellites. Midlist novelists of today may have a harder time remaining in print than did their predecessors, but with not-for-profit presses handling significant amounts of serious fiction and poetry, the conventional author will never disappear completely. What is uncertain is whether a critical mass of attention will continue to be paid to authors so that fallow periods in their careers will continue to receive scrutiny.

For now, the profile of the author is so conspicuous that true silence seems impossible. "There are no longer any silent men in the world today," wrote the Swiss philosopher Max Picard in 1948, "there is no longer even any difference between the silent and the speaking man, only between the speaking and the non-speaking man," neither of whom is truly silent (152). In such a world, our attention is drawn to the noise of the non-expressive artist. "The text always contains a certain number of signs referring to the author," Michel Foucault wrote (112), though he implied that, with the very concept of the author exposed as a mere construct, those signs might some day disappear. "Will the author in the modern sense prove to have been only a brief episode in the history of writing?" Martha Woodmansee asked in an analysis of authorial attribution ("Author Effect" 15). The future invites speculation. More than forty years ago, Marshall McLuhan observed: "We are today as far into the electronic age as the Elizabethans had advanced into the typographical and mechanical age. And we are experiencing the same confusion" (1). Making firm predictions about the fate of the author would be foolhardy. But this much is certain: in twentieth-century America, the concept of the author grew in strength—to almost ludicrous proportions. In a culture where silence was read as literature, the author function reigned.

Works Cited

Adams, Phoebe-Lou. Review of *Silences,* by Tillie Olsen. *Atlantic Monthly* Sept. 1978: 96.

Alexander, Paul. *Salinger: A Biography.* Los Angeles: Renaissance Books, 1999.

Allen, Brooke. "Love for Sale." *National Review* 14 June 1999: 34.

Alsen, Eberhard. *Salinger's Glass Family as a Composite Novel.* Troy, N.Y.: Whitston, 1983.

Alter, Robert. "Awakenings." *New Republic* 25 Jan. 1988: 33–37.

———. "The Desolate Breach between Himself and Himself." *New York Times Book Review* 16 Jan. 1994: 3, 29.

Amidon, Stephen. "Children of the Ghetto." *Sunday Times* (London) 23 Apr. 1995, sec. 7: 8.

Amis, Martin. *The War against Cliché: Essays and Reviews, 1971–2000.* 2001. New York, Vintage, 2002.

Anderson, Michael. "Talk the Talk, Walk the Walk." *TLS* 9 Aug. 2002: 7–8.

Atwood, Margaret. "Obstacle Course." Nelson and Huse 245–49.

Auchard, John. *Silence in Henry James: The Heritage of Symbolism and Decadence.* University Park: Pennsylvania State University Press, 1986.

Auster, Paul. *The Book of Illusions.* New York: Henry Holt, 2002.

Avant, John Alfred. Review of *Yonnondio: From the Thirties,* by Tillie Olsen. *New Republic* 30 Mar. 1974: 28–29.

Barrett, William. "Black and Blue: A Negro Céline." *American Century* June 1952: 100–104.

Barthes, Roland. *Mythologies.* Trans. Annette Lavers. 1957. London: Jonathan Cape, 1972.

———. *The Rustle of Language.* Trans. Richard Howard. Berkeley: University of California Press, 1986.

Bawer, Bruce. *Diminishing Fictions: Essays on the Modern American Novel and Its Critics.* Saint Paul, Minn.: Greywolf, 1988.

Belcher, William F., and James W. Lee, eds. *J. D. Salinger and the Critics.* Belmont, Calif.: Wadsworth, 1962.

Bellow, Saul. "Man Underground." *Commentary* 13 (1952): 608–10.

Benjamin, Walter. *Illuminations.* Trans. Harry Zohn. New York: Schocken, 1969.

Bernheim, Mark A. Review of *Tillie Olsen,* by Mickey Pearlman and Abby P. Werlock. *Studies in Short Fiction* 28 (1991): 235–37.

Bone, James. "Incest Key to Writer's Long Block." *Sunday Times* (London) 23 May 1998, sec. 1: 15.

Booth, Wayne C. *The Rhetoric of Fiction.* Chicago: University of Chicago Press, 1961.

Boucher, Sandy. "Tillie Olsen: The Weight of Things Unsaid." *Ms.* Sept. 1974: 26–30.

Boynton, H. W. "The Story of a Ghetto Childhood." *New York Times Book Review* 17 Feb. 1935: 7.

Braudy, Leo. *The Frenzy of Renown: Fame and Its History.* New York: Oxford University Press, 1986.

Bronsen, David. "A Conversation with Henry Roth." *Partisan Review* 36 (1969): 265–80.

Buelens, Gert. "The Multi-Voiced Basis of Henry Roth's Literary Success in *Call It Sleep.*" *Cultural Differences and the Literary Text: Pluralism and the Limits of Authenticity in North American Literature.* Ed. Winfried Siemerling and Katrin Schwenk. Iowa City: University of Iowa Press, 1996. 142–50.

Bukowski, Elizabeth. "The Author's Gone, So Whose Book Is It, Anyway?" *Wall Street Journal* 18 June 1999, w13.

Byam, Milton S. Review of *Invisible Man,* by Ralph Ellison. *Library Journal* 15 Apr. 1952: 716–17.

Callahan, John F. Introduction. *Juneteenth.* By Ralph Ellison. New York: Random House, 1999. xix–xxxi.

Cantwell, Robert. "The Literary Life in California." Letter. *New Republic* 22 Aug. 1934: 49.

————. "The Little Magazines." *New Republic* 25 July 1934: 295–97.

Castronovo, David. "Holden Caulfield's Legacy." *New England Review* 22.2 (2001): 180–86.

Cawelti, John. "The Writer as a Celebrity: Some Aspects of American Literature as Popular Culture." *Studies in American Fiction* 5 (1977): 161–74.

Chametzky, Jules. "Memory and Silences in the Work of Tillie Olsen and Henry Roth." *Memory, Narrative, and Identity: New Essays in Ethnic American Literatures.* Ed. Amritjit Singh, Joseph T. Skerrett Jr., and Robert E. Hogan. Boston: Northeastern University Press, 1994. 114–27.

Charvat, William. *The Profession of Authorship in America, 1800–1870.* Columbus: Ohio State University Press, 1968.

Chase, Richard. "A Novel Is a Novel." *Kenyon Review* 14 (1952): 678–84.

Chester, Alfred. "Salinger: How to Love without Love." *Commentary* 35 (1963): 467–74.

Clemons, Walter. "The Phantom of Cornish." *Newsweek* 23 May 1988: 73.

Coles, Robert. "Reconsideration: J. D. Salinger." *New Republic* 28 Apr. 1973: 30–32.

Collins, Thomas. "Stalking J. D. Salinger: A Mean Feat." *Newsday* 1 May 1988: 10.

Coombe, Rosemary J. "Author/izing the Celebrity: Publicity Rights, Postmodern Politics, and Unauthorized Genders." Woodmansee and Jaszi 101–31.

Covo, Jacqueline. *The Blinking Eye: Ralph Waldo Ellison and His American, French, German and Italian Critics, 1952–1971.* Metuchen, N.J.: Scarecrow, 1974.

Cowley, Malcolm. *The Dream of the Golden Mountains: Remembering the 1930s.* New York: Viking, 1980.

Craft, Brigette Wilds. "Tillie Olsen: A Bibliography of Reviews and Criticism, 1934–1991." *Bulletin of Bibliography* 50 (1993): 189–205.

Cruse, Harold. *The Crisis of the Negro Intellectual.* New York: Morrow, 1967.

Delbanco, Andrew. "Holden Caulfield Goes to Law School." *New Republic* 9 Mar. 1987: 27–30.

DeLillo, Don. *Mao II.* New York: Penguin, 1991.

DeSantis, Christopher C. " 'Some Cord of Kinship Stronger and Deeper than Blood': An Interview with John F. Callahan, Editor of Ralph Ellison's *Juneteenth*." *African American Review* 34 (2000): 601–20.

Dickstein, Morris. "Call It an Awakening." *New York Times Book Review* 29 Nov. 1987: 1, 33, 35.

———. "Henry Roth and the Currents of Time." *Washington Post Book World* 20 Feb. 1994: 6.

———. "No Longer at Home." *Times Literary Supplement* 5 Jan. 1996: 7.

Didion, Joan. "Finally (Fashionably) Spurious." *National Review* 18 Nov. 1961: 341–42. Rpt. in Laser and Fruman 232–34.

Dillon, David. "Art and Daily Life in Conflict." *Southwest Review* 64 (1979): 105–7.

Dowd, Maureen. "Leech Women in Love!" *New York Times* 19 May 1999, A23.

Eisenstein, Elizabeth. *The Printing Revolution in Early Modern Europe.* Cambridge: Cambridge University Press, 1983.

Ellison, Ralph. *The Collected Essays of Ralph Ellison.* Ed. John F. Callahan. New York: Modern Library, 1995.

———. *Conversations with Ralph Ellison.* Ed. Maryemma Graham and Amritjit Singh. Jackson: University Press of Mississippi, 1995.

———. *Going to the Territory.* 1987. New York: Random House, 1986.

———. *Invisible Man.* 1952. New York: Vintage, 1989.

———. *Shadow and Act.* 1964. New York: Vintage, 1972.

Ellison, Ralph, and Albert Murray. *Trading Twelves: The Selected Letters of Ralph Ellison and Albert Murray.* Ed. Albert Murray and John F. Callahan. New York: Modern Library, 2000.

Faulkner, Mara. *Protest and Possibility in the Writing of Tillie Olsen.* Charlottesville: University Press of Virginia, 1993.

Fiedler, Leslie. "Henry Roth's Neglected Masterpiece." *Commentary* 30 (1960): 102–7.

———. "The Many Myths of Henry Roth." Wirth-Nesher, *New Essays* 17–28.

———. "Neglected Books." *American Scholar* 25 (1956): 478.

Field, Michelle. "In Pursuit of J. D. Salinger." *Publishers Weekly* 27 June 1986: 63–64.

Fishkin, Shelley Fisher. "The Borderlands of Culture: Writing by W. E. B. DuBois, James Agee, Tillie Olsen, and Gloria Anzadúa." *Literary Journalism in the Twentieth Century.* Ed. Edward Sims. New York: Oxford University Press, 1990. 133–82.

———. "Reading, Writing, and Arithmetic: The Lessons *Silences* Has Taught Us." Hedges and Fishkin 23–48.

Foley, Martha. Foreword. *The Best American Short Stories 1971.* Ed. Martha Foley and David Burnett. Boston: Houghton Mifflin, 1971. ix–xi.

Folks, Jeffrey. "Henry Roth's National and Personal Narratives of Captivity." *Papers on Language and Literature* 35 (1999): 279–300.

———. Review of *Mercy of a Rude Stream,* vol. 4: *Requiem for Harlem,* by Henry Roth. *World Literature Today* 73 (1999): 150.

Forman, Seth. "On Howe, Ellison, and the Black Intellectuals." *Partisan Review* 66 (1999): 587–95.

Forrest, Emma. "Salinger's Daughter: Whining Bitch (Or 'How I Became the Voice of a Youth')." Kotzen and Beller 55–61.

Fosburgh, Lucey. "J. D. Salinger Speaks about His Silence." *New York Times* 3 Nov. 1974: 1, 69.

Foucault, Michel. *The Foucault Reader.* Ed. Paul Rabinow. New York: Pantheon, 1984.

Freedman, William. "A Conversation with Henry Roth." *Literary Review* 18 (1975): 149–57.

———. "Henry Roth in Jerusalem: An Interview." *Literary Review* 23 (1979): 5–23.

French, Sean. "The Rebirth of a Fallen Hero." *Times* (London) 13 Apr. 1995, 35.

French, Warren. *J. D. Salinger.* Boston: Twayne, 1963.

———. *J. D. Salinger.* Rev. ed. Boston: Twayne, 1976.

———. *J. D. Salinger, Revisited.* Boston: Twayne, 1988.

Friedman, John S. "On Being Blocked and Other Literary Matters: An Interview." *Commentary* 64.1 (1977): 27–38.

Friend, Tad. "Virtual Love." *New Yorker* 26 Nov. 2001: 88–99.

Frye, Joanne S. *Tillie Olsen: A Study of the Short Fiction.* New York: Twayne, 1995.

Fuller, Hoyt W. Review of *Shadow and Act,* by Ralph Ellison. *Negro Digest* Aug. 1965: 51–52.

Geismar, Maxwell. Critical introduction. *Call It Sleep.* By Henry Roth. Paterson, N.J.: Pageant Books, 1960. xxxvi–xlv.

———. "The Wise Child and the New Yorker School of Fiction." *American Moderns.* New York: Hill and Wang, 1958. 194–209. Rpt. in Grunwald 87–102.

Gelfant, Blanche H. "After Long Silence: Tillie Olsen's 'Requa.' " *Studies in American Fiction* 12 (1984): 61–69.

———. Review of *Tillie Olsen,* by Mickey Pearlman and Abby H. P. Werlock. *Western American Literature* 27 (1992): 236–37.

Genette, Gérard. *Paratexts: Thresholds of Interpretation.* Trans. Jane E. Lewin. 1987. New York: Cambridge University Press, 1997.

Goldstein, Bernice, and Sanford Goldstein. "Ego and Hapworth." *Renascence* 24 (1972): 159–67.

———. " 'Seymour: An Introduction'—Writing as Discovery." *Studies in Short Fiction* 7 (1970): 348–56.

Goldstein, Paul. *Copyright's Highway: From Gutenberg to the Celestial Jukebox.* New York: Hill and Wang, 1994.

Gollomb, Joseph. "Life in the Ghetto." *Saturday Review of Literature* 16 Mar. 1935: 552.

Goodwyn, Janet. Review of *Tillie Olsen,* by Mickey Pearlman and Abby H. P. Werlock. *Modern Fiction Studies* 88 (1993): 743–44.

Gottlieb, Annie. "Feminists Look at Motherhood." *Mother Jones* 1 Nov. 1976: 51–53.

———. Review of *Yonnondio: From the Thirties,* by Tillie Olsen. *New York Times Book Review* 31 Mar. 1974: 5.

Grumbach, Doris. "Tillie Olsen's Scrapbook." *Washington Post Book World* 6 Aug. 1978: 1, 4.

Grunwald, Henry Anatole, ed. *Salinger.* New York: Harper and Brothers, 1962.

Gwynn, Frederick L., and Joseph L. Blotner. *The Fiction of J. D. Salinger.* Pittsburgh: University of Pittsburgh Press, 1958.

Haederle, Michael. "Finally, a Time for No Regrets." *Los Angeles Times* 28 Feb. 1994, E1, E3.

Halkin, Hillel. "Henry Roth's Secret." *Commentary* 97.4 (1994): 44–47.

Hamilton, Ian. *In Search of J. D. Salinger.* New York: Random House, 1988.

———. *Keepers of the Flame: Literary Works and the Rise of Biography from Shakespeare to Plath.* London: Faber and Faber, 1994.

Harper, Howard M., Jr. *Desperate Faith.* Chapel Hill: University of North Carolina Press, 1967.

Harris, Lis. "In the Shadow of the Golden Mountain." *New Yorker* 27 June 1988: 84–92.

Hassan, Ihab. "Almost the Voice of Silence: The Later Novelettes of J. D. Salinger." *Wisconsin Studies in Contemporary Literature* 4 (1963): 5–20.

Hayes, Alfred. "Fine Recreation of Immigrant Boy's Childhood." *Daily Worker* 5 Mar. 1935, 5.

Hedges, Elaine, and Shelley Fisher Fishkin, eds. *Listening to Silences: New Silences in Feminist Criticism.* New York: Oxford University Press, 1994.

Heymann, C. David. "Salinger Is Alive." *Village Voice* 23 June 1975, 35–36, 38–40, 42.

Hicks, Granville. *The Great Tradition: An Interpretation of American Literature since the Civil War.* New York: Macmillan, 1935.

———. "Prose and the Politics of Protest." *Saturday Review* 24 Oct. 1964: 59–60.

Highsmith, Patricia. *Plotting and Writing Suspense Fiction.* 1983. New York: St. Martin's Press, 1990.

Hill, Iris Tillman. Review of *Silences,* by Tillie Olsen. *Georgia Review* 33 (1979): 958–61.

Howard, Jane. "The Belated Success of Henry Roth." *Life* 8 Jan. 1965: 75–76.

Howe, Irving. "Black Boys and Native Sons." *Selected Writings: 1950–1990.* New York: Harcourt Brace Jovanovich, 1990.

———. *Celebrations and Attacks: Thirty Years of Literary and Cultural Commentary.* New York: Horizon, 1979.

———. "Life Never Let Up." *New York Times Book Review* 25 Oct. 1964: 1, 60–61.

———. "A Negro in America." *Nation* 10 May 1952: 454.

Hyman, Stanley Edgar. *Standards: A Chronicle of Books for Our Time.* New York: Horizon, 1966.

Igi, Eka. "Note from a Non-Intellectual on Ralph Ellison (Commemorating the Non-Completion of His Second Novel)." *Black World* Apr. 1971: 97.

Ingrassia, Michelle. "The Author Nobody Met." *Newsweek* 31 May 1993: 63.

Jackson, Lawrence. *Ralph Ellison: Emergence of Genius.* New York: John Wiley and Sons, 2002.

Jaszi, Peter. "Towards a Theory of Copyright: The Metamorphoses of 'Authorship.' " *Duke Law Journal* (Apr. 1991): 455–522.

Jensen, Joan M. "Olsen's *Silences* and Women's Voices in the American West." *Frontiers* 18.3 (1997): 146–49.

Jewett, Sarah Orne. "A White Heron." *"A White Heron" and the Questions of Minor Literature*. By Louis A. Renza. Madison: University of Wisconsin Press, 1984. xiii–xxiii.

Johnston, George Sim. "Man of Letters." *Commentary* 82.6 (Dec. 1986): 71–74.

Kaganoff, Peggy. "Henry Roth." *Publishers Weekly* 27 Nov. 1987: 67–68.

Kaiser, Ernest. "A Critical Look at Ellison's Fiction and of Social and Literary Criticism by and about the Author." *Black World* 20.2 (Dec. 1970): 53–59, 81–97.

Kanfer, Stefan. "Call It Courage." *Los Angeles Times Book Review* 29 Oct. 1995: 10.

Kapp, Isa. "A Literary Life." *New Leader* 22 May 1978: 5–6.

Kawabata, Yasunari. *Japan the Beautiful and Myself*. Trans. Edward G. Seidensticker. New York: Kodansha International, 1969.

Kazin, Alfred. Introduction. *Call It Sleep*. By Henry Roth. New York: Farrar, Straus and Giroux, 1991. ix–xx.

———. "Neglected Books." *American Scholar* 25 (1956): 486.

Kellman, Steven G. "Requiem for Henry Roth." *USA Today Magazine* Mar. 2000: 75–76.

Kendall, Elaine. "A Neglected Writer Who Ran Out of Inspiration." *Los Angeles Times* 8 Dec. 1987, sec. 5: 12.

Kinsella, W. P. *Shoeless Joe*. Boston: Houghton Mifflin, 1982.

Knowles, A. Sidney, Jr. "The Fiction of Henry Roth." *Modern Fiction Studies* 11 (1965–66): 393–404.

Kostelanetz, Richard. "Ellison's Essays." *Sewanee Review* 73.1 (winter 1965): 171–72.

Kotzen, Kip, and Thomas Beller, eds. *With Love and Squalor*. New York: Broadway Books, 2001.

Kubica, Chris, and Will Hochman, eds. *Letters to J. D. Salinger*. Madison: University of Wisconsin Press, 2002.

Kurian, Elizabeth N. *A Religious Response to the Existential Dilemma in the Fiction of J. D. Salinger*. New Delhi: Intellectual Publishing House, 1992.

Langbaum, Robert. Review of *Invisible Man*, by Ralph Ellison. *Furioso* 7.4 (fall 1952): 58–66.

Langer, Elinor. Afterword. *Rope of Gold*. By Josephine Herbst. New York: Feminist Press, 1984. 431–49.

Laser, Marvin, and Norman Fruman, eds. *Studies in J. D. Salinger: Reviews, Essays, and Critiques of "The Catcher in the Rye" and Other Fiction*. New York: Odyssey Press, 1963.

Lashgari, Dierdre, ed. *Violence, Silence, and Anger: Women's Writing as Transgression*. Charlottesville: University Press of Virginia, 1995.

Leader, Zachary. "An East-Side Kid." *Times Literary Supplement* 25 Feb. 1994: 20.

LeClair, Thomas. "Missing Writers." *Horizon* Oct. 1981: 48–52.

Ledbetter, Kenneth. "Henry Roth's *Call It Sleep*: The Revival of a Proletarian Novel." *Twentieth Century Literature* 12 (1966): 123–30.

Lee, Don L. "I was born into slavery . . ." *Negro Digest* Jan. 1968: 44, 89.

Lee, Harper. *To Kill a Mockingbird*. 1960. New York: HarperCollins, 1999.

Leitch, David. "The Salinger Myth." *Twentieth Century* Nov. 1960: 428–35. Rpt. in Grunwald 69–77.

Leonard, John. Review of *Silences*, by Tillie Olsen. *New York Times* 31 July 1978, c15.

Levin, Meyer. "A Personal Appreciation." *Call It Sleep*. By Henry Roth. Paterson, N.J.: Pageant, 1960. xlvi–li.

Levine, Paul. "J. D. Salinger: The Development of the Misfit Hero." *Twentieth Century Literature* 4 (1958): 92–99. Rpt. in Belcher and Lee 107–15.

Lewis, R. W. B. "Ellison's Essays." Review of *Shadow and Act*, by Ralph Ellison. *New York Review of Books* 28 Jan. 1965: 19–20.

Lish, Gordon. "A Fool for Salinger." *Antioch Review* 44 (1986): 408–15.

[———]. "From Rupert—With No Promises." *Esquire* Feb. 1977: 83–87.

Lodge, David. *The Modes of Modern Writing*. Ithaca, N.Y.: Cornell University Press, 1977.

Lundquist, James. *J. D. Salinger*. New York: Frederick Ungar, 1979.

Lyons, Bonnie. "Henry Roth." *Twentieth-Century American-Jewish Fiction Writers*. Ed. Daniel Walden. Dictionary of Literary Biography, vol. 28. Detroit: Gale Research, 1984. 257–64.

———. *Henry Roth: The Man and His Work*. New York: Cooper Square, 1976.

———. "Interview with Henry Roth, March, 1977." *Studies in American Jewish Literature* 5.1 (1979): 50–58.

Maeterlinck, Maurice. *Before the Great Silence*. Trans. Bernard Miall. 1936. New York: Arno Press, 1977.

———. *The Treasure of the Humble*. Trans. Alfred Sutro. New York: Dodd, Mead, 1910.

Malcolm, Janet. "Justice to J. D. Salinger." *New York Review of Books* 21 June 2001: 16–22.

Margolick, David. "Whose Words Are They, Anyway?" *New York Times Book Review* 1 Nov. 1987: 1, 44–45.

Martin, Abigail. *Tillie Olsen*. Boise, Idaho: Boise State University Western Writers Series, 1984.

Materassi, Mario. Introduction. *Shifting Landscape: A Composite, 1925–1987*. By Henry Roth. Philadelphia: Jewish Publication Society, 1987. xv–xvii.

———. "Shifting Urbanscape: Roth's 'Private' New York." Wirth-Nesher, *New Essays* 29–59.

Mayberry, George. "Underground Notes." *New Republic* 21 Apr. 1952: 19.

Maynard, Joyce. "An 18-Year-Old Looks Back on Life." *New York Times Magazine* 23 Apr. 1972: 11, 76, 78–79, 82, 84–86.

———. *At Home in the World*. New York: Picador, 1998.

McCarthy, Mary. *The Writing on the Wall and Other Literary Essays*. New York: Harcourt Brace Jovanovich, 1970.

McHale, Brian. "Henry Roth in Nighttown, or, Containing *Ulysses*." Wirth-Nesher, *New Essays* 75–105.

McIntyre, John P. "A Preface for *Franny and Zooey*." *Critic* 20.4 (1962): 25–28.

McLuhan, Marshall. *The Gutenberg Galaxy*. Toronto: University of Toronto Press, 1962.

McNeil, Helen. "Speaking for the Speechless." *Times Literary Supplement* 14 Nov. 1980: 1294.

McSweeney, Kerry. *Invisible Man: Race and Identity.* Boston: Twayne, 1988.

———. "Salinger Revisited." *Critical Quarterly* 20.1 (1978): 61–68.

Meese, Elizabeth A. *Crossing the Double-Cross: The Practice of Feminist Criticism.* Chapel Hill, N.C.: University of North Carolina Press, 1986.

Michaels, Leonard. "The Long Comeback of Henry Roth: Call It Miraculous." *New York Times Book Review* 15 Aug. 1993: 3, 19–20.

Miller, James E., Jr. *J. D. Salinger.* Minneapolis: University of Minnesota Press, 1965.

Miller, Nancy K. "Arachnologies: The Woman, the Text, and the Critic." *The Poetics of Gender.* Ed. Nancy K. Miller. New York: Columbia University Press, 1986. 270–95.

Miller, Nolan. Review of *Silences,* by Tillie Olsen. Nelson and Huse 252.

Mills, Kay. " 'Surviving Is Not Enough': A Conversation with Tillie Olsen." *Los Angeles Times* 26 Apr. 1981, sec. 4: 3.

Morris, Wright. "The World Below." *New York Times Book Review* 13 Apr. 1952: 5.

Murray, John Middleton. "Herman Melville's Silence." *Critical Essays on Melville's Billy Budd, Sailor.* Ed. Robert Milder. Boston: G. K. Hall, 1989. 33–36.

Nadel, Alan. "Ralph Ellison and the American Canon." *American Literary History* 13 (2001): 393–404.

Nelson, Kay Hoyle. Introduction. Nelson and Huse 1–20.

Nelson, Kay Hoyle, and Nancy Huse. *The Critical Response to Tillie Olsen.* Westport, Conn.: Greenwood, 1994.

Nicholls, Richard E. "Henry Roth, 89, Who Wrote of an Immigrant Child's Life in *Call It Sleep,* Is Dead." Obituary. *New York Times* 15 Oct. 1995, 41.

Oates, Joyce Carol. Review of *Silences,* by Tillie Olsen. *The Critical Response to Tillie Olsen.* Nelson and Huse 245–49.

———. "Words of Love, Priced to Sell." *New York Times* 18 May 1999, A23.

Ohmann, Richard. *Selling Culture: Magazines, Markets, and Class at the Turn of the Century.* New York: Verso, 1996.

Olsen, Tillie. "The Iron Throat." *Partisan Review* 1 (Apr.–May 1934): 3–9.

———. "Requa-I." *The Best American Short Stories 1971.* Ed. Martha Foley and David Burnett. Boston: Houghton Mifflin, 1971.

———. "A Response." *Frontiers* 18.3 (1997): 159–60.

———. *Silences.* New York: Delacorte, 1978.

———. "The Strike." *Years of Protest: A Collection of American Writings of the 1930s.* Ed. Jack Salzman. New York: Pegasus, 1967. 138–44.

———. *Tell Me a Riddle.* 1961. New York: Delta, 1994.

———. *Yonnondio: From the Thirties.* 1974. New York: Delta, 1994.

Orr, Elaine. *Tillie Olsen and a Feminist Spiritual Vision.* Jackson: University Press of Mississippi, 1987.

Pattanaik, Dipti R. " 'The Holy Refusal': A Vedantic Interpretation of J. D. Salinger's Silence." *MELUS* 23.2 (1998): 113–27.

Patterson, Lyman Ray. *Copyright in Historical Perspective.* Nashville: Vanderbilt University Press, 1968.

Pearlman, Mickey, and Abby H. P. Werlock. *Tillie Olsen.* Boston: Twayne, 1991.

Perlman, Jim. Preface. *Strength to Your Sword Arm.* By Brenda Ueland. Duluth, Minn.: Holy Cow! Press, 1983. ix–xii.

Peters, Joan. "The Lament for Lost Art." *Nation* 23 Sept. 1978: 281–82.

Picard, Max. *The World of Silence.* Trans. Stanley Goodman. 1948. Chicago: Regnery, 1952.

Pinckney, Darryl. "The Drama of Ralph Ellison." *New York Review of Books* 15 May 1997: 52–60.

Pinsker, Sanford. "Against the Current." *Washington Post Book World* 15 Mar. 1998: 1, 14–15.

———. "The Re-Awakening of Henry Roth's *Call It Sleep.*" *Jewish Social Studies* 28 (1966): 148–58.

———. "Roth Redux." *Congress Monthly* June/July/Aug. 1994: 20–21.

———. "The Torments of Literary Consciousness." *Congress Monthly* May/June 1995: 1.

Pogrebin, Robin. "A Deep Silence of 60 Years, and an Even Older Secret." *New York Times* 16 May 1998, B9, B12.

Polster, Karen L. "Tillie Olsen." *Contemporary Jewish-American Novelists.* Ed. Joel Shatzky and Michael Taub. Westport, Conn.: Greenwood Press, 1997. 242–51.

Pratt, Linda Ray. "Mediating Experiences in the Scholarship of Tillie Olsen." *Frontiers* 18.3 (1997): 130–34.

Prescott, Orville. "Books of the Times." *New York Times* 16 Apr. 1952, 25.

Quinn, Judy. "A Spotlight on Salinger." *Publishers Weekly* 12 July 1999: 26–27.

Rabinowitz, Paula. *Labor and Desire: Women's Revolutionary Fiction in Depression America.* Chapel Hill: University of North Carolina Press, 1991.

Ranchan, Som P. *An Adventure in Vedanta (J. D. Salinger's The Glass Family).* Delhi: Ajanta, 1989.

Renza, Louis A. *"A White Heron" and the Question of Minor Literature.* Madison: University of Wisconsin Press, 1984.

Review of *Call It Sleep,* by Henry Roth. *New Masses* 12 Feb. 1935: 27.

Review of *Invisible Man,* by Ralph Ellison. *Time* 14 Apr. 1952: 112.

Review of *Silences,* by Tillie Olsen. *Yale Review* 68 (1978): vi–x.

Ribalow, Harold M. "Henry Roth and His Novel *Call It Sleep.*" *Wisconsin Studies in Contemporary Literature* 3.3 (1962): 5–14.

———. "The History of Henry Roth and *Call It Sleep.*" *Call It Sleep.* By Henry Roth. Paterson, N.J.: Pageant, 1960. xi–xxxv.

Rich, Adrienne. *On Lies, Secrets, and Silence: Selected Prose 1966–1978.* New York: W. W. Norton, 1979.

Rideout, Walter B. " 'O Workers' Revolution . . . The True Messiah.' " *American Jewish Archives* 11 (1959): 157–75.

———. *The Radical Novel in the United States 1900–1954: Some Interrelations of Literature and Society.* Cambridge, Mass.: Harvard University Press, 1956.

Rifkind, Donna. "Call It Irresponsible." *New Criterion* Feb. 1988: 75–76.

Roberts, Nora Ruth. *Three Radical Women Writers: Class and Gender in Meridel Le Sueur, Tillie Olsen, and Josephine Herbst.* New York: Garland, 1996.

Rose, Mark. *Authors and Owners: The Invention of Copyright.* Cambridge, Mass.: Harvard University Press, 1993.

Rosen, Jonathan. "The 60-Year Itch." *Vanity Fair* Feb. 1994: 36–46.

Rosenbaum, Ron. "The Man in the Glass House." *Esquire* June 1997: 48–53, 116–21.

Rosenfelt, Deborah. "From the Thirties: Tillie Olsen and the Radical Tradition." *Feminist Studies* 7 (1981): 371–406.

———, ed. *"Tell Me a Riddle."* New Brunswick, N.J.: Rutgers University Press, 1995.

Rosenheim, Andrew. "Growing Up Absurd in America." *Times Literary Supplement* 14 Apr. 1995: 20.

Roth, Henry. *Call It Sleep.* 1934. New York: Farrar, Straus and Giroux, 1991.

———. *Mercy of a Rude Stream.* Vol. 1: *A Star Shines over Mt. Morris Park.* New York: St. Martin's, 1994.

———. *Mercy of a Rude Stream.* Vol. 2: *A Diving Rock on the Hudson.* New York: St. Martin's, 1995.

———. *Mercy of a Rude Stream.* Vol. 3: *From Bondage.* New York: St. Martin's, 1996.

———. *Mercy of a Rude Stream.* Vol. 4: *Requiem for Harlem.* New York: St. Martin's, 1998.

———. *Shifting Landscape: A Composite, 1925–1987.* Ed. Mario Materassi. Philadelphia: Jewish Publication Society, 1987.

Sale, Roger. "The Career of Ralph Ellison." *Hudson Review* 18 (1965): 124–28.

Salinger, J. D. *The Catcher in the Rye.* 1951. New York: Bantam, 1964.

———. *Franny and Zooey.* 1961. New York: Bantam, 1964.

———. "Hapworth 16, 1924." *New Yorker* 19 June 1965: 32–113.

———. *Nine Stories.* 1953. New York: Bantam, 1964.

———. *Raise High the Roof Beam, Carpenters and Seymour: An Introduction.* 1963. New York: Bantam, 1965.

Salinger, Margaret A. *Dream Catcher.* New York: Washington Square, 2000.

Samet, Tom. "Henry Roth's Bull Story: Guilt and Betrayal in *Call It Sleep.*" *Studies in the Novel* 7 (1975): 569–83.

Samuels, David. "Marginal Notes on *Franny and Zooey.*" *American Scholar* 68.3 (1999): 128–33.

Schultz, Lydia A. "Flowing against the Traditional Stream: Consciousness in Tillie Olsen's 'Tell Me a Riddle.' " *MELUS* 22.3 (1997): 113–31.

Schulz, Max F. "Epilogue to *Seymour: An Introduction:* Salinger and the Crisis of Consciousness." *Studies in Short Fiction* 5 (1968): 128–38.

Schwartz, Delmore. "The Wrongs of Innocence and Experience." *Partisan Review* 19 (1952): 354–59.

Seed, David. "Keeping It in the Family: The Novellas of J. D. Salinger." *The Modern American Novel.* Ed. A. Robert Lee. New York: St. Martin's Press, 1989. 139–61.

Severo, Richard. "Henry Roth Is Dead at 89; Wrote Novel *Call It Sleep.*" Obituary. *New York Times* 14 Oct. 1995, 27.

Shechner, Mark. "The Unquiet Past of Henry Roth." *Chicago Tribune Books* 19 Feb. 1995, sec. 14: 1, 14.

Shulman, Alix Kates. "Overcoming Silences: Teaching Writing for Women." *Harvard Educational Review* 49 (1979): 527–33.

Silverberg, Mark. "A Bouquet of Empty Brackets: Author-Function and the Search for J. D. Salinger." *Dalhousie Review* 75 (1995): 222–46.

Smith, Dinitia. "Salinger Letters Are Sold and May Return to Sender." *New York Times* 23 June 1999, B1+.

Sollors, Werner. " 'A World Somewhere, Somewhere Else': Language, Nostalgic Mournfulness, and Urban Immigrant Family Romance in *Call It Sleep*." Wirth-Nesher, *New Essays* 127–88.

Sontag, Susan. *Against Interpretation*. 1966. New York: Anchor, 1990.

———. *Styles of Radical Will*. 1969. New York: Anchor, 1991.

Spivak, Gayatri Chakravorty. "Displacement and the Discourse of Woman." *Displacement: Derrida and After*. Ed. Mark Krupnick. Bloomington: Indiana University Press, 1983. 169–95.

Staples, Brent. Review of *The Collected Essays of Ralph Ellison*, ed. John F. Callahan. *New York Times Book Review* 12 May 1996: 6–7.

Stashower, Daniel M. "On First Looking into Chapman's Holden: Speculations on a Murder." *American Scholar* 53 (1983): 373–85.

Stein, Joel. "The Yips." Kotzen and Beller 170–76.

Steiner, George. *Language and Silence: Essays on Language, Literature, and the Inhuman*. 1967. New Haven, Conn.: Yale University Press, 1998.

———. "The Salinger Industry." *Nation* 14 Nov. 1959: 360–63. Rpt. in Laser and Fruman 113–18.

Stimpson, Catharine R. "Tillie Olsen: Witness as Servant." *Where the Meanings Are*. New York: Methuen, 1988. 67–76.

Stolz, Craig. "Salinger: An Explanation." *City Paper* (Washington, D.C.) 8 May 1987, 13+.

Strauch, Carl F. "Salinger: The Romantic Background." *Wisconsin Studies in Contemporary Literature* 4 (1963): 31–40.

Streeter, Thomas. "Broadcast Copyright and the Bureaucratization of Property." Woodmansee and Jaszi 303–26.

Strout, Cushing. Review of *Going to the Territory*, by Ralph Ellison. *Black American Literature Forum* 23 (1989): 808–14.

Swados, Harvey. "Must Writers Be Characters?" *Saturday Review* 1 Oct. 1960: 12–14, 50.

Syrkin, Marie. "Revival of a Classic." *Midstream* 7 (1961): 89–93.

Szalay, Michael. *New Deal Modernism: American Literature and the Invention of the Welfare State*. Durham, N.C.: Duke University Press, 2000.

Teachout, Terry. "Salinger Then and Now." *Commentary* 84.3 (1987): 61–64.

Timberg, Scott. "Composer Speaks Out on His Cagey Use of Silence." *Los Angeles Times* 27 Sep. 2002, home ed., F1.

Tomaševskij, Boris. "Literature and Biography." 1923. Rpt. in *Twentieth-Century Literary Theory: An Introductory Anthology*. Ed. Vassilis Lambropoulos and David Neil Miller. Albany: SUNY Press, 1987. 116–23.

Toth, Susan Allen. Introduction. *Strength to Your Sword Arm*. By Brenda Ueland. Duluth, Minn.: Holy Cow! Press, 1993. xiii–xxv.

Trueblood, Valerie. Review of *Silences*, by Tillie Olsen. Nelson and Huse 253–54.

Ueland, Brenda. *If You Want to Write*. 1938. Saint Paul, Minn.: Schubert Club, 1983.

———. *Me*. 1939. Saint Paul, Minn.: Schubert Club, 1983.

Walling, William. "Ralph Ellison's Invisible Man: 'It Goes a Long Way Back, Some Twenty Years.' " *Phylon* 34 (1973): 4–16.

Walker, Alice. *In Search of Our Mother's Gardens*. San Diego: Harcourt Brace Jovanovich, 1983.

Warren, Robert Penn. "The Unity of Experience." *Commentary* 39.5 (1965): 91–96.

Washington, Peter. *Fraud: Literary Theory and the End of English.* London: Fontana, 1989.

Webster, Harvey Curtis. "Inside a Dark Shell." Review of *Invisible Man,* by Ralph Ellison. *Saturday Review* 12 Apr. 1952: 22–23.

Weil, Robert. Afterword. *Mercy of a Rude Stream,* vol. 4: *Requiem for Harlem.* By Henry Roth. New York: St. Martin's, 1998. 273–82.

Wenke, John. *J. D. Salinger: A Study of the Short Fiction.* Boston: Twayne, 1991.

West, Anthony. "Black Man's Burden." *New Yorker* 31 May 1952: 93–96.

Whiteside, Thomas. *The Blockbuster Complex: Conglomerates, Show Business, and Book Publishing.* Middletown, Conn.: Wesleyan University Press, 1981.

Wideman, John Edgar. "What Is Afro, What Is American." *New York Times Book Review* 3 Aug. 1986: 15.

Williams, Christian. "J. D. Salinger's Day in Court." *Washington Post* 6 Nov. 1982, C1–C2.

Wilson, Christopher P. *The Labor of Words: Literary Professionalism in the Progressive Era.* Athens: University of Georgia Press, 1985.

Wirth-Nesher, Hana. "Call It Sleep: Jewish, American, Modernist, Classic." *Judaism* 44 (1995): 388–98.

———. "Facing the Fictions: Henry Roth's and Philip Roth's Meta-Memoirs." *Prooftexts* 18 (1998): 259–75.

———, ed. *New Essays on "Call It Sleep".* New York: Cambridge University Press, 1996.

Wolfe, Tom. "Lasting Impressions." *Esquire* Dec. 1981: 60.

Wood, James. "The Water and the Preacher." *New Republic* 28 June 1999: 38–42.

Woodmansee, Martha. "The Genius and the Copyright: Economic and Legal Conditions of the Emergence of the 'Author.'" *Eighteenth-Century Studies* 17 (1984): 425–48.

———. "On the Author Effect: Recovering Collectivity." Woodmansee and Jaszi 15–28.

Woodmansee, Martha, and Peter Jaszi, eds. *The Construction of Authorship: Textual Appropriation in Law and Literature.* Durham, N.C.: Duke University Press, 1994.

Wren, Paul. "Boy in the Ghetto." *New Republic* 27 Feb. 1935: 82.

Wyatt, David. *Prodigal Sons: A Study in Authorship and Authority.* Baltimore, Md.: Johns Hopkins University Press, 1980.

Yalom, Marilyn. *Women Writers of the West Coast: Speaking of Their Lives and Careers.* Santa Barbara, Calif.: Capra, 1983.

Yardley, Jonathan. "Sharper Than a Serpent's Tooth." *Washington Post* 1 Sep. 2000, C1, C3.

Index

Barthes, Roland, 6, 9, 13, 29, 41, 102; "The Death of the Author," 3, 40; *Mythologies*, 2

Batt, Mike, 1, 12

Baudelaire, 23

Beckett, Samuel, 111

Before the Great Silence (Maeterlinck), 9, 96–97

"Belated Success of Henry Roth, The" (Howard), 51

Bellow, Saul, 55, 118; *The Adventures of Augie March*, 78

Benjamin, Walter, 134

Bernheim, Mark A., 43

Best American Short Stories anthology (1957), 20

Billy Budd, Sailor (Melville), 133

Bird, 124–25

Black Boy (Wright), 119

"Black Boys and Native Sons" (I. Howe), 124

Black World, 128

Blotner, Joseph L., 112

Bone, James, 87

Book of Illusions, The (Auster), 9

Booth, Wayne C., 10

Bottom Dogs (Dahlberg), 55

Boucher, Sandy, 32

Boynton, H. W., 54, 81

Brawley, Tawana, 42

Brightness Falls (McInerney), 9

Broder, Rose, 72, 77, 86–87

Bronsen, David, 58

Buelens, Gert, 58

Bukowski, Elizabeth, 130

Burroughs, William S., 111

Byam, Milton S., 118

Cage, John, 1, 13

California Congress of Industrial Organization's Women's Auxiliary, 19

Call It Sleep (H. Roth): as based on lost identity, 63; "The Cellar" section of, 81–82; critical reviews of, 12, 53–61, 65, 76, 81–87; David Schearl character in, 54, 63, 69, 81–84; as high modernist work, 11, 48, 56; influence of Joyce on, 53, 58–59, 61; innate literary talent shown in, 1–2; Oedipal/sexual themes of, 74, 81–83, 85–86; "The Rail" section of, 82; Roth interview on, 50; Roth on lyrical impulses of, 57–58; Roth's inability to write after, 51–52; scholarly studies based on assumptions about, 46, 47; as youthful indulgence by Roth, 67. *See also* Roth, Henry: Works

Callahan, John F., 122, 130

Capote, Truman: *Answered Prayers*, 90; "Handcarved Coffins," 8; *In Cold Blood*, 8; *The Muses Are Heard*, 8

Castronovo, David, 111

Catcher in the Rye, The (J. Salinger), 2, 90, 103, 104, 111–12

Caulfield, Holden (J. Salinger fictional character), 104

Cawelti, John, 6

Caxton, William, 3

"Cellar, The" (*Call It Sleep*; H. Roth), 81–82

censorship, 3–4, 19, 23

Cerf, Bennett, 17

Chafetz, Chap, 52

Chametzky, Jules, 35

Charvat, William, 6

Chester, Alfred, 109

Cicero, 6

Coles, Robert, 94

Collected Essays (R. Ellison), 123, 128, 130

"Commemorating the Non-Completion of His Second Novel" (Igi), 128

Commentary, 52, 74, 118

commodification of silence, 1. *See also* silences

Communist Party: growing disillusionment with, 120; McCarthyism and, 19–20; Olsen's interest in, 19–20; on "proletarian writers," 58; Roth's membership in, 45, 52, 63–64; *Silences'* oblique entries regarding, 28

Company of Stationers of London, 3, 4

Congress of American Writers (1935), 17

Cooper, James Fenimore, 6

copyright: early history of, 3–4; extension of period of protection, 134; as new form of property, 3

Copyright in Historical Perspective (Patterson), 3

copyright law: covering screenplays and product packages, 134–35; extended protection under, 133–34; shift of, toward corporate entities, 12–13; U.S. implementation of international, 4–5

Country of Pointed Firs, The (Jewett), 16

Covo, Jacqueline, 125

Craft, Brigette Wilds, 31

Crane, Stephen, 5, 7, 124, 135

Crown Publishing, 38, 39

Cruse, Harold, 120

Cummings, E. E., 8

Dahlberg, Edward, 55

Daily Worker, 83

Daughter of Earth (Smedley), 33

Davis, Angela, 128

Davis, Rebecca Harding, 24, 33

"De Daumier-Smith's Blue Period" (J. Salinger), 106

"Death of the Author, The" (Barthes), 3, 40

Defoe, Daniel, 4

"delayed preface" (R. Ellison), 121–22, 128–29

Delbanco, Andrew, 100

DeLillo, Don, 89; *Mao II,* 96

Derrida, Jacques, 40, 41

Devine, Frank, 89

Dickens, Charles, 4

Dickstein, Morris, 73, 80

Didion, Joan, 111

Dillon, David, 35

Diving Rock on the Hudson, A (H. Roth), 61, 64, 71, 72, 78, 83, 87

Do the Right Thing (film), 42

Donne, John, 6

Dos Passos, John, 17

"Down at the Dinghy" (J. Salinger), 107

"Dun Dakotas, The" (H. Roth), 52

Ecclesias (H. Roth's fictional character), 69, 73–74, 76, 85

"18-Year-Old Looks Back on Life, An" (Maynard), 99

Eisenstein, Elizabeth, 2–3, 5

Eliot, T. S., 11; *The Waste Land,* 48, 57, 58, 60, 65, 67, 119

Ellison, Fanny, 123, 130

Ellison, Ralph: efforts of, to explain own writing, 129–30; essays and book reviews by, 90, 124–25, 129–30; examining silence of, 1; "the Hickman project" of, 119–22; hostility of black intellectuals toward, 126–29; interviews given by, 123, 129–30; "later preface" and "delayed preface" to works of, 121–22, 128–29; literary legacy of, 130–31; literary status given to, 2; scholars on work of, 121–26; silence of, following *Invisible Man,* 12, 50; squabble between Howe and, 124, 128; on white versus Negro values, 123; "you-know-what" question posed by, 117–18. Works: *Collected Essays,* 123, 128, 130; *Going to the Territory,* 119, 121, 122, 123, 127, 128–29; *Juneteenth,* 130; "The Novel as a Function of American Democracy," 119; *Shadow and Act,* 121, 122, 123, 124, 125, 126–27, 128; "Slick Gonna Learn," 127; "Tell It Like It Is," 127; "The World and the Jug," 124. See also *Invisible Man* (R. Ellison)

Enormous Room, The (Cummings), 8

Eppes, Betty, 100

"Equipment for Pennies" (H. Roth), 47

Esquire magazine, 88, 93

influences on, 57; loss of identity by, 63, 64; obituary of, 61; on sexual involvement with sister, 61, 62, 68. Works: "At Times in Flight," 52; *A Diving Rock on the Hudson*, 61, 64, 71, 72, 78, 83, 87; "The Dun Dakotas," 52; "Equipment for Pennies," 47; *From Bondage*, 72; "The Meaning of *Galut* in America Today," 66; "No Longer at Home," 66; *Requiem for Harlem*, 72, 78; *A Star Shines over Mt. Morris Park*, 58, 68, 69–70, 74, 76, 85, 86; "Where My Sympathy Lies," 63–64. See also *Call It Sleep* (H. Roth); *Mercy of a Rude Stream* (H. Roth); *Shifting Landscape* (H. Roth)

Roth, Muriel, 67, 76

Roth, Philip, 55, 95; *Operation Shylock*, 8; *Portnoy's Complaint*, 8; *Zuckerman Unbound*, 8

Roth, Rose (later Broder), 72, 77, 86–87

Sale, Roger, 125–26

Salinger, Dorris, 95

Salinger, J. D.: accused of using silence to gain fame, 96–103; compared to Olsen, 132; critical analysis using content of published works, 103–9; critical analysis using form of published works, 109–16; critical reviews of, 112–16; hypotheses on silence of, 95–96; literary marketplace shaped by silence of, 1, 2, 9; move of, to legally block Hamilton's biography, 91, 98–99, 100–101; professional literary status of, 12; refusal of, to anthologize works, 95; unique author persona of, 89–90; on vulnerability to opportunists, 88–89. Works: *The Catcher in the Rye*, 2, 90, 103, 104, 111–12; "De Daumier-Smith's Blue Period," 106; "Down at the Dinghy," 107; "Franny," 103, 104, 107, 112; *Franny and Zooey*, 90, 103, 104, 106–7, 109, 111, 112; "Hapworth 16,

1924," 107, 113–14; *Nine Stories*, 90, 96, 112; "A Perfect Day for Bananafish," 103, 107; "Raise High the Roof Beam, Carpenters," 92, 103, 107, 112; *Raise High the Roof Beam, Carpenters and Seymour: An Introduction*, 90; "Seymour: An Introduction," 92, 103, 107, 112–13; "Teddy," 103; "Uncle Wiggly in Connecticut," 107; "Zooey," 103, 104–5, 106, 107–9, 112, 113

Salinger, Margaret, 116

Samet, Tom, 83–84

Samuels, David, 109

Schearl, David (H. Roth's fictional character), 54, 63, 69, 81–84

Schultz, Lydia A., 35

Schulz, Max F., 113–14

Scott, Sir Walter, 4

Seed, David, 115

Selling Culture (Ohmann), 5

Selsberg, Andy, 94

Severo, Richard, 79

"Seymour: An Introduction" (J. Salinger), 92, 103, 107, 112–13

Shadow and Act (R. Ellison), 121, 122, 123, 124, 125, 126–27, 128

Shenandoah, 52

Shifting Landscape (H. Roth), 45–50, 62, 67, 74; "At Times in Flight," 52; critical response to, 47, 49–50; "The Dun Dakotas," 52; editing of, 46, 47; "Equipment for Pennies," 47; "The Meaning of *Galut* in America Today," 66; "No Longer at Home," 66; purpose of, 45–46; introduction to, 47, 48; "Where My Sympathy Lies," 63–64; as written explanation for Roth's silence, 11, 48–49, 52–53, 63, 75, 87

Ship of Fools (Porter), 90

Shulman, Alix Kates, 35, 38

Silence in Henry James (Auchard), 9

silences: commodification of, 1; efforts to tell truth about, 41–43; as form of speech, 132; generating legitimate